THE EMERGENCE OF MINORITIES IN THE MIDDLE EAST

THE EMERGENCE OF MINORITIES IN THE MIDDLE EAST

THE POLITICS OF COMMUNITY IN FRENCH MANDATE SYRIA

♦ ♦ ♦

BENJAMIN THOMAS WHITE

EDINBURGH
University Press

This book is dedicated to my father, Brian White, wishing that he could have seen it finished; and to my mother, Rita White, who will.

© Benjamin Thomas White, 2011, 2012

First published in 2011 by
Edinburgh University Press Ltd
22 George Square, Edinburgh EH8 9LF
www.euppublishing.com

This paperback edition 2012

Typeset in Sabon by
Servis Filmsetting Ltd, Stockport, Cheshire, and
printed and bound in Great Britain by
CPI Group (UK) Ltd, Croydon CR0 4YY

A CIP record for this book is available from the British Library

ISBN 978 0 7486 4187 1 (hardback)
ISBN 978 0 7486 8540 4 (paperback)

The right of Benjamin Thomas White to be identified as author of this work has been asserted in accordance with the Copyright, Designs and Patents Act 1988.

An early version of chapters 1 and 2 of this book appeared as 'The nation-state form and the emergence of "minorities" in Syria' in *Studies in ethnicity and nationalism*, vol. 7, no. 1 (2007), pp. 64–85. A short segment of chapter 4 first appeared as 'Addressing the state: the Syrian 'ulama' protest personal status law reform, 1939', a 'quick study' in *International Journal of Middle Eastern Studies*, vol. 42, no. 1 (2010), pp. 10–12. Material from that chapter also appeared in a different form in 'Frontières et pouvoir d'État. La frontière turco-syrienne dans les années 1920 et 30' (with Seda Altuğ), *Vingtième siècle. Revue d'histoire*, no. 103 (2009/3), pp. 91–104. The author would like to thank the editors of these journals for permission to reuse this material.

CONTENTS

Map 1. Syria c.1936	vi
Map 2. The Far Northeast of Syria in the 1930s	vii
Outline Chronology of the French Mandate, 1919–39	viii
Acknowledgements	xi
Introduction	1

Part I

1. Minorities, Majorities and the Nation-state	21
2. 'Minorities' and the French Mandate	43

Part II

3. Separatism and Autonomism	69
4. The Border and the Kurds	101

Part III

5. The Franco-Syrian Treaty and the Definition of 'Minorities'	131
6. Personal Status Law Reform	162
Conclusion: Minorities, Majorities and the Writing of History	209
Select Bibliography	213
Index	233

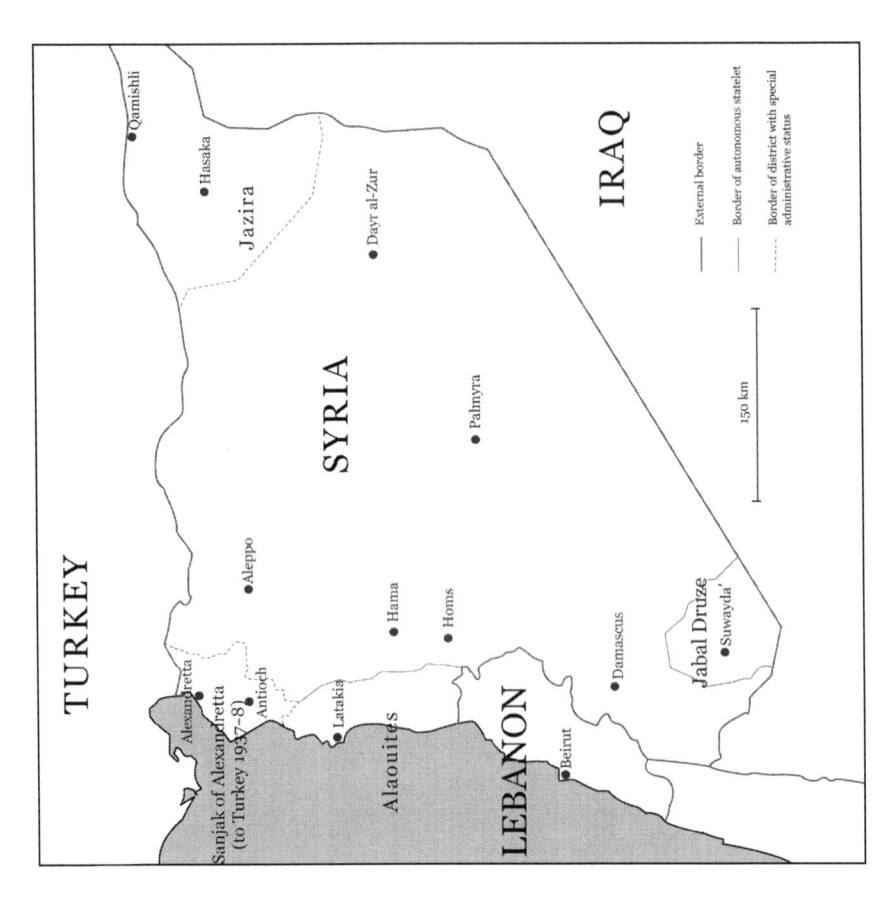

Map 1 Syria c. 1936.

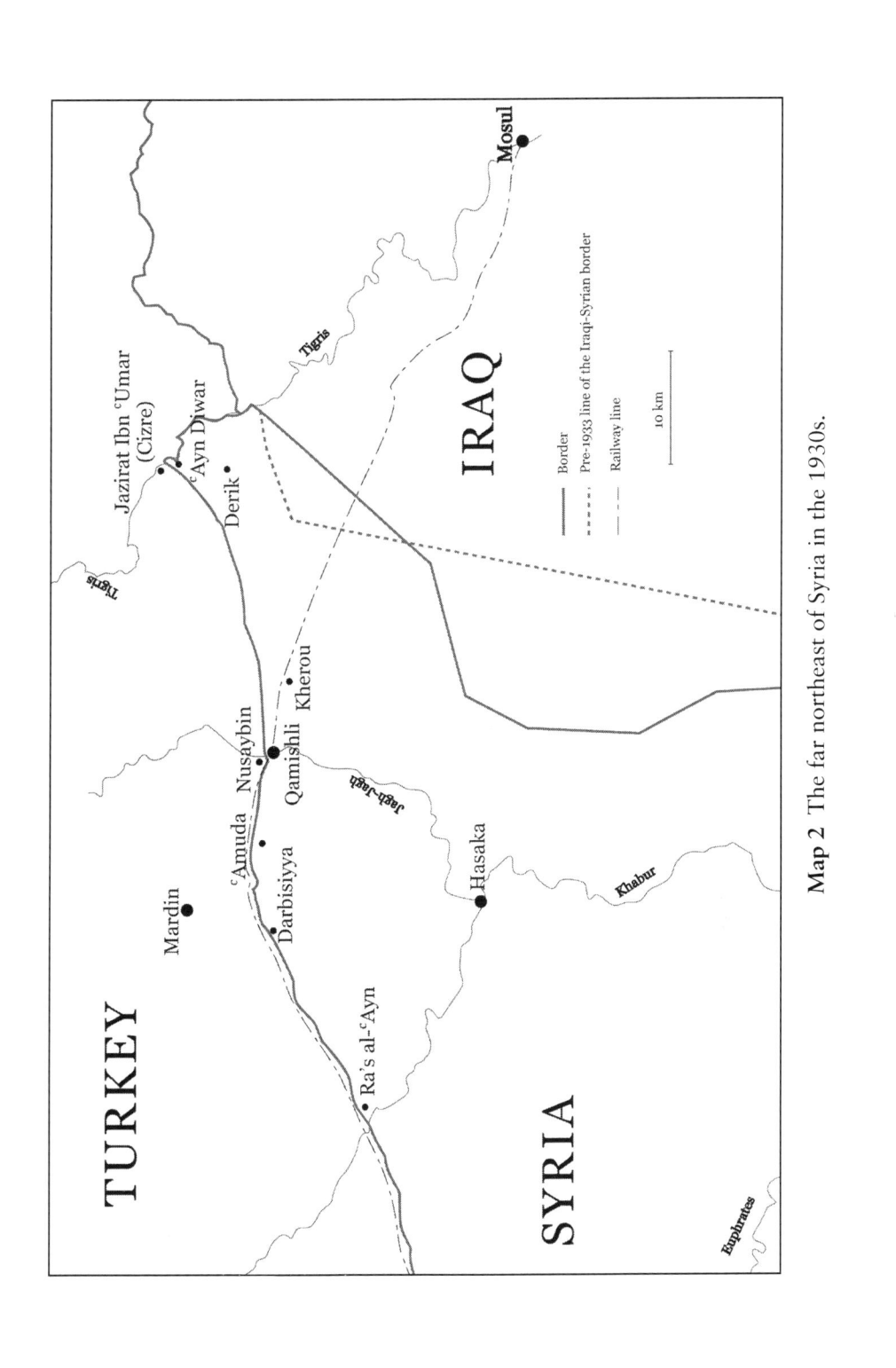

Map 2 The far northeast of Syria in the 1930s.

OUTLINE CHRONOLOGY OF THE FRENCH MANDATE, 1919–39

Year	Events	High Commissioners (date of appointment)
1917–19	Allied occupation of Arab provinces; end of First World War; end of Ottoman rule in Arab provinces; Faysali rule in Damascus.	Georges-Picot (9 Apr. 1917) Gouraud (8 Oct. 1919)
1920	July: Battle of Maysalun; French occupation of Damascus; flight of Faysal. August–September: formation of Greater Lebanon; state of Aleppo; territory of the ʿAlawis; state of Damascus. To 1921: armed opposition to French rule continues in Alaouites and region of Aleppo. French authority spreads slowly across the mandate territories over the course of the decade.	
1922	March: autonomy of Jabal Druze. June: 'Syrian Federation' links states of Aleppo and Damascus; state of the ʿAlawis (an accidental change of name – and status – for the territory). July: Mandate over Syria and Lebanon granted to France by League of Nations.	

Outline Chronology

Year	Events	High Commissioners
1923		Weygand (19 Apr. 1923)
1924	Syrian Federation replaced by state of Syria (unifying states of Aleppo and Damascus); 'Alawi state autonomous.	
1925	July: 'Druze Revolt' begins; quickly spreads across southern and central Syria and into Lebanon.	Sarrail (2 Jan. 1925)
	October: bombardment of Damascus.	Jouvenel (10 Nov. 1925)
1926–7	Armed insurgency continues to spring 1927; put down by massive reinforcement of French military presence, with much loss of life.	Ponsot (3 Sep. 1926)
1928	April: elections to Constituent Assembly in Syria.	
	Summer: Constituent Assembly meets, draws up constitution that does not acknowledge French presence, is suspended by High Commissioner for six months then *sine die*.	
1930	May: Ponsot permanently dissolves Assembly, promulgates a constitution more acceptable to French.	
1931–2	Parliamentary elections (December–January); negotiations between High Commission and Syrian government for Franco-Syrian treaty begin under Ponsot, but unsuccessfully.	
1933	Negotiations continue under Martel.	Martel (16 Jul. 1933)
	November: draft treaty agreed by Syrian government, text blocked in Parliament. Parliament suspended.	
1934	November: Parliament suspended *sine die*.	
1936	Serious unrest in Damascus and other cities in late winter/spring. France agrees to negotiate treaty with Syrian nationalist delegation, which leaves for Paris in March.	

Year	Events	High Commissioners
(1936 cont'd)	May: Popular Front government in France – a real outcome to negotiations suddenly becomes possible.	
	September: treaty signed. Return of delegation.	
	November: legislative elections.	
	December: Druze and ʿAlawi statelets placed under authority of Damascus by decree of High Commission; National Bloc government of Jamil Mardam Bek takes office; Syrian parliament ratifies Franco-Syrian treaty.	
1937	July: Franco-Turkish agreement on Sanjak of Alexandretta.	
	November: Sanjak of Alexandretta becomes independent from Syria as Republic of Hatay. Still under French mandate, its administration begins to adopt Turkish republican norms (law, currency).	
1938	December: French government refuses to ratify Franco-Syrian treaty.	Puaux (27 Oct. 1938)
1939	February: fall of Mardam Bek government, triggered by controversy over personal status law reform. Syrian politics at crisis point.	
	June: formal end of French mandate in Hatay, which becomes a province of Turkish Republic.	
	July: Druze and ʿAlawi regions return to direct French rule; so does the Jazira. Constitution suspended, parliament dissolved.	
	September: outbreak of Second World War; state of emergency declared in Syria.	

ACKNOWLEDGEMENTS

The main funding for this project was a generous doctoral scholarship from the Carnegie Trust for the Universities of Scotland, supplemented by several helpings of funding for research trips. The master's degree that preceded it was funded by the then Arts and Humanities Research Board; an MA scholarship from the British Society for Middle Eastern Studies allowed me to live a little that academic year. Small grants came from several Oxford sources: the Faculty of Modern History, the Middle East Centre, and St Antony's College. I also benefited from Socrates/Erasmus funding for an academic exchange with the Université de Provence – Aix-Marseille I. I would like to thank all of these funding bodies for their support, and to acknowledge the help of their administrative staff, especially Jackie Gray of the Carnegie Trust.

Several institutions hosted me over the course of my research. In the Oxford Venn diagram I stood at the overlap of the Middle East Centre, St Antony's College, and the Faculty of Modern History. In Aix, I was attached to the Institut de Recherches et d'Études sur le Monde Arabe et Musulman (IREMAM). On two extended trips to Syria I had the good fortune to be a *chercheur associé* at the Institut français du Proche-Orient in Damascus (IFPO-Damas), an invaluable institutional base. In the middle of my doctoral research I was given the opportunity to take a year off and teach at the Department of Islamic and Middle Eastern Studies of the University of Edinburgh. The final year or so of my doctorate was spent in Paris, where I once again found an institutional home, this time the Institut d'histoire du temps présent (IHTP). This book found its publisher while I was back in Edinburgh as a postdoctoral research fellow at the Centre for the Advanced Study of the Arab World; it was completed on another postdoctoral fellowship, in the Department of Near Eastern Studies at Princeton. The academic and administrative staff of all these institutions have my heartfelt gratitude.

My research was carried out at the Centre d'archives diplomatiques, Nantes; the Bibliothèque Nationale de France, Paris; the library of IFPO-Damas; Maktabat al-Asad (the Syrian national library), Damascus; Markaz al-watha'iq al-tarikhiyya (the Historical Documents Centre), Damascus; the Service Historique de l'Armée de Terre, Vincennes; and the Quai d'Orsay. The personnel of the Centre d'archives diplomatiques, the Markaz al-watha'iq al-tarikhiyya, and the IFPO library deserve particular thanks – the latter two not just for their professional assistance but for their endless willingness to clarify linguistic points ('*Su'āl lughawī?*'). I have been fortunate to present my work at a number of seminars and conferences. These are too many to list, but I am grateful for all the helpful suggestions and criticism I have received.

Among my many debts I acknowledge with special gratitude the advice and support of my supervisor, Eugene Rogan, and my examiners, Peter Sluglett and John Darwin. In Britain, I must also thank Judith Brown, John Chalcraft, Carole Hillenbrand, Elisabeth Kendall and Yasir Suleiman. In France, Randi Deguilhem, Gérard Khoury, André Raymond, Nadine Méouchy, Lenka Bokova and Pierre Fournié all offered valuable help. The IHTP offered not just office space, but paid employment once my funding had run out: my thanks go to all its staff, particularly Anne-Marie Pathé and Henry Rousso.

A number of people in Syria helped me directly, by discussing, informing, or facilitating my research. Others helped indirectly: by giving me the benefit of their expertise in Arabic, or listening kindly and patiently to my innumerable stumbling attempts to explain my work in that language; or by informing my understanding of Syria's past by letting me take part in their present. Some of these people are scholars, others are not. In ordinary circumstances, it would have been a pleasure to acknowledge my debts to them individually. However, at the time of writing (May 2011), the political situation in Syria is so uncertain that an association with a foreign historian writing about a touchy subject could carry risks, even when the book concerned stops at the beginning of the Second World War. At risk of excessive caution, then, it seems best to thank these people anonymously.

All of my family and friends (many of whom are, in the way of these things, also academics) have contributed to this book in some way. A full list would be very long, but special thanks go to Andrew Arsan, Timothy Bradford, Andrea Brazzoduro, Jessica Carlisle, Anna Clarke, Yann Gayet, Maggy Hary, Caroline Izambert, John Knight, James McDougall, Jessica Marglin, Karam Nachar, Joe Nankivell, Andrew Newsham, Ana Santos, Marion Slitine, Andromeda Tait, Annie Tindley, Saeko Yazaki and Ben Young. Without Peter Whitby's assistance with computers, this book would have been written by hand. If there's an innermost circle, of close friends who also bore the brunt of discussing and re-reading virtually all of this book, then Seda Altuğ and

Thomas Pierret are in it. I take full responsibility for whatever shortcomings remain.

It is customary for the final acknowledgement to go to one's life partner. Malika Rahal isn't mine, which makes the scale of her contribution over the last few years all the more remarkable. (She did the maps, too.)

INTRODUCTION

Let me start with what this book is not. When I began my research, I planned to study minorities in French mandate Syria. Everyone who had written about the mandate seemed to agree that the French in Syria used the minorities – in some eyes even created them – in order to offset the opposition of the nationalist majority.[1] Studying these communities would therefore allow me to understand better the confrontation between two ideologies that have shaped our time: imperialism and nationalism.

My original plan was to consider several specific minorities, defined along religious or linguistic lines (or both), to see how these different variables affected their relationships with the majority, the nationalists and the imperial power. This would provide insight into the aggressively divisive policies put in place by the French in Syria, and the imperialist conception of the colonised society as hopelessly divided that underpinned those policies. At the same time, it would illuminate the means whereby Syrian Arab nationalism constructed the Syrian Arab nation. While I was sceptical of the imperialist claim that religious or linguistic cleavages in Syrian society were primordial, permanent, and insurmountable, and that religious or linguistic identity determined political identity, I was also aware that such cleavages are not negligible, especially to the development of nationalism. A numerical majority of the inhabitants of the new state were Sunni Muslims, but that majority was divided by language; a numerical majority were Arabic-speakers, but that majority was divided by religion. Sunni Muslim Arabic-speakers – sharing both language and religion – were a numerical majority, but a much smaller one: nationalism would need to appeal beyond this group to achieve a solid base in Syrian society. Since French imperialism imposed divisions on that society precisely to hinder the appeal of nationalism outside this group, examining Syrian Arab nationalist responses to those divisions – whether seeking to reassure minorities of their place within the nation, on the one hand, or threatening them, even denying their existence, on the other – would help us understand how the ideology functioned. Such a study would thus find its place in the comparative history of both imperialism and nationalism.[2]

I still think that such a study would be a good idea. This book, however, is not quite it. It does answer some of my original questions about how different variables affected the position of different minorities relative to the French and to the nationalists; but my underlying research questions slowly shifted, because quite early on in my archival research I noticed something unusual. The secondary literature about French mandate Syria used the term 'minority' freely, and confidently attributed analytical force to it: certain groups behaved in such a way because they were 'minorities'. But in the archives of the French mandate themselves, and in other contemporary texts on the mandate, it was used fairly infrequently until around 1930 – when it quickly became very widespread. This provoked two questions: when did people start thinking of themselves or others as 'minorities', and for that matter as 'majorities'? And why?

I therefore put inverted commas around both terms, so to speak, and my research project changed. Using French mandate Syria as a case study, I now hoped to trace the emergence of these categories and understand the historical context that made them meaningful – which, I have come to conclude, is the context of the modern nation-state: states with a supposedly eternal 'national' territory over which state authority is uniformly applied, and deriving their legitimacy from some version of the principle of representativity expressed in the claim to share a cultural identity with a numerical majority of their population. The book that I have actually written is not about minorities, as such: it does not explain how minority X was instrumentalised by the French, or how minority Y resisted the High Commission's blandishments and rallied to Syrian Arab nationalism. Instead, it explains why, and when, certain groups within Syria – a nation-state in formation – came to be described, by insiders and outsiders, as 'minorities', and what that meant. By the same token, it traces the emergence of the concept of 'majority' in the country. These two paired concepts are frequently used by historians (and others) to describe the societies we study, but they may be misleading: they deserve to be critically analysed.

The book argues that it is anachronistic to understand the communitarian politics of French mandate Syria in terms of minorities and a majority: doing so implies the prior existence of a Syrian Arab nation-state with a coherent majority. The definition of the Syrian state's territory, its binding together as a coherent unit[3] by common institutions, and its separation from surrounding areas by the new borders that partitioned the recently vanished Ottoman Empire were all developments of the mandate period, and gradual developments at that. As Syria passed from being part of a non-national dynastic empire whose legitimacy still derived chiefly from the maintenance of a religious order, to being a nation-state that was supposed to represent its population, a fundamental redefinition of the state took place. Until these changes were at least partly accepted by the population, the idea of a single group constituting (and constituting itself as) a 'majority' with a right to dominate 'Syria' is questionable.

As we have seen, Sunni Muslim Arabic-speakers were a numerical majority in Syria as a whole. But it is hard to argue from first principles the existence of a Sunni Muslim Arabic-speaking majority in any meaningful political sense. During the mandate period, that numerical majority might include a notable in Aleppo, whose political loyalty was to the Ottoman caliphate; a preacher in Dayr al-Zur, who wanted his town to be detached from Syria and incorporated into an Iraqi nation-state; still another in Homs arguing for Islam as the basis of state law in Syria not because Muslims outnumbered non-Muslims in the state, but simply because Islam was the true religion and only legitimate source of law; or a nomad in the Syrian desert, who regarded the settled population as legitimate prey. We will meet some of them, not just at the outset of the mandate period but well into the 1930s. The fact that they happened to speak (dialects of) a common language and share certain tenets of religious faith did not automatically make them fellow members of a coherent Syrian majority. Only when the developing Syrian state came to enframe the political ambitions of these different actors, and nationalist ideology constituted them as a single group within the state, did some Syrians begin to harness their political ambitions to the term 'majority'. And when they did, their definitions of it differed, and may have been contradictory, because the majority they usually identified tended to be either Arab, including diverse religious groups, or Sunni, including speakers of several languages. Even then, whether the 'majority' existed as anything other than a politically useful fiction may be questioned.

It was the development of the nation-state form in the mandate period, I argue, that made the concepts of 'minority' and 'majority' meaningful in Syria. But if the communitarian nature of French policy in Syria is widely recognised in the literature, the modernity – and historical contingency – of the concept of 'minority' are not. Works that clearly grasp and express this are rare.[4] One reason for this is that by the time the mandate ended, the concept was well developed in Syria: even works written soon afterwards, by observers who had experienced Syria under the mandate, adopted it to understand the functioning of mandatory rule – not just in its final decade, when the term had certainly achieved widespread currency, but from the start.[5] (For that matter, primary sources from the later mandate period do the same thing.) Since the concept retains its power in the societies from which modern historians and social scientists come, Syrians included, they too have used it. But, as I will argue, adopting these terms and attributing analytical force to them masks the very important development that was the creation of a modern nation-state in Syria. This is by no means unique to the Syrian case: as soon as it had emerged, the concept was being projected back into the past in all sorts of cases. My argument concerns not only the French mandate in Syria, but also the comparative study of minorities.

In the first instance, then, the aim of the book is to refine our understanding of the politics of community in Syria under the mandate. But it will become clear that attempting to understand why the concept of minority came into widespread use has led me to concentrate on the form and practices of the modern state, and the responses they engendered among Syrian society – without taking these forms and practices for granted, or making prior assumptions about the responses they provoked. In this I join some of the recent scholarship on the Levant in modern times.[6] Keith Watenpaugh's work on Aleppo examines the effect of modernity on the 'architecture of community' in the city during and before the mandate period; Ussama Makdisi's work on Ottoman Lebanon, too, looks at the effects of modern state-building on communal identity. Both see modern communal identities as having been in many senses produced, and certainly profoundly altered, by modern state development – not as primordial 'givens' snarling this process.[7]

Beyond its examination of the Syrian case, I hope that my specific focus on the aspects of modern state development that give meaning to the concept of 'minority' will provide a robust and generalisable analytical framework for comparative study.[8] This, I hope, will function on two levels and overcome several kinds of exceptionalism. First, it allows existing studies that concentrate on particular minorities in the Middle East to be incorporated into a single framework.[9] There are good reasons for concentrating on a specific community, but too narrow a focus may encourage one kind of exceptionalism: the assumption that the minority under study is exceptional in the way they have related to the state(s) in which they live. An extreme form of this is the 'nation denied' model, in which the minority is taken to constitute a nation in the exceptional situation of having been – unlike its oppressors – denied the state that every nation should have by right. This is a model that accepts nationalist ideology from the outset, and typically examines its subject in comparison only with 'nations' that do have states.[10] Without wanting to deny the specificity of different minorities, it is both possible and useful to draw a sustained comparison between them.

Doing so illuminates similar processes of state development in the region, and allows us to see not only that individual minorities are not exceptional for having been deprived of a state, but also that minorities themselves are not exceptional. Minorities are integral to the development of modern nation-states, not awkward groups that do not properly fit into them. Meanwhile, by examining the emergence of minorities and majorities as a dynamic, dialectical process, this framework avoids the primordialism which underpins bad scholarship in this field and often creeps even into good. A glance at some of the more tendentious works available shows that this is an effort worth making.[11]

The second level for comparative study is that of nation-state development under different conditions and in different states, not only in the Middle East: the framework I propose can be applied to the emergence of minorities (and thus to the development of states) anywhere. A particularly useful comparison would be between nation-state formation in the Levant, under mandate, and the contemporary formation of nation-states in eastern and central Europe. To take only one obvious example, the role of the debate about treaty guarantees for minorities in the construction of both minorities and a majority, studied here with reference to the Franco-Syrian treaty, could very well be compared with the debate about the minorities treaties in European states. Here, too, a kind of exceptionalism is avoided: the notion that the Middle East is an exception in the number, treatment, or sensitivity of its minorities.

So the book is not, in the end, about the confrontation of French imperialism and Syrian Arab nationalism. But in an indirect way it contributes to our understanding of them. The development of the nation-state form in Syria placed constraints on the French, but it also opened up opportunities for them. It certainly affected the intersection of French imperial policy and the politics of community in Syria. At the same time, the book proposes a way of studying the development of nationalism from outside the ideology itself, but inside the state-form that gives it meaning.

Major Sources

The most important archives for the study of the French mandate in Syria are those of the High Commission. Since the High Commission belonged to the Ministère des Affaires étrangères, these are now held at the Centre d'archives diplomatiques in Nantes. Inevitably, they are incomplete: apart from the ordinary work of triage carried out by archivists at the time, substantial portions of the Commission's records – especially on political affairs in the 1930s – were deliberately destroyed by the Vichy High Commissioner, Dentz, on the approach of Free French and British forces in 1941; more were lost at the mandate's end during the inelegant French withdrawal. Some may yet be found.[12]

Nonetheless, the surviving records amount to thousands of boxes: the richest available source for the mandate 'on the ground', so to speak. This book is concerned with the institutional restructuring of the Syrian state that took place under the supervision of the High Commission, and how Syrian society responded; the material contained in the archives on the relationship between the mandatory authorities and the society they sought to rule over is therefore extremely valuable. It gives a good picture of French official thinking on specific policies – why this administrative division was desirable, why that reform was necessary – and specific problems – what to do about refugees, how to deal with Turkish complaints about the border. From these a broader picture emerges, both of the general framework of the mandate and its institutions and of the set of attitudes that underlay French policy. In some senses the most informative aspect of the records may be the gaps in them – by which I mean not the lacunae resulting from loss or destruction, but the things that French officials chose not to say, or did not even think of saying. To take one highly pertinent example, documents on a startling diversity of subjects find it necessary to emphasise the absence of unity in Syrian society, its 'non-nationness'; the language of minorities, when it developed, fitted neatly into this rhetoric. But to my knowledge, no mandate functionary ever questioned the (eminently questionable) unity or nationhood of French society. This dichotomy deserves comment as one of the clearest signs of the category distinction French officials made between colonising and colonisable societies – a distinction that historians should not reproduce. It also has implications for our understanding of the imperial project as a unifying factor in French politics and society, at a time when these were riven by deep divisions.[13]

Syrians, meanwhile, left an impression on the French archives both indirectly and directly. Most of the material generated by the mandate administration naturally related to the administration of the mandate: that is, the government of Syrians. Government is never frictionless, however much governments might wish that it were. We can therefore learn a lot about how Syrians dealt with the mandatory authorities from the records the latter kept. Syrians figured constantly in French considerations, especially (but not only) when they objected to the way in which they were being governed. Much of the material in the French archives, however, was generated by Syrians directly: letters, petitions, newspaper articles. Crucially, then, the archives can tell us how Syrians presented themselves politically, whether to the High Commission or to the League of Nations – how they understood their own society.

There are reservations, of course. The archives were constructed subjectively, and may tell us more about who the French wanted to listen to than about who was actually important: one might cite the extraordinary prominence of the Christian patriarchs as the High Commission's favoured interlocutors among the Christian communities, or the near absence of sustained correspondence with Muslim religious figures. Also, how people presented themselves and their communities to the authorities was not necessarily how they presented themselves to other Syrians. A nationalist politician might address the High Commission on behalf of a Syrian Arab nation, but to an assembly at a Damascus mosque as a Muslim defending Islam: pitching oneself correctly to an audience is neither unusual nor blameworthy. In particular, we should be very careful, for example, when reading the account given of his community by a Kurdish notable, an Orthodox patriarch, a Catholic deputy, or a nationalist journalist not to assume that we are getting an image of it that its members would recognise. Again, the most informative aspect of the records may be the gaps in them. Still, such reservations must be brought to any historical source; they are what permits meaningful analysis, and despite their blank spots the High Commission archives provide plenty of material to digest.[14]

The other main French public archives for the Mandate are at La Courneuve and Vincennes. While Nantes holds the High Commission's archives, including material received from the ministry in Paris, the new archival centre at La Courneuve holds material generated by the ministry itself. However, the collection here is also incomplete. Most importantly, almost all political documentation for the period 1932–40 was destroyed on the orders of the ministry's secretary-general ahead of the German occupation of Paris;[15] this includes all the ministry's records of the 1936 negotiations for a Franco-Syrian treaty, which would have been especially valuable to this book. In the end, since the archives at Nantes contained so much – including duplicates of much of what is held in Paris – for diplomatic material I concentrated on the archives there.

The archives of the Service Historique de l'Armée de Terre at Vincennes are another matter. Again, there are gaps: in this case, not material that was destroyed prior to an enemy advance, but rather material that was not destroyed in time. Tens of thousands of boxes, including some from the Armée du Levant in Syria, were seized by the Germans and taken to Berlin, from where they were taken to the Soviet Union at the end of the Second World War. Post-Cold War diplomatic agreements saw some, but not all, of this material returned to France.[16] The division between military and political affairs is not entirely clear for the French mandate: on the one hand, the Armée du Levant was under the orders of the High Commission, which belonged to the Ministère des Affaires étrangères; on the other hand, many of the mandate's French functionaries (especially its intelligence officers), not to mention several High Commissioners, were army officers on secondment.[17] In theory, at least, documents relating to the political and diplomatic aspects of the military's role in Syria were archived by the High Commission; the military archives received material, above all, on operational matters.[18] This proved very useful, especially for understanding the slow spread of French authority into remoter areas of the mandate territories, or the recruitment and functioning of troops from 'minority' communities.

If the French archives for the mandate are characterised by large gaps, the Syrian archives for the period are more gap than archive. The Historical Documents Centre (*Markaz al-wathā'iq al-tārīkhiyya*) in Damascus has remarkably complete records for the Ottoman period, and much less for the post-Ottoman period.[19] The holdings for the mandate are patchy and unsystematic. However, they represent a vital complement to the French archives, since only here are any substantial records held for the Syrian administration as opposed to the High Commission – and most of the business of government was done by a Syrian bureaucracy, police force, gendarmerie and judiciary, even if the hands of French advisers were heavily felt. Where records survive, then, they provide important information about the bureaucratic and institutional 'shape' of the Syrian state under French rule. From Damascene police reports, provincial governors writing to the interior ministry, or officials on a tour of inspection in rural areas, we can gain a valuable picture of the ways in which the state apparatus touched the lives of Syrians across the country – despite the unsystematic nature of the collection, and even when the reasons why such items were kept are not the reasons why they are interesting today. For example, barely any of what must have been a mountain of daily reports produced by the police stations in Damascus have survived. To judge from markings in blue pencil on those that did, the reason why a few were kept was because they were from days when (presumably nationalist) activists had disrupted the foreign-owned tramway. But those few are enough to give us useful information: they tell us where the city's police stations were, and that the General Police Directorate (*Mudīriyyat al-shurta al-cāmma*) collated information on the crimes and misdemeanours with which each station dealt; they describe some of those incidents, from stabbings to public drunkenness, brawls to rapes, or the murder of a baby girl; they give a vague idea of how the police dealt with each one – for example, when someone had been injured they usually noted how long their recovery was expected to take.[20]

Frequently, then, such documents can shine a narrowly focused but intense beam of light on a particular subject. For someone trying to write a narrative history of some aspect of Syrian life under mandate, the scant and arbitrary nature of these sources might be frustrating, like trying to perceive the design of a vast mosaic from spots of torchlight falling here and there on random clusters of tesserae. But for this book, which concentrates on general, structural aspects of state development in Syria, the information in these sources may prove more illuminating – as the same torch, shone around the room, might at least tell you where the walls and ceiling are.

The most important of my published sources is the Syrian nationalist press of the mandate period. I will begin with some reservations about the usefulness of this source for this project: these will help identify where it can indeed be useful. First, at the risk of stating the obvious, newspapers are much better at telling us what journalists and editors thought than what opinions were widely held in society. I would nuance Souheil al-Malazi's assessment that the nationalist press 'bore on its shoulders the mission of expressing the wishes of the people, and their desire for freedom':[21] this was the vision that the press had of itself. What readers really thought is harder to say; what the illiterate majority thought, who heard the news read aloud, or by word of mouth, or not at all, harder still. Historical work on the press in the Middle East has tended to concentrate on production and to neglect reception: more attention has been given to what journalists wrote than to those who read their articles, and how they read them – which is, of course, much harder to study.[22] The press was also heavily centred on the cities, and especially Damascus: of daily and weekly titles appearing in Syria during the mandate, more than half were published in Damascus, and more than half of the remainder in Aleppo.[23] The audience that nationalist journalists claimed to be addressing was Syrian, but in reality most of their readership was concentrated in Damascus and a few other cities, where nationalist feeling was strongest and most articulate. Again, this is not to dismiss nationalist claims automatically as untrue; but they should be understood as claims, not verities. It is prudent to assume that rather than expressing the wishes of the nation entire, nationalist newspapers reflected the views of an urban, nationalist public.

It was initially frustrating to realise that nationalist newspapers were chiefly useful as a source for the study of nationalist discourse, which was not my subject. But, as my interest in state development grew, it became clearer that the nationalist press could be a valuable source for understanding how an ideology can be used to harness the state, how the modern state apparatus, in turn, lends itself to the ideology of nationalism, and how the two together transform the relationship between state, society, and territory in ways that are directly relevant to the emergence of minorities. The enormous abundance of documentation, combined (paradoxically) with patchy coverage, meant that a systematic survey was neither feasible nor necessarily useful. Instead, I identified particular periods and subjects which were likely to offer an illumination of nationalist attitudes on the minorities question: these included the great revolt of the mid-1920s; the treaty negotiations of 1933–6; the Alexandretta crisis, a little later; the arrival of refugees from Turkey in the 1920s and from Iraq in the 1930s.

I read articles on these subjects taken from a number of different titles, selected because all – by the standards of the time – had a relatively large circulation and influence.[24] For the early mandate years I used material from *al-Muqtabas*, the newspaper founded by Muhammad Kurd 'Ali in the late Ottoman period and edited during the mandate by his brother Ahmad. After its closure in 1928 it was replaced by *al-Qabas*, whose editor, Najib al-Rayyis, stayed close to the National Bloc until the end of the 1930s.[25] A harder line of nationalism was represented by *al-Ayyām*, which at its founding in 1931 was also associated with the Bloc, but moved into the Shahbandarist nationalist opposition from 1935;[26] while a more inclusive understanding of the Syrian nation emerged from *Alif Bā'*, the 'semi-official daily newspaper of Damascus'.[27] Since my understanding of the 'minorities question' changed so radically in the course of my research, I have used less of this material in the book than I expected – mostly as it related to the question of a Syrian national territory. But I derived from it a much keener awareness of the ideology of Syrian Arab nationalism, and of the functioning of nationalist ideology in general, with all its inevitable contradictions and *non dits*.

French published sources, meanwhile, also became less relevant than I had expected as my research questions shifted away from French imperialism and more towards the nation-state form in Syria. Nonetheless, a range of books and articles published by French writers during, and about, the mandate were important for a wider understanding of French imperialist attitudes to Syrian society, the place of the Syrian mandate in French conceptions of empire and the place of empire in modern French politics and society. So, too, were the debates about Syria in the French National Assembly, set down in the *Journal officiel* – and the rarity of those debates. On some subjects, notably the question of Franco-Syrian treaty negotiations and their role in the more systematic application in Syria of the concept of 'minority', this material is clearly present in the finished book: I consider at length the changing use of the concept in the colonialist bulletin *L'Asie française*, which I surveyed for the entire inter-war period. But even material that in the end went unused nonetheless influenced my thinking throughout.

French High Commissioners, 1920–39

Although this is not a diplomatic history of the mandate, I refer to the senior French officials frequently enough to make a brief overview of the successive High Commissioners worthwhile.

The first French High Commissioner to rule over Damascus as well as Beirut was General Gouraud. He was the first of three military High Commissioners, being replaced by generals Weygand (from April 1923 to November 1924) and Sarrail (until November 1925). Sarrail, whose time in office was terminated after the outbreak of the great revolt, was succeeded by a civilian, Henry de Jouvenel. Jouvenel stayed an even shorter time in Beirut, returning to France to pursue his political career in September 1926.

The first years of the mandate were thus marked by a rapid turnover of High Commissioners: it was not until Jouvenel's successor, Henri Ponsot, arrived in Beirut that some administrative stability was reached at the High Commission. Ponsot stayed in office for seven years, until July 1933; his replacement, Damien de Martel, stayed in office for over five, retiring in October 1938. The fact that he retired, rather than being recalled, marks a contrast to the political turmoil of the High Commission in the 1920s. The final High Commissioner to govern in the period of this study was Martel's replacement, Gabriel Puaux, who was in office when the Second World War began.[28] After the fall of France a Vichy administration was put in place, but expelled by a joint British/Free French invasion in 1941; thereafter, nominal authority rested with the ranking French officer in Beirut, but a 'fake' independence was granted to Syria and Lebanon in 1943, while actual authority rested with the all-too-real British military occupation. It is because of this extreme political complexity that I chose to focus – other things being equal – on the inter-war years.

It should be noted that the relative stability at the High Commission in the 'long' decade of 1927–38 is in sharp contrast to the tumultuous comings and goings of governments in the metropole, in perhaps the most divided and unstable period of modern French politics.[29] The point made by Andrew and Kanya-Forster about the Third Republic before the First World War is worth bearing in mind for the inter-war period also:

> The ministries of the Third Republic, often precarious, usually preoccupied by domestic affairs, rarely attempted to impose Cabinet control over foreign and colonial policy. Major decisions could be taken by a single minister and approved by Cabinet without serious discussion, or even implemented without Cabinet approval at all. Ministerial instability sometimes left the permanent officials in control of policy . . .[30]

Administrative Divisions

French rule in Syria was marked throughout by a policy of territorial division: what Syrians referred to as *tamzīq* or *tajzi'a*. In July 1920, Robert de Caix, the colonial lobbyist turned mandate official, suggested dividing the mandate territories – an area smaller than mainland Britain – into as many as eleven statelets.[31] The next month, the most important and lasting division was made: Greater Lebanon, a much-expanded version of the Ottoman autonomous district of Mount Lebanon, was declared. The existence of Lebanon and Syria as separate entities was enshrined by the mandate charter itself in 1922; all the other divisions imposed on the mandate territories were within the newly constituted 'Syria', and all but one proved to be temporary (see Map 1, p. vi, which shows the most important divisions for this book).

The 'Syria' of the mandate charter had already been divided into several constituent parts. The main body of the interior was made up of the states of Damascus and Aleppo, while the coastal mountains between the Lebanese border and Latakia, which had been under French occupation for longer than Damascus, were also constituted as a separate statelet. I will refer to this simply as the Alaouites, as French officials often did, and presumably for the same reason: to avoid confusion over that statelet's multiple changes of name: Territoire des Alaouites; État des Alaouites; Gouvernement de Lattaquié, when the French wanted to de-emphasise the statelet's communitarian basis; État des Alaouites again, when they wanted to re-emphasise it.[32] Using the French term also avoids confusion between the statelet itself and the ʿAlawis who made up most of its population.

To these three, another was added in 1922 when the Jabal Druze was detached from the state of Damascus. The states of Damascus and Aleppo were united from the beginning of 1925 as the state of Syria. The other two statelets, however, remained administratively separate until the 1940s, with the exception of the years of nationalist rule, 1936–9, when they were placed under the authority of the Syrian government in Damascus. I discuss the grounds on which these divisions were made, including the presence in the coastal mountains and the Jabal Druze of what have been termed 'compact minorities', in Chapters 2 and 3.

When looking at the map of these divisions, two important caveats should be borne in mind. First, for most of its length, the neat line of Syria's external border existed only on maps in the early years of the mandate. For much of its length, this remained true for decades. Secondly, the impression a map gives of a stable geographical unit under the uniform authority of a state – never a wholly accurate reflection of reality – is particularly misleading here: for example, permanent French military posts and regular patrols in the north-eastern regions of Syria began only in the later 1920s, in some zones even the 1930s. That these two points are related should be evident; Chapters 3 and 4 investigate them in depth.

Several subdivisions within the state of Syria should also be mentioned. First, the uncultivated steppe of the Syrian desert was administered, to the extent that it was administered at all, by the military Contrôle Bédouin.[33] The Sanjak of Alexandretta, although part of the state of Aleppo and then Syria, had autonomous status because it was home to a substantial Turkish-speaking community; Turkish was an official language there, alongside French and Arabic. In 1936, while the autonomous statelets of the Alaouites and the Jabal Druze came under the authority of a Syrian government for the first time, the Sanjak of Alexandretta's gradual, permanent detachment from Syria began: the combination of pressure from Turkey and the increasingly Turkish nationalist outlook of the sanjak's Turkish-speakers[34] led first to its becoming 'independent', then to its annexation by Turkey. Many of its Arab and virtually all of its Armenian inhabitants fled in the process. Finally, by the mid-1930s the far northeast of Syria – the Jazira – was both more firmly fixed under state authority and considerably more populous as a result of immigration by Kurds and Christians fleeing Turkey and Christians fleeing Iraq. This influx, with French support, had also transformed the region's economy. The Haute-Djézireh or upper Jazira was therefore upgraded to a full governorate. The inhabitants of the region were not, however, keen to be placed under the authority of the Syrian government in Damascus in 1936; in 1939, when the Druze and 'Alawi statelets were 'de-incorporated' from Syria, the Jazira too was placed under direct French control as an autonomous region.

Despite these divisions, the state apparatus put in place by the French was in many ways unified: within Syria as a whole Damascus was the 'senior' city; if the various statelets each had their own flag, their inhabitants shared a common, Syrian nationality, as well as a common currency and a common external tariff.[35] As I argue throughout the book, both implicitly and explicitly, if the French did their best to hinder the development of a 'nation' in Syria, they were nonetheless obliged to construct a state: the tension between these two aims ran through the mandate period. Politics in Syria under the mandate was largely a contest over control of that state apparatus. Syrian Arab nationalists wanted to control the entire state apparatus, and in the period 1936–9 they were permitted to – up to a point. Syrians who favoured cooperation with the French, and opposed the nationalists, were also usually concerned with controlling the state apparatus, or at least the part of it that touched them. As a mandate state, Syria was meant to be an expression of its inhabitants' right to self-determination – a nation-state, even if the identity of the Syrian nation remained to be defined.

A word about the 'ordinary' administrative subdivisions within Syria: the state was divided into governorates (*muḥāfadha*) and sanjaks, which were further divided by caza (*qadḥā'*) and district (*nāhiya*). The senior local official at each level was the governor (*muḥāfidh*) for governorates and sanjaks, the *qā'immaqām* for cazas and the *mudīr* for districts. Future instances of these words will be written without italics or diacritics.

Structure

The book is divided into three parts. In Part I (Chapters 1 and 2), I make a general argument then apply it to French mandate Syria; in Parts II (Chapters 3 and 4) and III (Chapters 5 and 6), I offer specific case studies illustrating the argument. Since the structure of this book is thematic, not narrative, an outline chronology is included for quick reference (see p. viii).

Chapter 1 explains the circumstances in which the concept of minority emerged in international public discourse, as the nation-state became the standard state form after the First World War. Having identified the historical origins of the concept, it shows how its usage has escaped those origins – to the detriment of its analytical usefulness. It explains why minority is a distinctively modern concept, and outlines various aspects of modern nation-state development which give it meaning.

Chapter 2 reconsiders the concept's place in the history and historiography of the French mandate in Syria. While French policy in Syria was certainly divisive, simply describing it as 'divide-and-rule' and assuming that the divisions involved were those between a majority and minorities is not satisfactory. The mandatory authorities certainly saw many divisions in Syrian society and sought to exploit and exacerbate them, but the category of 'minority' was not systematically attached to those divisions – not at first, at least, and in some cases hardly at all. By outlining how certain groups came to be identified as 'minorities' (or not), the chapter offers an insight into French imperialist attitudes towards Syrian society and the groups within it, and the policies that those attitudes informed. It also broaches the question of why the category came into use, contrasting it to the older Ottoman category of *millet* or religious community,[36] and links my general argument in Chapter 1 to its specific application in Syria.

Part I thus establishes my general analytical framework (Chapter 1) and the parameters of my specific empirical enquiry (Chapter 2). The rest of the book presents four thematic chapters, each offering a case study of one aspect of state development in French mandate Syria to illustrate how that development led to the emergence of 'minorities'. They form two pairs. Part II considers the development of a coherent national territory in Syria, taking a critical look at the question of separatism (Chapter 3) and the definition of the state's borders (Chapter 4). Part III addresses the transformation of the post-Ottoman state's legal institutions. First, it considers the development of a new body of international law regarding minorities, and the debate over its application to Syria (Chapter 5). Then, it examines France's multiple failed attempts to reform personal status law in Syria (Chapter 6), showing how legal change – even abortive legal change – encouraged some actors to see themselves as 'minorities', and others to present themselves for the first time as representatives of a 'majority'.

Notes

1. Philip S. Khoury, *Syria and the French Mandate: The Politics of Arab Nationalism, 1920–1945* (London: I. B. Tauris, 1987), p. 58; Michael Provence, *The Great Syrian Revolt and the Rise of Arab Nationalism* (Austin, TX: University of Texas Press, 2005), p. 50. The same interpretation can be found in textbooks: Robert Aldrich, *Greater France. A History of French Overseas Expansion* (London: Palgrave, 1996), pp. 208–12; William L. Cleveland, *A History of the Modern Middle East*, 3rd edn (Oxford: Westview Press, 2004), pp. 218–23. See also Chapter 2.
2. My main, well-founded worry was that the focus on minorities might lead some to assume a prejudged hostility on my part towards Syrian nationalism in particular. Nationalist claims deserve to be examined with the same sceptical inquisitiveness wherever they are made.
3. Despite the administrative divisions imposed by the French, see below.
4. Among them are Elie Kedourie, 'Ethnicity, majority, and minority in the Middle East', on the concept in general, and Nelida Fuccaro, 'Minorities and ethnic mobilisation: the Kurds in northern Iraq and Syria', on a specific minority.
5. Albert H. Hourani, *Syria and Lebanon: A Political Essay* (Oxford: Oxford University Press, 1946), and on the Arab world more generally *Minorities in the Arab World* (London: Oxford University Press, 1947); Stephen H. Longrigg, *Syria and Lebanon under French Mandate* (London: Oxford University Press, 1958).
6. Deserving mention here is the research programme on the mandates at the Institut français d'études arabes de Damas in the late 1990s and early 2000s which resulted in the publication of two substantial collective works edited by Nadine Méouchy and Peter Sluglett (see Bibliography).
7. Keith D. Watenpaugh, *Being Modern in the Middle East. Revolution, Nationalism,*

Colonialism, and the Arab Middle Class (Princeton, NJ: Princeton University Press, 2006); Ussama Makdisi, *The Culture of Sectarianism: Community, History, and Violence in Nineteenth-century Ottoman Lebanon* (London: University of California Press, 2000), and 'Ottoman orientalism', *The American Historical Review* (2002), 107(3) (accessed online), on Ottoman modernity more generally.

8. This was refined by my discussions with participants at a 'thematic conversation' I organised at the Middle East Studies Association's annual conferences in 2006 and 2007, and a panel I ran at the British Society for Middle Eastern Studies annual conference in 2005, both under the title 'Majorities and minorities in the Middle East and North Africa'.

9. Such studies are numerous. Examples that are particularly relevant to the Syrian case include David McDowall, *A Modern History of the Kurds*, 3rd rev. edn (London: I. B. Tauris, 2004); or Khaldun S. Husry, 'The Assyrian Affair of 1933' (I and II), *International Journal of Middle East Studies* (1974), 5(2): 161–76, and 5(3): 344–60, and Sami Zubaida, 'Contested nations: Iraq and the Assyrians', *Nations and nationalism* (2000), 6(3): 363–82.

10. The term comes from the title of David McDowall, *The Kurds: A Nation Denied* (London: Minority Rights Group, 1992), though his *A Modern History of the Kurds* is somewhat more careful in its assumptions.

11. Such as Mordechai Nisan, *Minorities in the Middle East : A History of Struggle and Self-expression* (Jefferson, NC: McFarland, 1991).

12. Pierre Fournié and François-Xavier Trégan, 'Outils documentaires sur le mandat français', in Méouchy and Sluglett (eds), *The British and French Mandates*, pp. 45–53.

13. As Rod Kedward puts it, 'Colonialism was universally projected in France as an epic adventure in the realization and growth of French identity ... The level of tacit agreement on colonial matters in the period 1900–1914, and well beyond, was itself a rare facet of French political life.' *La vie en bleu: France and the French since 1900*, paperback edn (London: Penguin, 2006), p. 15.

14. From the point of view of this book, perhaps the most frustratingly absent records are those of the High Commissioner's representatives – delegates, assistant delegates, or governors – in Damascus, Aleppo, Latakia and Suwayda'. We have some of what they sent to Beirut, but nothing that they produced for internal consumption, or preferred not to forward.

15. This was Aléxis Léger, better known today as the poet Saint-John Perse.

16. Martin C. Thomas, 'French intelligence-gathering in the Syrian mandate, 1920–40', *Middle Eastern Studies* (2002), 38(1): 1–32, quote at 2. (The fact that the partial return amounted to 40,000 boxes shows the size of the original haul.)

17. A prosopography of the Service des renseignements du Levant is contained in Jean-David Mizrahi, *Genèse de l'État mandataire. Services des Renseignements en Syrie et au Liban dans les années 1920* (Paris: Publications de la Sorbonne, 2003), pp. 183–288.

18. See introduction to the inventory of Archives du Levant, sub-series 4 H (1917–46).

19. At the time of my research in Damascus the Centre's staff had recently prepared an archival law, the country's first, for the Syrian administration. Whether it would be passed, or, having been passed, applied, was not certain.
20. A number of such reports can be found in MWT, *wathā'iq al-dawla*, sijill 2, under *wizārat al-dākhiliyya – al-amn al-ʿāmm – taqārīr*. The murder of a baby girl, whose body was found in a garden off Baghdad Street, is recorded on 5 September 1936 in a report under call number 6.
21. Souheil al-Malazi, *al-Tabāʿa wal-sihāfa fi Halab* (Damascus: Dār Yaʿrub lil-dirāsāt, 1996), p. 198 – nonetheless a valuable work, particularly on technical questions and on the role of the Armenian community in the Aleppo press.
22. Ami Ayalon's work is a very honourable exception.
23. Shams al-Dīn al-Rifāʿī, *Tārīkh al-sihāfa al-sūriyya, al-juz' al-thānī: al-intidāb al-faransī hattā al-istiqlāl, 1918–1947* (Cairo: Dār al-Maʿārif, 1969), pp. 161–4.
24. Ami Ayalon, *The Press in the Arab Middle East: A History* (Oxford: Oxford University Press, 1995), ch. 6. Nasir Denaria's help in locating these articles, among stacks of bound volumes and kilometres of microfilm, was invaluable.
25. Najib al-Rayyis, *Yā dhalām al-sijn (1920–1952). Al-aʿmāl al-mukhtāra 1* (London: Riad el-Rayyes, 1994), p. 27 (introduction by Jūzīf Ilyās).
26. Khoury, *Syria and the French Mandate*, pp. 269, 573. The newspaper introduces itself in its first issue: *al-Ayyām*, 10 May 1931.
27. Khoury, *Syria and the French Mandate*, p. 136. After discussing a fiery article from *al-Ayyām* with me, one of my (Christian) teachers in Damascus said he understood why his father preferred *Alif Bā'*.
28. A complete list of French High Commissioners and their dates in office can be found in the introduction to SHAT, *Inventaire des archives du Levant. Sous-série 4 H (1917–1946)*, the source for dates in this paragraph. These reflect the official period in office; in practice, High Commissioners usually arrived in Beirut some time after their appointment – Puaux was appointed in October 1938 but did not reach Lebanon until early January 1939.
29. 'Fifteen cabinets under the presidency of Gaston Doumergue, 1924–1931; three in the eleven months of Paul Doumer's presidency before his murder in 1932; seventeen under Albert Lebrun, between 1932 and 1940 – though only eleven prime ministers and ten ministers of foreign affairs led the musical chairs.' Eugen Weber, *The Hollow Years: France in the 1930s* (London: Sinclair-Stevenson, 1995) p. 111.
30. C. M. Andrew and A. K. Kanya-Forstner, 'The French "colonial party": its composition, aims and influence, 1885–1914', *The Historical Journal* (1971) 14(1): 99–128 at 127.
31. Turkish- and Kurdish-speaking zones, a Lebanese statelet, and 'eight or nine autonomies' in the remainder. Gérard D. Khoury, *Une tutelle coloniale: le mandat français en Syrie et au Liban. Ecrits politiques de Robert de Caix* (Paris: Éditions Bélin, 2006), pp. 248–70, quote at 261.
32. On one occasion its name changed by accident: the High Commissioner's decree of 28 June 1922 linking the statelets of Syria as a federation mentioned an État des

Alaouites that did not exist – the entity concerned was the *Territoire* des Alaouites. The High Commission noticed its mistake the next month and issued another decree retrospectively upgrading the territory to a state as of 28 June (Takla 2004: 80).

33. Khoury, *Syria and the French Mandate*, pp. 58–9; Thomas, 'French intelligence-gathering'.
34. This should not be taken for granted. In the 1920s the sanjak was a refuge for Turks loyal to the vanished Ottoman Empire and opposed to Mustafa Kemal's nationalist republic. In other parts of northern Syria, notably the city of Aleppo, substantial turcophone communities became increasingly Arabised during the mandate as Syrians.
35. In the words of Roger Owen and Şevket Pamuk, 'from an economic point of view . . . the whole area [of 'Syria'] was governed more or less as a single unit'. *A History of the Middle East Economies in the Twentieth Century* (London: I. B. Tauris, 1998), p. 64.
36. The term can refer to Muslims, but by the nineteenth century this was not the normal usage. Later instances of this word will not be italicised. It is pronounced *mil-LET*.

PART I

CHAPTER

1

MINORITIES, MAJORITIES AND THE NATION-STATE

Introduction

The eleventh edition of the *Encyclopaedia Britannica*, published in 1910–11, does not contain an entry for 'minorities'. By the fourteenth edition of 1929 the entry on minorities runs to eleven pages, mostly discussing the post-First World War peace settlements and the League of Nations.

Minorities seem to have come out of nowhere; or rather, the term 'minority' does. As late as 1914 it hardly existed in its modern sense of a group 'distinguished by common ties of descent, physical appearance, language, culture or religion, in virtue of which they feel or are regarded as different from the majority of the population in a society'[1] – a distinction usually understood to have political significance. But in the immediate post-war period the term suddenly emerged as a key concept in the mainstream of international public discourse, and by the end of the twentieth century it was applied to a bewildering range of groups in widely differing situations around the world. Moreover, once in circulation, the term was freely applied to past societies: Jews in medieval Europe, for example, or non-Muslims in the Islamic empires. The resulting theoretical confusion has been great. The term is frequently – indeed, almost always – used as if it were a neutral, objective category; as if certain groups within any given society are self-evidently 'minorities'. This is not the case. Still more unsafe is the assumption, implicit in the use of the term 'minorities', that 'majorities' exist as unproblematic entities.

'Minority': Origins of a Slippery Concept

The use of the word 'minority' in the modern sense – meaning a culturally defined group within a polity whose members face legal, political, or social disadvantages because of their cultural belonging – is relatively recent. It first appeared in the mid-1800s, and referred most often to religious groups. At that time, though, this sense seems not yet to have been clearly distinguished from the more narrowly political meaning of a group holding distinct political views that are not shared by a majority of political actors – this, in any case, is the impression given by the nineteenth-century uses of the word cited in the *Oxford English Dictionary* (*OED*).[2] It was an important concept in democratic political theory, but while there is some theoretical overlap, it is not congruent with the sense of a minority group within society at large.

The broader meaning became suddenly more distinct, and widespread, in the years around the First World War – as the example of the *Encyclopaedia Britannica* shows. The *OED*'s first citations for the locutions *national* and *ethnic minorities* were in 1918 and 1945, respectively; in French, *Le Robert* cites the equivalent terms in 1908 and 1931. At the root of this change is the assumption that groups defined by some aspect of their culture will permanently form a political minority because their cultural identity defines their attitudes across a wide range of political issues, especially regarding their relationship with the state.[3]

That assumption belongs to the age of nationalism and modern states – as was recognised early on by the *Encyclopaedia of the Social Sciences* (*ESS*) (1930–5), which noted that the 'enormous extension of the competence of the state into cultural and economic spheres has considerably decreased the sphere of the non-political'. As a result, the 'distinction between political and non-political ... is fraught with much practical difficulty'.[4] Expressions of cultural identity which would previously have been politically neutral were now taken as signs of loyalty or disloyalty to the state, a change that indicates a fundamental transformation of the state itself. Despite understanding that the development of modern states has affected the situation of national groups within any given state, however, this article assumes their existence as coherent and distinct groups to be independent of both the state and of nationalism.[5]

Of course, the concept of 'minority' did not achieve currency in international political discourse simply because people had thought of it in the abstract as a problem of statecraft in the age of nationalism. The concept solidified at a particular historical moment because it was seen to describe the situation of certain groups at that moment, and the groups concerned were the 'national minorities' of central and eastern Europe. The re-drawing of the map of post-war Europe, justified in terms of the principle of the self-determination of peoples, had turned the continent into a crowded patchwork of new nation-states, each associated with one particular 'people' or nationality. Members of other nationalities resident in those states were in a new situation, summed up by the opening definition of the 1935 article in the *ESS*:

> The term national minority is applied to a distinct ethnic group with an individual national and cultural character living within a state which is dominated by another nationality and which is viewed by the latter as the particular expression of its own identity.[6]

That is, they had become minorities because they were now resident in states which had majorities; whereas, previously, these groups had mostly been living in multinational or, rather, non-national, states. (That a state could be viewed as the 'particular expression' of a nationality's identity was a novelty that was not fully understood.) However, the term 'minorities' was not applied to all groups resident in these states but not belonging to the 'state people'.[7] The *ESS* offered various criteria by which to define minorities: in this case, for example, small and geographically dispersed groups were not to be considered 'minorities'.[8] Similar attempts to provide objective criteria by which a group can be properly identified as a 'minority' (or not) are a common feature of reference works down to the present time. Since minorities are subjective, not objective, groups, as a rule such criteria only multiply inconsistencies – though they do share a common tendency to assume that the groups concerned are objective, discrete and primordial units. However, whereas later reference works differ wildly in the groups they take to be minorities, at this early stage a common defining characteristic was visible. While commentators did raise, with varying degrees of unease, the possibility of applying the term to various other groups, they concentrated on groups that had been recognised as such in international law.[9] How did that recognition come about?

The powers involved in re-drawing the map of Europe, the United States among them, were aware that creating new states or expanding existing ones in accordance with the principle of self-determination of peoples would itself create new problems and risks of war: national groups were intermingled, not distributed in neat blocs across the landscape. Granting a state to a given people on a given territory where that people was in a majority created the problem of how to manage relations between the state and the 'state people', on the one hand, and everyone else, on the other: the 'minorities problem'. The assumptions implicit in this characterisation of a problem – that populations are primordially separated into clearly-bounded, coherent units, and that one state can represent only one such unit – are highly questionable, but they were not widely questioned at the time: they underlay the politics of the period as they underlie these reference works. One possible 'solution' to the problem was population transfer. The largest-scale attempt was that between Greece and Turkey; the 'enormous sacrifices in life and health' involved,[10] not to mention huge political, practical and moral difficulties, discouraged its widespread adoption elsewhere before the Second World War, though other, smaller attempts were made or considered in the 1920s and 1930s. (For the historian, the exchange of often Turkish-speaking Greek Orthodox Christians for sometimes Greek-speaking Muslims is a warning not to assume that 'national' groups exist as self-evident and discrete units: it took Greece and Turkey enormous effort to forge those populations into 'Greeks' and 'Turks'.[11])

Population transfer having been generally rejected as a solution, measures were instead taken to secure the rights of the new minorities through international law. Beginning with the June 1919 treaty whereby Poland's independence was recognised by the Allied and Associated Powers, a body of law arose to protect 'minority rights'. The League of Nations, once it was established, oversaw existing treaties and made similar treaty guarantees a condition of membership for new states.[12]

Despite the (fairly) good intentions behind the establishment of this body of law, its defects were obvious. The fact that it was applied to some states and not others caused great resentment.[13] Minorities could not themselves complain that their rights had been infringed: such complaints had to be raised by a state or the League on their behalf. Nor was it clear exactly what constituted a 'minority', though as a rule simple realpolitik meant that only groups belonging to a nationality that itself possessed a state elsewhere were officially recognised: as noted above, these are the groups described as minorities in scholarly work of the period.[14] These are defects in the very framework of the law: in practice, the institutional working of the League meant that it granted no real protection.[15] On the whole, the minorities treaties only exacerbated the perception of each state concerned that its minorities were disloyal – that their primary loyalty was to the (often hostile, sometimes neighbouring) state within which their own nationality was the majority.[16] Nevertheless, the concept of 'minority' was now in widespread circulation thanks to this body of law. It was commonly agreed to be meaningful, even if discord reigned as to its proper application.[17]

Although the early works consulted here were aware that the international law of minorities was novel, and to an extent that 'minority' identities had been made salient by recent political transformations, they already assumed that the term, being accurate in their present, could also be applied to the past – that if a group was a 'minority' today, it was one yesterday too. This was a mistaken assumption. Even at this stage, so soon after the emergence of the concept, its historical origins were being lost – with important consequences for its analytical usefulness. Once it existed, the term acquired its own inertia: it was applied to the past; it was adopted by groups not covered by the treaties to describe their own situation; and it was used by scholars to describe yet other groups in both present and past.

Some of this was foreseen by the League's rapporteur on minorities, who in 1926 advised against the generalisation of the minorities regime to other states:

> The introduction into the laws of all countries of provisions protecting minorities would be enough to cause them to spring up where they were least expected, to

provoke unrest among them, to cause them to pose as having been sacrificed, and generally to create an artificial agitation of which no one had up to that moment dreamed.[18]

This is too cynical in its presumption that 'minorities', outside the states where they had already been recognised, would be purely artificial and opportunistic. But it does reflect the way in which the usage of the concept, once it existed, could not be restricted. Insofar as it was open to be adopted as a means of gaining some sort of advancement or protection, the concept encouraged a wide range of groups (especially disadvantaged ones) to constitute themselves as 'minorities'. However, in one respect the rapporteur was quite mistaken: the generalisation of such legal protections was mostly irrelevant to this process. Once the concept of 'minority' was in circulation, the possibility was open for groups anywhere to adopt it to describe their own situation, whether they were covered by minority guarantees or not. (Once again I am leaving aside the obvious question: what makes a 'group'?) Likewise, the way was open for outsiders to start to define certain groups as minorities, not always for benign purposes.

The Emergence of 'Minorities'

The proliferation of the term 'minority' both inside and outside the academy derives from its rhetorical force, not from its analytical usefulness. I have already indicated that after the First World War the working definition in international law, taken up by scholars, largely excluded groups that were not represented by a state of their own elsewhere, even when their situation closely resembled that of the recognised minorities. Attempts to provide objective criteria for defining 'minorities' – though often made with the best of intentions – have not increased the analytical force of the term.

One problem is that it is difficult to define a group as a minority by opposition to a majority within a state on cultural grounds alone, simply because many such groups exist without any sense of being a 'minority'. This problem has led some commentators to stress that minorities are defined not just by their collective belonging, but also by the collective disadvantages they face. However, measures of disadvantage rarely apply only to groups that can be defined as 'minorities' on cultural lines. The article on minorities in the *International Encyclopedia of the Social Sciences* (*IESS*)[19] suggests that 'a minority's position involves exclusion or assignment to a lower status in one or more of four areas of life: the economic, the political, the legal, and the social-associational'[20] – domains of exclusion that may equally apply, collectively, to members of the working class, and to their children. Such concentration on disadvantages faced by 'minorities' risks taking for granted the existence of a coherent and uniformly privileged majority, thereby obscuring the realities of power distribution within a society, and especially within the majority.[21] This is emphatically not to say that some minorities in modern societies do not suffer real and durable collective disadvantages; but we should be aware that the notion of 'majority' can do ideological work, and so – by reinforcing it – can the notion of 'minority'.[22] This point holds *a fortiori* in non-democratic states: the public aggrandisement of the 'nation' or the 'majority', and the identification and perhaps persecution of 'minorities', are powerful ideological tools permitting closed and unaccountable regimes of all kinds to curtail the political rights of their citizens, while presenting themselves as an expression of the popular will.[23]

The surprisingly common claim that 'a minority need not be a numerical minority',[24] which presumably derives from the legal notion of the minor, is also problematic. It is fairly clear from the etymological sources that in our sense the term derives not from this legal concept but from the numerical political meaning – a minority of voters within a representative assembly.[25] In any case, if oppressed groups are a numerical majority, why bother calling them a 'minority' when 'oppressed group' is more accurate?[26] Especially since such groups are likely to mobilise politically around the fact that they are a numerical majority – one example, commonly cited as a minority before 1994, being black South Africans.[27] The term 'minority' became meaningful precisely because being a numerical minority was what made certain groups subordinate, and it serves no useful purpose to extend it to numerical majorities.

Objective criteria for defining 'minorities' are unlikely to be found, and the search for them has not been particularly helpful. It may be appropriate to jettison the term as an analytical category, and it is certainly appropriate to examine it carefully for the ideological baggage it carries, especially in implying the existence of a 'majority'. This book, however, is not directly concerned with whether 'minority' stands up as a valid category of analysis when used by scholars, nor with particular minorities as objective groups within Syrian society. It is concerned with the history of the concept itself: what were the political conditions that made it meaningful to those who used it – as they would not have done previously – in Syria during the French mandate; how and why did particular actors deploy it? These questions help us recover the historicity of the concept, and with it that of the majority.

That such an effort is worthwhile – indeed, necessary – is demonstrated by any number of examples of the usage of the concept by scholars. One such comes in the *IESS* article on minorities, which makes the following claim:

> Some [European national minorities] are of very ancient origin, and their minority status has not changed appreciably in centuries, such as the Basques in Spain and the Greeks in Turkey, who also use a language different from that of the majority in their respective countries.[28]

To say of the Greeks in Turkey that 'their minority status has not changed appreciably in centuries' is, simply, wrong. One might first note that until the nineteenth century the terms 'Greek' and 'Turkey' would have had limited significance to Greek Orthodox Christians living in the Ottoman Empire – certainly it was by religion rather than language or 'nationality' that this group was identified by the Ottoman state, and many Anatolian 'Greeks' spoke Turkish as their language of ordinary use until after the population transfer. One important change in this group's status which has occurred since 1800 is the 'nationalisation' of Greek identity (and its closer association with the Greek language) after the establishment of an independent Greece – an event which also radically altered the prospects of 'Greeks' remaining in the empire. State-building reform in the empire and its republican successor, meanwhile, fundamentally changed the relationship between state and society, a process which also brought into being a 'Turkish' majority where once there had been Ottoman rulers and 'Turk' peasants. Finally, as a part of this process, the number of Greek Orthodox Christians in the Ottoman Empire/Turkish Republic declined precipitously both proportionately and absolutely, leaving the remaining 'Greeks' as a much smaller group relative to a much more cohesive 'majority' in an actively nationalist, Turkifying state. These are altogether appreciable changes in the group's status. Comparable changes have no doubt affected the Basques in both Spain and France.

All of this history is elided if the historical origin of the concept of 'minority' is forgotten – if, once applied to a group in the modern period, it is assumed to be a valid description of that group in the past. There is a real danger of anachronism in too carelessly adopting 'minority' as a category of analysis. It is in order to avoid such confusion that the remainder of this chapter attempts to recover the historical origins of the concept of 'minority', and find a more limited, but more satisfactory, way of using the concept to understand the past.

I have already alluded to the reasons why the existence of numerically inferior, culturally defined groups within states became politically salient, and resulted in the emergence of the concept of the 'minority'. These reasons lie in the related development of modern states and nationalism. In a sense, there was no articulated concept of 'minority' prior to the modern period because minorities did not exist: the concept acquires meaning only once certain conditions associated with the existence of modern nation-states have been fulfilled. This is, obviously, not to say that the communities that later became minorities did not exist, but rather that the term 'minority' does not usefully describe their place in relation to the wider society and to the state.

In this section I outline some of the conditions that gave the term meaning. The Ottoman Empire, the historical backdrop to the rest of this study, provides many of my examples. However, my purpose in this book is to provide a case study in support of a general comparative argument, not to give an isolated account of a particular place, diverting enough but of strictly local interest. Therefore, I freely bring in examples from other parts of the world. In doing so, I want to avoid the mistaken assumption that the history of state-building in the later Ottoman Empire and post-Ottoman Middle East is one of catching up (or failing to catch up) with European states. As they underwent this process of transformation, the Ottoman Empire and the states that replaced it were not catching up with norms that had already been established in European states. The emergence of minorities (and majorities, and nation-states) took place in the Ottoman and post-Ottoman Levant at the same time as it occurred in much of Europe – not later. As Selim Deringil remarks in his study of the ideology of the late Ottoman state, the Ottoman experience paralleled 'the broad sweep of change that was taking place in European societies as a whole at the same period'.[29] If this becomes particularly clear when the empire is compared with the other European dynastic empires, it nonetheless frequently holds for a comparison with states further west too. The conditions in which the terms 'minority' and 'majority' become meaningful developed quite recently everywhere.

Philosophically, the most important precondition for the emergence of minorities is the existence of a concept of representative government. Under what Niyazi Berkes calls the medieval view of society, the ruler did not represent the ruled: he represented the will of God.[30] In the Ottoman case, it is hardly controversial to observe that for most of its existence the state made no claim to represent the population. A divinely appointed sultan had no need to represent his subjects, though he certainly claimed the right to rule over them. This is not to claim that the sultan's subjects passively accepted his authority; but when that authority was challenged, as it frequently was, it was not on the grounds that the sultan had failed to 'represent' a 'majority' of the population. More usually it was on the grounds that he had failed to ensure the stable balance of the correct social 'order' (*nizam*).[31]

Representative government fundamentally alters the relationship between rulers and ruled. Propelling the spread of a concept of representative government is the state's need to make ever greater direct demands on the population. The population, naturally, bargains hard in return for concessions from the state.[32] It is no longer seen as legitimate for states to have no other link to the populations they rule than the coercive extraction of surplus. Previously it was acceptable – indeed, necessary – for the ruling ideology to be one that sharply differentiated between rulers and ruled: 'To be Ottoman was ... to maintain an imperial difference between sultan and subjects.'[33] But now, an ideology of cohesiveness develops as the terrain on which this bargaining can take place. This is not a purely top-down development: it arises from the compromise between pressure from above and resistance from below. The notion of representativity is part of this ideology of cohesiveness: the state is no longer above the people, but of the people.[34] Dynastic states lose their raison d'être at this stage if the monarchy cannot identify itself with the population.[35]

The notion of representative government is not imposed from above: rulers adopt it in response to pressure from below. The representation involved, however, does generally spread from top to bottom, as the sections of the population with which the state must deal directly gradually widens from dominant elites to the whole of the population; that is, as the state's direct demands fall on ever wider sections of society, from aristocrats and perhaps clergy in the first instance to an urban bourgeoisie and other property-holders, to all adult males, and eventually (in the twentieth century, under the impulse of the mobilisation of entire populations for total war) to all adult women also.[36] It is when the concept of representativity is widened to embrace the entire population at the level of individual households (represented through their adult males) that the terms 'majority' and 'minority' start to apply to the whole population, rather than to members of a town or communal council, or all property-owning voters.[37]

It must be emphasised here that the concept of representative government does not imply democracy. What is at issue is whether the state claims to represent the population: whether that representation is democratic or not is irrelevant. Kemal Atatürk was no democrat, but he based his legitimacy entirely on his claim to represent the Turkish 'people'. The claim to be representative is frequently used by states and rulers precisely to foreclose the possibility of any real democratic representation – a similar point to the one made above about the concept of the 'majority'. The fact that many non-democratic regimes call themselves democratic simply shows the rhetorical power of that concept in buttressing the notion of representativity.

In the Ottoman Empire, as elsewhere, the concept of representative government spread to touch the entire population in the nineteenth century.[38] While Ottoman sultans by no means abandoned the claim to divine right and to religious legitimation, the state sought to widen its repertoire of legitimating practices. (Both of these statements apply to other European monarchies that survived the century: British monarchs retained the claim to reign *deo gratia*, although the British state no longer legitimated itself purely by that claim.) This widening was the aim of the *tanzimat* reforms, which for the first time introduced the notion that the state represented as well as ruling the population. Later changes in the empire's ruling ideology – notably a renewed use of Islam as a basis for legitimation under Abdülhamid II (discussed below) – retained the notion of representation. It would be wrong to see this development as an adoption of foreign practices. The internal dynamic of state–society relations drove reform, even if external pressure made it imperative.

The concept of representative government is, as noted earlier, part of an ideology of cohesiveness that creates a terrain on which the interaction between state and society – with demands and resistance emanating from both sides – is played out. But it is only one part of that ideology. For the population to take seriously the state's claim to represent it, the relationship between them must be defined: who, precisely, does the state claim to represent?

One part of this process of definition is the establishment of fixed borders, territorially defining the population upon which the state can make demands – and vice versa. But in the modern period, the demands made by both sides have steadily increased: states demand individual income tax, general conscription, attendance at school; populations demand a greater say in how revenue is spent, healthcare, education. This is the stuff of politics in modern states, and the population's mere residence on the state's territory has not usually provided a strong enough connection to bear the weight of such politics. A stronger link is needed, usually based on shared culture: the state demonstrates that it is of the people by sharing their 'national identity'; this, in turn, provides the population with a basis for making their demands.

The pressure to create such a cultural link may come from the state (as in France) or from segments of the population in opposition to the state (as with separatist nationalisms in the Austro-Hungarian Empire): both trends can be observed in the Ottoman case. Either way, it makes the relative numbers of different culturally defined groups increasingly salient. When such pressure comes from the state there is an obvious benefit in assuming or idealising a cultural identity that is shared by, or at least acceptable to, a majority of the population. Likewise, if members of a culturally defined group come to see the ruling state as alien, and therefore reject it as not representing them, their likely response will either be to take over the state for themselves (if the group, as they constitute it, represents a numerical majority within the existing state) or to try and break away and form a new state within which they are a numerical majority. Charles Tilly shows how these two currents strengthen each other, with

> the attempt of rulers to commit their subjects to the national cause generating resistance on the part of unassimilated minorities, [and] the demand of unrepresented minorities for political autonomy fostering commitment to the existing state on the part of those who benefit most from its existence.[39]

In either case, number becomes increasingly important. As states old and new come to present themselves as sharing the identity of a 'majority', those culturally defined groups that fall outside the definition of national identity adopted by the state but inside its geographical borders become 'minorities'. Since populations are rarely homogeneous, with territories of any size containing culturally diverse populations, 'minorities' appear almost everywhere.

The link between the concepts of representative government and national identity is easy to see.[40] Their development together is what allowed the *ESS* to describe a Europe, after the First World War, where each state was viewed by a given 'nationality' as 'the particular expression of its own identity':[41] in other words, nation-states. But as cultural identity became more salient in the relationship between state and society, it also became more likely to mark lines of conflict between them. In the pre-modern era it was sometimes problematic for religiously-legitimated states to rule over populations belonging to a different faith; in modern times there are far more potential points of disagreement, since 'nations' define themselves using varying combinations of language, ethnicity, geography, religion and (supposed) shared history, and the state's activities have expanded into cultural fields. The terms 'minority' and 'majority' having already become relevant at the level of the entire population, this is when their extended meaning as permanent political groupings defined by their cultural identity emerges.[42]

So far, this analysis has been presented as if, in these circumstances, pre-defined groups already exist. This is a misleading simplification: social groups are also produced, or produce themselves, through this process, and cultural identities refashioned or (re)invented – the example of the 'Greeks' in Turkey, or indeed the 'Turks', illustrates this. Notably, boundaries between culturally defined groups often harden as they become associated with political identities relative to the state, much more so in the modern period than previously. This is always a dialectic process in which different groups define themselves in relation to one another and the state, with the state sometimes serving as the instrument of one group. In the definition of a 'majority' and 'minorities', each side of the process depends on the other.

The Ottoman state did not – for most of its history – claim a cultural affinity between itself and all groups within the population, any more than it claimed to represent a 'majority'. In a religiously-legitimated monarchy, whether or not the ruler shares the language or 'ethnicity' of the ruled is irrelevant.[43] Nor need he even share their religious beliefs, since he draws his right to rule from his own religion. Religious differences may become politically salient in the relationship between ruler and ruled, as in Europe during and after the Reformation, but this is by no means inevitable.[44] The empire claimed an Islamic identity which it shared with a substantial part of the population, but whether that part was a numerical majority or minority of the population was irrelevant. The Arab caliphates had ruled over a majority of non-Muslims for centuries; so did the Ottomans in their Balkan provinces. Indeed, since the early Ottoman sultans won substantial territories in the Balkans before they expanded into the Levant, Arabia and Egypt, 'before the sixteenth century they probably ruled over more Christians than they did Muslims'.[45] Islamic law provided a place in the social and political order for non-Muslims, and although this was a structurally subordinate place it was nevertheless guaranteed by the state. And, of course, non-Muslims were not subordinated because they were a minority (often they were not), but because they were non-Muslims. Under this system of government, whose ordering principle was religious (with no direct reference to number), ethnic identity had very limited political salience. The

Ottoman state required that its servants speak Ottoman Turkish, not that they be 'Turks'. State functions were assigned to members of the different religious communities, not to members of 'ethnic' or 'national' groups.

It was only in the nineteenth century that this began to change, as the empire – like other states – shifted towards an idea of representative government. At the same time as the state came under pressure from separatist nationalisms that presented it as alien to 'their' nationality – mobilisations which, at the risk of repetition, themselves involved constituting a new form of political identity – it also adopted measures to promulgate a cultural identity of its own. The Ottomanism of mid-century, the Hamidian Islamism that followed it and, eventually, the current of Turkish nationalism can all be seen in this light, with separatist nationalisms acting as both a counter-current and an example. Ottomanism was a culturally diffuse concept, based on a putative shared loyalty to the institutions of the state and residence on the territory. Its vagueness was deliberate: Ottomanism was concerned with overcoming the growing centrifugal forces within the empire, particularly among Christian populations, and therefore needed to be as inclusive as possible – in a sense, to forestall the emergence of minorities by making everyone a part of an Ottoman nation. (It also existed alongside an older and sometimes oppositional concept of the Islamically-legitimated state which would prove to be both resilient and flexible.) Other states in comparable situations in this period adopted similar solutions: the Austro-Hungarian Empire, for example, tried to build a sense of national identity based on loyalty to the emperor and shared belonging to the 'Imperial Fatherland', as well as through the multiplication of bureaucratic institutions to give every part of the population a stake in the state apparatus.[46] While the vagueness of Ottomanism was necessary given the diversity of the empire's population, it made the concept less effective as a mobilising ideology in the face of the more exclusive separatist nationalisms that developed, and attracted foreign support, within the population.

One reason for Islam's renewed prominence as a source of legitimacy and as a cultural identity linking state and society as a whole in the later nineteenth century was that in this period Muslims finally became an overwhelming numerical majority in the empire.[47] This was partly the result of the loss of most of the Balkan provinces, especially after the 1877–8 war with Russia: the Christian populations remained in the newly formed Balkan states, while large numbers of Muslim refugees fled from them into the remaining territory of the empire.[48] (Many others were massacred.) Starting in mid-century, Russian control in the Caucasus was also consolidated, causing a substantial wave of Muslim immigration to the empire.[49] For these reasons, the number of Christians in the empire fell sharply in this period, both proportionately and absolutely, while that of Muslims increased.[50] We can begin to speak meaningfully of a Muslim majority in the empire by the late nineteenth century: not only because, in numerical terms, there certainly was one, but because the state was self-consciously claiming to represent that majority and to promote Islam as a more robust cultural link between itself and the population than Ottomanism. However, given the numerous ethnolinguistic divisions within the Ottoman Muslim community it remains dangerous to assume that the Muslim majority was a coherent political grouping: the various ethnolinguistically-based nationalisms already developing within that community would soon demonstrate that it was not.

Several other developments that mark the transformation of the state in the modern period can be seen as preconditions to the emergence of 'minorities' and a 'majority'. They spread over the boundary between philosophy and political geography. As we have already seen, the concepts of representative government and national identity develop together; these factors, too, develop as part of the same process.

As the concept of representative government spreads, for example, it is embodied in common institutions operating across the entire territory and touching the entire population. Most important, perhaps, is the institution of common citizenship, but also included are such essential parts of a modern state as a judicial system which operates in more or less the same way across the territory, and on all individuals within it; a state education system with a common curriculum and a state language;[51] and such 'representative' institutions as may exist as a link between state and population (whether truly representative or not). These either replace or subsume to one state-wide framework the multiple local and regional institutions of varying power and influence which are common in pre-modern states – where, under the tenuous sovereignty of one ruler, different groups within the population, or different regions, may for example be subject to quite different legal systems.[52] Much of the process of Ottoman reform in the last century of the empire's existence can be interpreted in this way: consider, for example, the standardisation of law under the *mejelle*, which attempted to reduce discrepancies both in local customary law and in the communal law of the millet system, and also hoped (unsuccessfully) to overcome the exceptional status of the mixed courts; or the development of a common Ottoman citizenship, which attempted to standardise the relationship between members of different millets and the state. Concentrating on the fact that the tanzimat enshrined legal equality for non-Muslims, scholarly literature has often ignored the fact that these reforms also introduced a concept of equal citizenship for all Muslims, too.

Ussama Makdisi has drawn the contrast between the tanzimat period and earlier phases of the relationship between Ottoman state and population: 'After the nineteenth century, Ottoman reformers sought to nationalize (Ottomanize) the empire and ultimately to absorb the margins into a cohesive and uniform Ottoman modernity.'[53] While far from wholly successful, these reforms did fundamentally alter the relationship between individual Ottomans and the state. They also mirror transformations of the state in other countries in this period: Britain, for example, where the emancipation of Catholics and later Jews occurred at around the same time, or the United States, where slavery was abolished towards the end of the tanzimat period – an extension of citizenship that led to a far greater 'crisis of the state' than anything the tanzimat provoked.

Just as important to the development of a sense of national identity is the development of a public sphere going beyond educated elites. Benedict Anderson's lastingly influential analysis has shown how important this is to the development of modern nationalism.[54] This is somewhat more distinct from the state than the kinds of institution mentioned above, but in a sense they contribute to it. Institutions such as citizenship or an education system act to establish the sense of commonality (of interest and experience) on which a public sphere going beyond a local level depends. They also, thereby, work strongly to stake out 'national' boundaries within the public sphere. And such institutions also create cadres who are among the public sphere's most active participants: thus the schoolteacher as the iconic figure of the French Third Republic.

Even in the modern period, we have already seen that the formulations 'minority' and 'majority' may gloss over divisions within a society and obscure the very different relationships that individuals or groups within the majority and the minorities have with the state. In the pre-modern period, the absence of common institutions and a public sphere makes it hard to see what meaning the term 'majority' could have had at the level of the population as a whole. It implies a perception of commonality of interest and experience which self-evidently does not, and cannot, exist of itself. The developments outlined here, and no doubt others besides, are necessary before that perception can exist. Whether that perception is true or false is another question.

Developing alongside the common institutions described above is the notion of uniform state authority over a permanent national territory, replacing the formally and informally differentiated state authority and weaker philosophical link between state and territory that were normal prior to the modern period.[55] Because modern states do claim a uniform sovereignty over the entire territory, and in many cases possess the means to enforce that claim (or at least punish those who challenge it), it is hard to remember that until recently states did not – and could not – make such claims. In these circumstances, culturally-differentiated groups in areas away from the main centres of state authority were not under anything like the same pressure to conform to state-imposed norms that they are today.

To an extent the same goes even in centres of state authority, because that authority was more likely to bend itself to, or at least accommodate, local factors than it was to impose common norms. For example, by comparison with the Balkan mountains, the Jabal Hawran, or the Arabian desert, Ottoman authority was strong in Salonica, Damascus and Mecca; but the three cities operated under very different regimes. At the level of the city it would be possible to argue, without having to make heroic assumptions at the level of the empire about the coherence of a non-Jewish majority and the uniform authority of a non-Jewish state, that the small Jewish community of Damascus constituted a 'minority' in more than a numerical sense. Whether the same could be said of the Jews of Salonica, a city which they dominated not only numerically but also economically and socially (at all levels), and where 'the docks stood silent on the Jewish Sabbath',[56] is doubtful. As state authority comes to be more uniformly applied, through the instrument of a state apparatus that functions more uniformly at the level of the entire territory and population, and as common institutions and a public sphere at the state-wide level develop, communities of all kinds gain a sense of their place relative to a greater whole.

The geographical limits of that whole are set by an important development in political geography: the establishment of fixed borders with a state's authority on either side, a process closely related to the spread of the state's physical presence across its territory. This is relevant to the emergence of 'minorities' because, within each state, it restricts to that state the field of political action open to subordinate communities. If a subordinate community under threat can simply pack its bags and head west of its own free will, as it were, then it has a freedom of action which a minority group within a modern state does not have, however traumatic such a migration may be in practice. Among countless examples are successive waves of nomadic migrations west out of central Asia under pressure from the east; English Dissenters fleeing for America; Boers moving north through southern Africa at the time of the British occupation of the Cape; or Caucasian Muslims fleeing to the Ottoman Empire to escape Russian imperial expansion in the nineteenth century. Modern minorities under threat have a much more limited range of options: flight, individually or en masse, can only take them to another nation-state where they may be assimilated to the majority (at best), become an immigrant minority, or remain as stateless refugees (at worst).[57]

The establishment of fixed borders, like many other of the developments described above, is underpinned by the extension of modern communications: a transformation in physical geography that permits some approximation in reality of the uniform application of state authority, for example, as well as the establishment of a common public sphere. The extension of the state's real authority over its entire territory and population brings communities which might previously have been semi-autonomous into permanent and direct contact with the state, and fixes them within a state structure where they are in a minority.[58] For the Ottoman Empire, the Druzes of Mount Lebanon and the Hawran are an obvious example; less obviously, because a larger and more diverse community, it is unlikely that the Christians of the Ottoman Balkans would have considered themselves to be a minority before the nineteenth century at the very earliest – if they ever did. Muslims may have been a majority, though not an overwhelming one, in the empire as a whole; but before the spread of modern communications the empire did not act as a whole, and in the Balkans the Christians were a numerical majority. It was in the period of the tanzimat that infrastructural developments (railways, telegraphs, steamships) started to tie the territory together – putting the state apparatus more firmly, and more immediately, under the direct control of the centre, and simultaneously giving the population more direct access to the central state.[59] Similar processes were occurring in other European states at the same time, as Eugen Weber has perhaps most famously described.[60]

It is difficult to separate out these preconditions, or to say with any certainty which way causation runs between them. The processes involved contribute to and reinforce one another. Moreover, it should be apparent that these preconditions – and the list is not exhaustive – are ideals, not realities. Many of them could never be fully achieved. Even today, the authority of the most powerful states is not uniform across the territory, weakening in remote rural areas or urban areas whose populations are hostile to state intrusion.[61] In other states the differentiation is greater, and may be extreme. There are also frequently exceptions to supposedly common state institutions: witness the peculiar and possibly unconstitutional status relative to Congress of Washington, DC; the exceptions to French citizenship once applied to Algerian Muslims – nonetheless French subjects – under the *code de l'indigénat*; or the inconsistencies arising from devolution in the United Kingdom (the 'West Lothian question'). Such exceptions, whether made for particular regions or particular groups within the population, often represent practical solutions to the problem of government – but they may pose serious existential questions for the state. Sometimes it is the very creation of a common institution which causes the problem, as when formal citizenship or nationality laws institutionalise the exclusion or subordination of certain residents within a territory – one example being immigrants and their offspring, down to the third resident generation and counting in Germany. Such institutions inevitably create exceptions, and the argument over where to draw their limits underlies much of modern politics. If most borders, meanwhile, are now clearly delineated on maps, they frequently remain porous: state authority is rarely uniform along their length.[62] Above all, national identity usually escapes precise definition.

What is important, however, is not that these ideals exist in reality, but that states, their rulers and their citizens act as if they exist. In the era of the nation-state, this is largely the case. Taken altogether, the adoption of these ideals as something approaching norms represents a radical transformation of the state – a transformation which has taken place across the globe over the last two centuries. It is not final – the current preoccupation of scholars and journalists with 'globalisation' is one indicator of this – but it is the framework for this study.

It is this transformation of the state which gives meaning to the twin concepts of majority and minority, understood as groups within a population: terms which emerged in a specific, contemporary context. This transformation has so profoundly marked our era that it is difficult to imagine how different the past was – to imagine, for example, that political categories which are fundamental to us could have been literally unthinkable so short a time ago. But outside the specific, contemporary context of the nation-state it is difficult to see what meaning these two concepts could have. Put simply, the burden of proof is on anyone who claims that majority is a valid term of analysis when applied to the past to show how a coherent 'majority' could possibly have been constituted without all these various developments that we take for granted in modern states; likewise for 'minority'. Each of these terms implies a relationship between the state and the population – above all, between the state and the supposed majority – which simply did not exist previously. The concepts would have been meaningless to residents of the Ottoman Empire for most of its long history. Neither are they useful from the historian's point of view until late in the day, since the conditions which make them meaningful were absent. Those conditions were developing in the later Ottoman period. But it was not until the mandate period, when these concepts became fully developed in international political discourse, that individual actors began consciously to refer to themselves as members of a majority or a minority.

The argument that majority and minority are not meaningful concepts outside the context of a modern nation-state also has a 'reverse implication': namely, that tracing the emergence and development of these concepts is a useful way of studying the development of modern nation-states, without adopting (knowingly or not) the categories that the nation-state itself creates. Paradoxically, focusing on minorities as central to the state permits us to get beyond a state-centred analysis, because instead of assuming the existence of powerful state norms it enables us to see how those norms gradually developed and imposed themselves. This is a worthwhile task, since the nation-state form has shaped recent world history. As Benedict Anderson puts it, 'When the forty-two founding members of the League of Nations assembled in 1920, they inaugurated an era in which the nation became the only internationally legitimate state form.'[63] This book proposes to use the concept of 'minority' not as an analytical category, but as a subject of study in its own right – one that will shed light on the process of state formation in the modern Middle East and elsewhere.

Notes

1. Alan Bullock *et al.*, *The Harper Dictionary of Modern Thought* (London: Harper & Row, 1988), 'Minorities'.
2. Henceforward *OED*.

3. Kedourie, 'Ethnicity, majority, and minority in the Middle East'.
4. *Encyclopaedia of the Social Sciences*, 1930–5 (henceforward *ESS* 1935): 'Minorities, National' – the only minorities covered by this encyclopaedia. The following entry, 'Minority Rights', is mostly a discussion of the rights of minorities of voters vis-à-vis the majority in democratic political theory, not minority rights in the modern sense.
5. This is not surprising: the article's author, Max Hildebert Boehm, was a prominent German *Volk* sociologist whose ideas (notably *Volksgemeinschaft* – the *Volk* as a primordial entity sharing common interests) were well adapted to the corporatist ideology of the Nazi regime. Boehm was appointed to a professorship under the Nazis, whom he enthusiastically supported. (Christa Kamenetsky, 'Folklore as a political tool in Nazi Germany', *Journal of American Folklore* (1972), 85(337): 221–35; E. K. Francis, 'Minority groups – a revision of concepts', *British Journal of Sociology* (1951), 2(3): 219–29, 254, n. 1.)
6. *ESS* 1935: 'Minorities, National'.
7. Arendt takes the term 'state people', with due reservations, from the texts of the post-First World War peace treaties: *The Origins of Totalitarianism*, ch. 9.
8. It is notable that the criteria established by Boehm, while by no means restricted to German minorities in central and eastern Europe, would confer on them clear 'minority' status. Boehm's assertion of the rights of such minorities to privileged contact with the 'mother country' stands out in this respect as presaging subsequent traumas.
9. See, e.g., *Encyclopaedia Britannica* 1929: 'Minorities'; *EES* 1935: 'Minorities, National'. The 1975 *Grand Larousse de la langue française* cites its own 1931 edition as a source when it defines 'minority' in this sense: 'En termes de droit international, communauté qui, à l'intérieure d'un État, représente un petit nombre d'individus qui ont en commun un certain nombre de caractères (race, langue, religion).'
10. *ESS* 1935: 'Minorities, National'
11. See, among others, Bruce Clark, *Twice a Stranger: How Mass Expulsion Forged Modern Greece and Turkey* (London: Granta, 2006); Anastasia Karakasidou, *Fields of Wheat, Hills of Blood: Passages to Nationhood in Greek Macedonia, 1870–1990* (London: University of Chicago Press, 1997), chs 5–7; and the articles in Renée Hirschon (ed.), *Crossing the Aegean: An Appraisal of the 1923 Compulsory Population Exchange between Greece and Turkey* (Oxford: Berghahn, 2003).
12. Mark Mazower, 'Minorities and the League of Nations in Interwar Europe', *Daedalus* (1997), 126(2): 47–63. These treaties drew on the historical precedent of nineteenth-century treaties that, without describing such groups as 'minorities', included clauses on the status of religious groups.
13. Howard B. Calderwood, 'International affairs: The proposed generalization of the minorities régime', *The American Political Science Review* (1934), 28(6): 1088–98.

14. Jews were a partial exception in that, despite lacking any such legal safeguards, they were widely accepted to constitute a 'minority' in the states concerned – a semi-official recognition that can be ascribed to the active, but ultimately unsuccessful, participation of Jewish delegations during the post-First World War peace negotiations. Arendt terms them the *'minorité par excellence'*: *The Origins of Totalitarianism*, pp. 289–90.
15. An account of the institutional barriers is given in *ESS* 1935: 'Minorities, National'.
16. The presence of inverted commas should generally be assumed around the words minority, majority and nationality. For the functioning and failings of the treaties, and their implications, see Arendt, *The Origins of Totalitarianism*, pp. 269–76.
17. Chapter 5 discusses this body of law and its application to Syria.
18. Quoted in Calderwood, 'The proposed generalization of the minorities régime', p. 1092. The rapporteur was citing, approvingly, the opinion of Dutch senator Baron Wittert van Hoogland.
19. Henceforward *IESS*, 1968 successor to the earlier *ESS*.
20. *IESS* 1968: 'Minorities'.
21. Ellis Ernest Cashmore *et al.*, *Dictionary of Race and Ethnic Relations*, 4th edn (London: Routledge, 1996): 'Minorities'.
22. Barton Meyers, 'Minority group: an ideological formulation', *Social Problems* (1984), 32(1): 1–15.
23. Dr James McDougall kindly drew my attention to this point, with a forceful analysis of North African politics.
24. Paul Clarke and Joe Foweraker (eds), *Encyclopedia of Democratic Thought* (London: Routledge, 2001), 'Minorities'.
25. See also Kedourie, 'Ethnicity, majority, and minority in the Middle East'.
26. Meyers, 'Minority group', is not alone in making this point.
27. E.g., in *IESS* 1968: 'Minorities'.
28. *IESS* 1968: 'Minorities'.
29. Selim Deringil, *The Well-Protected Domains: Ideology and the Legitimation of Power in the Ottoman Empire, 1876–1909* (London: I. B. Tauris, 1998), p. 8.
30. Niyazi Berkes, *The Development of Secularism in Turkey* (Montreal: McGill University Press, 1964), pp. 8–10.
31. Inalcik and Quataert also discuss the role of *nizam*: 'the general principle was adhered to that each individual should remain in his own status group so that equilibrium in the state and society could be maintained': *An Economic and Social History of the Ottoman Empire, 1300–1914* (Cambridge: Cambridge University Press, 1994), p. 17.
32. Charles Tilly, *Coercion, Capital and European States, AD 990–1992*, revised paperback ed. (Oxford: Blackwell, 1992), especially ch. 4. NB: It would be a mistake to assume a singularity of purpose on the part of the entire population, or indeed the entire state apparatus, in this process.
33. Makdisi, 'Ottoman orientalism', para. 12.
34. When colonial states made the same demands on the population without

representation, the opposition came to justify itself precisely by claiming to represent the population.

35. For the British case, see Linda Colley's account of the reign of George III: by the time he died, it was 'axiomatic that royal celebration should ideally involve all political affiliations, all religious groupings and all parts of Great Britain: in other words, that it should at least *seem* to be authentically national and not sectional celebration': *Britons: Forging the Nation, 1707–1837*, 2nd edn (London: Yale University Press, 2005), p. 231.
36. Tilly, *Coercion, Capital and European States*.
37. Kedourie, 'Ethnicity, majority, and minority in the Middle East'.
38. A classic account of this can be found in Roderic H. Davison, 'The advent of the principle of representation in the government of the Ottoman empire', in *Essays in Ottoman and Turkish History, 1774–1923: The Impact of the West* (London: Saqi Books, 1990), pp. 96–111. Davison concentrates on elected institutions, a narrower meaning of representation than that outlined here. I suspect he also overestimates the extent to which representation was a 'Western' import rather than something driven by internal dynamics of the Ottoman state–society relationship.
39. Tilly, *Coercion, Capital and European States*, pp. 116–17. I am making the slightly different point, however, that groups come to be defined as 'minorities' through this process.
40. Again, there is nothing to stop a profoundly unrepresentative regime legitimating itself by claiming some kind of representativity – the concept of national identity makes this easier.
41. ESS 1935: 'Minorities, National'.
42. Kedourie, 'Ethnicity, majority, and minority in the Middle East'.
43. Cf. Benedict Anderson on the 'dynastic realm': *Imagined Communities: Reflections on the Origin and Spread of Nationalism*, rev. edn (London: Verso, 1991), pp. 19–22.
44. Even when religion does become salient in the relationship between ruler and ruled, it is not necessarily correct to assume that a 'majority' dynamic is at work – that it has become impossible for a ruler belonging to a 'minority' faith to rule over a 'majority' belonging to another. It may well be more accurate to say that the religion not of a majority but of certain influential groups – aristocrats, urban middle classes, an established clergy – is what matters.
45. Mark Mazower, *Salonica, City of ghosts: Christians, Muslims, and Jews, 1430–1950* (London: HarperPerennial, 2005), p. 25.
46. Deringil, *The Well-protected Domains*, pp. 16–17; Norman Stone, *Europe Transformed 1878–1919*, 2nd edn (Oxford: Blackwell, 1999), p. 236.
47. Hasan Kayali, *Arabs and Young Turks: Ottomanism, Arabism and Islamism in the Ottoman Empire, 1908–1918* (London: University of California Press, 1997), ch. 1; Albert H. Hourani, *A History of the Arab Peoples* (London: Faber & Faber, 1991), p. 309. Deringil, *The Well-protected Domains*, examines Ottoman self-legitimation in this period.

48. Kemal Karpat, 'The status of the Muslim under European rule: the eviction and settlement of the Çerkes', in *Studies on Ottoman Social and Political History: Selected Articles and Essays* (Leiden: Brill, 2002), pp. 647–75; Inalcik and Quataert, *An Economic and Social History*, p. 782, who also note (p. 792) a lesser but not insignificant contribution to the shifting balance: the increase in emigration to the Americas in the later decades of the nineteenth century. Most emigrants were Christians.
49. Inalcik and Quataert, *An Economic and Social History*, pp. 794–5; Karpat, 'The status of the Muslim', p. 72. Karpat notes that some of the Circassians fled twice: from the Caucasus to the Balkans in the 1860s, and from the Balkans to Anatolia and the Levant in the 1870s. James Meyer argues that the Russian Empire generally tried to keep hold of its Muslim population, and notes that some (though not many) migrants returned to Russia temporarily or permanently. Others retained their Russian citizenship and used it to gain access to Russian consular protection in the Ottoman Empire: 'Immigration, return, and the politics of citizenship: Russian Muslims in the Ottoman empire, 1860–1914', *International Journal of Middle East Studies* (2007), 39(1): 15–32.
50. Kayali, *Arabs and Young Turks*, ch. 1.
51. The process of language standardisation is clearly a crucial one, but far too large a subject to go into detail here. Étienne Balibar brilliantly links language and school, and shows that the development of a national language is marked by the stratification of 'levels of language' within one language: Étienne Balibar, 'The nation form: history and ideology', in É. Balibar and I. M. Wallerstein, *Race, Nation, Class: Ambiguous Identities* (London: Verso, 1991), pp. 86–106, especially 97–9.
52. In *Empire of Difference: The Ottomans in Comparative Perspective* (Cambridge: Cambridge University Press, 2008), Karen Barkey offers a sophisticated account of (flexibly) structured difference along these lines as the factor underpinning the Ottoman Empire's success and longevity.
53. Makdisi, 'Ottoman orientalism', para. 8.
54. Anderson, *Imagined Communities*.
55. See Chapter 3. Balibar places the transformations discussed here earlier, with the development of absolute monarchy that 'brought with it effects of monetary monopoly, administrative and fiscal centralization and a relative degree of standardization of the legal system and internal "pacification". It thus revolutionized the institutions of the *frontier* and the *territory*': 'The nation form', p. 87, emphasis in original. I take the point, but would argue that (1) it is more likely to hold for France than for other states and (2) if these processes began earlier, they reached a new intensity in modern states – notably revolutionary France.
56. Mazower, *Salonica*, p. 8. This was the case as late as 1912.
57. Hannah Arendt expresses this problem in her stark description of inter-war Europe, with its 'migrations of groups who, unlike their happier predecessors in the religious wars, were welcomed nowhere and could be assimilated nowhere. Once they had left their homeland they remained homeless, once they had left their

state they became stateless; once they had been deprived of their human rights they were rightless, the scum of the earth.' *The Origins of Totalitarianism*, p. 267.
58. See Chapters 3 and 4.
59. On the impact of the telegraph in this respect, e.g., see Eugene Rogan, 'Instant communication: the impact of the telegraph in Ottoman Syria', in Thomas Philipp and Birgit Schaebler (eds), *The Syrian Land: Processes of Integration and Fragmentation. Bilād al-Shām from the 18th to the 20th Century* (Stuttgart: Franz Steiner Verlag, 1998), pp. 113–28.
60. Eugen Weber, *Peasants into Frenchmen: The Modernization of Rural France, 1870–1914* (London: Chatto & Windus, 1977).
61. James Scott shows that this point holds even in cities designed on a grid pattern, for maximum 'legibility' and accessibility, in powerful modern states: *Seeing like a State: How Certain Schemes to Improve the Human Condition have Failed* (London: Yale University Press, 1998), p. 56, n. 12.
62. This has been the case since the Ottoman–Persian Treaty of Zuhab in May 1639, 'the oldest explicit demarcation based on geography rather than on purely the clarification of judicial rights between states. Unfortunately, the wording of the treaty was vague, and the reality on the ground was a wide and porous autonomous zone that tribesmen crossed at will, despite the existence of border posts scattered along a nominal frontier line.' Peter Barber and Tom Harper, *Magnificent Maps: Power, Propaganda and Art* (London: The British Library, 2010), p. 116.
63 Anderson, 'Nationalism'.

CHAPTER

2

'MINORITIES' AND THE FRENCH MANDATE

Introduction

The accusation of having mutilated Syrian unity ... is laid against us by Arabizers who call themselves patriots and whose design is evident: adversaries of the mandate, what they want is an independent Syria where the 1,500,000 Muslims would subjugate the half-million Christians. If this state of affairs came about, it would not only be the end of western influence in the Orient: it would be the opening of an era of disorders and massacres. Greater Lebanon is a rampart against invasive panarabism and Islamic persecution. The institution of the mandate had precisely the aim of preventing, in the anarchic unchaining of fanaticisms, the most frightful religious war.[1]

This extract from Robert de Beauplan's 1929 work *Où va la Syrie?* is fairly typical of French imperialist writings on Syria in the 1920s. Rejecting the notion of a territorially or socially unified Syria – 'the Syrian nation is a myth', Beauplan affirms elsewhere[2] – it stresses the religious divisions within Syrian society and assumes a latent persecuting fanaticism on the part of Syria's Muslims. It justifies the French presence, and the administrative divisions France had imposed in the mandate territories, as the only thing standing between Syrian Christians and massacre. It cites the mandate in support of French rule. And, despite referring to the numerical inferiority of the Christians, it lacks any explicit reference to minorities.

This chapter places the emergence of 'minorities' in Syria in the context of the French mandate. It focuses on the interplay between two distinct factors: first, the policies the French put in place in Syria in order to structure, and exacerbate, the divisions between Syria's diverse communities; and, second, and more profound in its effects, the transition to a nation-state form.

If the Ottoman Empire remained a dynastic empire to the end, the states that replaced it – Syria among them – were constituted as nation-states representative of their populations from the outset, and recognised as such by the League of Nations. In that formal, institutional sense the end of the First World War was a decisive turning point in the Middle East, though the break between what went before and what came after was less radical than that might imply. Like other states in Europe and elsewhere, the Ottoman Empire in the nineteenth century had adopted many of the characteristics of a nation-state, as the previous chapter described; and, as elsewhere, the transition to a nation-state form masked many continuities.

In the new nation-states of the post-war period in central and eastern Europe, and in what became the Republic of Turkey, the relationship between each state and its new minorities was essentially bilateral, despite external intervention by the League of Nations – through the minorities treaties – and other states interested in populations belonging to 'their' state people. In Syria and the other states of the Levant, however, the relationship between the new states and their (new) minorities was mediated by a third factor: imperial occupation. Rather than being recognised as a fully independent nation-state by the League, Syria was provisionally recognised as independent and placed under the mandatory tutelage of France. But although state development in mandate-era Syria was, without doubt, animated and ordered by the imperial power, it is harder to ascribe the norms this process followed to French imperialism alone. States inside and outside Europe adopted them in the modern period, whether imperial powers or not, and to a great extent the 'national' practices and institutions that shaped state development in mandate Syria were continuations of Ottoman trends.

Within this context, the chapter discusses the place of the concept of 'minority' in the relationship between France and Syria. Doing this with a critical understanding of the concept and its historicity allows us to refine earlier analyses of French policy in Syria as one of 'divide-and-rule' based on using 'minorities' to offset the 'majority'. The concept came into common use in both French and Syrian writings later than one might think, and was used not only as a justification for French domination in Syria (on the grounds of 'protection of minorities'), but as a means for certain groups in Syrian society to advance their own interests relative to the mandatory authorities, the Syrian state and society at large. The discussion of the concept of 'minority' is placed in a wider analysis of the French imperialist vision of Syrian society which shows how that vision affected French policy in Syria, and how French policy, in turn, affected Syrian society. This casts light on the contradictions created by French attempts to order Syrian society along religious lines within the secular state form of the nation-state.

Examining this question also offers us a way of assessing the continuities and discontinuities between the Ottoman and post-Ottoman periods in Syria. The communities that emerged as 'minorities' during the mandate cannot simply be mapped back onto the millets or Christian and Jewish communities of the Ottoman period. A minority is a modern phenomenon, a millet pre-modern, though by 1914 the Ottoman millets were already marked by the effects of the transformation of the state. Even those religious communities that did previously exist as millets saw their relationship to the state and the wider society alter significantly as they became minorities in the new Syrian nation-state; other minorities, with no prior history as millets, also emerged. In many cases neither the Syrian minorities nor the French understood the significance of the transformation that had occurred – unsurprisingly, since it was a slow, uneven, and difficult process that had begun long before. Frequently, Syrians recognised the import of their changed circumstances before their French rulers did.

Divide and Rule: But on what Grounds?

Many sound historical works have demonstrated that French officials approached Syria with a communitarian understanding of Syrian society, and on this basis adopted a divisive communitarian politics. Philip Khoury's classic political history of the mandate offers numerous examples in the framework of a general argument about the shape of mandatory politics, as do earlier works by Albert Hourani and Stephen Longrigg.[3] An influential article by Edmund Burke relates this aspect of French policy in Syria to imperial experiences elsewhere, showing that it fitted into the 'associationist' model of imperial rule developed in Morocco, where the French emphasised – and institutionalised – the division between Arabs and Berbers.[4]

Other works have shown how the dynamic functioned either with regard to specific events or specific communities. Communitarian patterns of recruitment into the local armed forces, for example, have been widely discussed, as have their effect on politics in independent Syria. Philip Khoury outlines the pattern; other scholars have nuanced the picture, like Nacklie Bou-Nacklie, or discussed recruitment from specific groups or into specific formations, as in Jean-David Mizrahi's account of the formation of the 'Circassian squadrons'.[5] (The policy pre-dated the mandate, indeed, with French recruitment of an initially mostly Armenian *Légion d'Orient* to fight against the Ottomans during the First World War.[6]) Patrick Seale discusses the participation of ʿAlawis in the armed forces of the mandate in his account of the rural ʿAlawi background of Hafiz al-Asad – an account which certainly takes 'minorities' to be the basis of French policy.[7] The effects of this pattern of recruitment on independent Syria have also been noted elsewhere: tellingly, Khoury closes his account of the mandate by discussing it, while Eyal Zisser's discussion of the 'Alawis' passage 'from ethnic minority to ruling sect' also draws the link.[8] The use of irregular troops from Armenian, Circassian and other communities in the repression of the 'Great Revolt' of 1925-7 is also well-known.[9] It is against the contemporary French interpretation of the revolt as a sectarian outburst instigated by feudal notables that Michael Provence argues that the uprising brought together different communities and different socioeconomic classes – that it was, in a sense, the crucible in which a Syrian nation was forged.[10]

Communitarianism did not only mark French military policy. The administrative division of Syria along communal lines is discussed in the general histories of the mandate; the so-called 'compact minorities' and the statelets attributed to them by the French have also been the specific subject of scholarly studies.[11] France's relations with Syria's refugee communities have been studied, too,[12] and with the Kurds – a community including recently arrived refugees and long-established residents.[13] French policy 'ethnicised' groups whose boundaries and communal identity had not previously been clear.[14] This understanding of Syrian society as primordially divided was materialised in the form of countless postcards and photographs of communal 'types', often playing out typical 'scenes'.[15]

My aim here is not to dispute the well-supported position that French policy had a communitarian basis, but rather to nuance the argument that France's policy of 'divide and rule' was based on cultivating close links with minority groups in order to offset the opposition of the majority – the terms that are commonly used in this literature.[16] Although not entirely inaccurate, this interpretation is unsatisfactory. It assumes that at the start of the mandate there was a coherent majority in Syria from which other groups can be easily distinguished as minorities – an unsafe assumption, since these concepts became meaningful in Syria only in the mandate period, and then only gradually. This interpretation also implies that minorities as such figured in the French imperialist vision of Syrian society. But if they were present at all, 'minorities' played a limited part in French rhetoric about Syrian society at the outset of the mandate. Sketching out the future organisation of Syria just before the French occupation of Damascus in 1920, the senior official, Robert de Caix, certainly used the term: in a long document proposing multiple divisions for the mandate territories, he called the 'protection of minorities' a 'primordial task of the mandatory Powers'. But this was in the final section, after a detailed survey of the areas claimed by France (and the many divisions within their population) in which the word appears little.[17] For the most part, in the early years of the mandate French writers focused on sectarian divisions in Syria without necessarily attaching the term 'minority' to them. Writing in 1929, Beauplan began his chapter on the division of Syria by referring specifically to de Caix and his 'great idea' of 1920 'which today still dominates our whole policy in the Levant' – but he proceeded to describe that policy without using the word 'minority' once.[18] This indicates the weak hold of the concept at that time. It spread gradually in both French and Syrian usage as the 1920s and 1930s progressed. By the mid-1930s it was common in both French and Syrian writings about Syria – but it was not applied in the same way to all communities that were numerical minorities.

Simply seeing French policy as one of manipulating or instrumentalising minorities carries other risks. First, it tends to assume the power and agency of the coloniser while overlooking the agency of the colonised – with the possible exception of the nationalists who opposed France. In fact, even individual members of 'minority' communities who were strongly pro-French were far from being passive tools of imperialism: they were agents who made their own choices, and were quite capable of putting pressure on France to advance their own interests. Second, it overlooks the diversity of responses to the French presence between and within particular 'minorities': in every community – the 'majority' as well as the 'minorities' – there was a range of responses to French imperialism. And third, it ignores the significant differences in the way the French treated different 'minorities': significant both in the sense that they were large, and that they reveal much about the imperial understanding of Syrian society. As we will see, in their effort to divide and rule, French officials in Syria gave most weight to religious divisions. Although they did exploit Syria's ethnolinguistic divisions, it was in a less extensive, less formalised way. The gradual and incomplete change from a sectarian to a minoritarian understanding of Syrian society – in both French and Syrian sources – reflects the transformation of that society. By analysing the French imperial understanding of Syrian society on which this policy of divide and rule was based, I hope to offer a more nuanced account of how it functioned. My analysis starts with a brief account of the contemporary European understanding of the Ottoman millet system, in which the French understanding of post-Ottoman Syrian society was rooted.

European Understandings of the Ottoman Millet System

According to the classical European understanding of the millet system, the non-Muslim communities of the Ottoman Empire were divided up according to their religion: Greek Orthodox Christian, Armenian Christian and Jewish. Each of these communities was given political autonomy, under the authority of the Patriarch in the first two cases and the Chief Rabbi in the last. The head of each community was a senior official of the Ottoman administration resident in Constantinople; the first holders of these posts had been appointed by Mehmet the Conqueror immediately after the city fell to him in 1453. The millets were discrete units, administered by their respective religious hierarchies through which they interacted with the state, for example, by paying tax; each had its own legal system for personal status law. There was little interaction between the non-Muslim millets, or between them and the Muslim population.

This understanding of the system has been extensively revised in the last thirty years.[19] It is too dependent on the view from Constantinople: it assumes that the formal legal relationship of the millets in Constantinople was reflected throughout the empire. Moreover, it anachronistically projects the state of affairs existing at the apogee, and under the influence, of European expansion in the empire back into the Ottoman past. Thus, it presents the 'system' as being more systematic than it in fact was. The formal relationship between the non-Muslim peoples of the empire and the state varied considerably from place to place and over time, rather than being set in stone from 1453; the very concept of the millet as a specific community of non-Muslim Ottoman subjects developed much later than that.[20] If the Ottoman authorities even in the empire's heyday were unable to impose central control over the population (assuming that such a thing was even considered desirable then), it is unlikely that the Patriarch's authority over the Greek Orthodox of Homs, say, was especially effective. His spiritual authority might be acknowledged, but in temporal matters diversity was the rule. The Jewish community of Salonica – the largest in the empire – consistently rejected the authority of the chief rabbi in Istanbul.[21] The clergy's role in actual administration of the community was probably smaller than was once thought. Within the non-Muslim communities, religious subdivisions gradually came to be recognised by the establishment of new millets, for example, the Armenian Protestant millet recognised by the Sultan in 1850 under British pressure. There were fourteen officially recognised millets by 1914, while several religious communities that were (broadly speaking) Muslim but were distant from the Ottoman state's official interpretation of Sunni Islam – notably, for our purposes, the Druzes and 'Alawis of the Levant – behaved as unofficial millets, a term I explain below.

The danger of describing Ottoman society in terms of the millet system is that, by assuming a systematic organisation of state–society relations, we may overlook the ad hoc and constantly developing nature of those relations, especially at the local level away from Constantinople. It is better to acknowledge that the millet system was not systematic: it constantly adapted to meet new circumstances. The complicated reality of interaction between the religious communities of the empire, and between individual non-Muslims and the state, is obscured by the assumption that it was extremely limited. Likewise, the diversity of the empire's populations, both Muslim and non-Muslim, is obscured by the assumption that only religious divisions mattered, when even within the main religious groupings there were many more cleavages, both religious and ethnolinguistic. In the transformation of the Ottoman communities, ethnolinguistic divisions gained a primacy they had never had under the millet system.

Although by the nineteenth century European perceptions of Ottoman society were influencing how that society perceived itself, the millet ideal was not merely a creation of European scholarship: the millets themselves traced their lineage back to the conquest of Constantinople.[22] This reflects an historical irony. Under the ideal of the millet system, religion was the main marker of identity, religious law was paramount and religious hierarchies wielded temporal authority over the non-Muslim communities on behalf of the Sultan. These three phenomena had probably never been as prevalent in practice as in theory – but the ideal crystallised at exactly the point when they began to wane definitively, in favour of ethnic/national identities, secular law and the secularisation of political authority within the millets.

For the purposes of this book, however, the most important thing to bear in mind about the classical ideal of the millet system as outlined above is that this was the understanding that French officials under the mandate brought to Syrian society: they believed that it was a society already divided along religious lines into numerous mutually suspicious and insular communities, and that religious identities trumped all other kinds – a tenacious misconception about the Middle East. 'Each community is a little people, jealous of its personality, which has its chief, national and religious at the same time; they are so many nations, and in effect they carry that name.'[23] Therefore, the political divisions they sought to impose followed religious lines – divisions that applied both to the territory and to the population under mandate. In categorising the population by religion in censuses the French authorities followed Ottoman precedent; the same could be argued for the use of religious communal law to divide the population, although the French extended official recognition in this way to communities that had previously lacked it. Likewise, while the administrative division of the mandate territories along religious lines had some precedent in the late Ottoman era – namely, the special administrative status granted to the *mütesarrifiye* of Mount Lebanon in the 1860s – it went far beyond that precedent. Syrian society reacted to these administrative and judicial divisions in unpredictable ways.

A Religious Ordering of Society within a Secular Nation-state Form

The emergence of minorities in Syria took place within the framework of a new nation-state form created by the Allied powers after the First World War. This state and France's role in it both derived legally from Article 22 of the League of Nations Covenant, which enshrined the principle of 'mandates'. Clause 4 states that:

> Certain communities formerly belonging to the Turkish Empire have reached a stage of development where their existence as independent nations can be provisionally recognised subject to the rendering of administrative advice and assistance by a Mandatory until such time as they are able to stand alone.[24]

Simultaneously, therefore, the mandate both justified French occupation and legitimated Syrian nationalism – which, developing from pre-war Arabism, was already a rising force.

James Gelvin has shown how the emir Faysal's short-lived regime attempted to mobilise the population using a nationalism defined from above, while a popular nationalism with rather different priorities emerged in Syria's larger cities.[25] This national feeling was not universal: it should not, for example, be taken as expressing the will of a coherent majority. (Later chapters will elaborate on this point.) It was sufficiently dynamic, however, to represent the main challenge to French rule. Colonial rule provided a rallying point for nationalism even as colonial policies undermined it, and the nation-state form in itself encouraged nationalism even if Syrian nationalism felt cramped by the borders imposed in the post-war peace settlement. Within those borders, the emergence of minorities (as opposed to millets) was inevitable. Even without the Sykes–Picot agreement and the mandate, a Syrian nation-state of some form would still have appeared, with its own borders, nationalism and 'minorities', to seek recognition by the League of Nations – as the example of the Turkish Republic suggests.

Despite this new, explicitly national framework of the Syrian state, the French attempted to reinforce religious divisions: particularly, by distributing seats to representative bodies on religious communal grounds; extending legal autonomy in matters of personal status to communities which had not previously been autonomous; and granting territorial autonomy to certain religiously defined groups. That is, by extending what remained of the Ottoman millet system – as they understood it. This policy adhered to the colonial theories of Marshal Lyautey, whose principle of *association* as opposed to *assimilation* had been developed in Morocco.[26] Rather than attempting to assimilate Syrian society to French norms, the mandatory authorities would rule by association with that society, through native governments and laws. Ottoman legal reforms since the mid-nineteenth century had reduced legal distinctions between Muslim and non-Muslim subjects, but in the important area of personal status law religious distinctions still obtained.[27] The continued competence of communal religious courts in this area was ensured by Article 6 of the mandate charter, including the line: 'Respect for the personal status of the various peoples and their religious interests shall be fully guaranteed.' On this basis, personal status law was crucial to French efforts to divide Syria's communities religiously.

Examples are numerous. Before the mandate even officially began, the High Commission established separate 'Alawi religious courts on the authority of a judgement from an amenable Muslim legal scholar that the 'Alawis were not heretical Muslims but a distinct religious community.[28] A later High Commissioner, Damien de Martel, issued a decree on religious law – *Arrêté no. 60/L.R.*, of 13 March 1936 – requiring the communities to submit their own communal statute for governmental approval, based on their religious texts and traditions. This remained in abeyance due to Sunni Muslim opposition, but French efforts to formalise the position of religious communities continued – even when the community was so small it had no religious authorities competent to draw up its own communal law, as with the Isma'ilis.[29]

What were the reasons for this policy of extending, not reducing, the religious divisions of Ottoman law? It derived from the French authorities' religious understanding of Syrian society, itself influenced by France's historical links with the Christian communities. Maintaining these communities as client groups – above all, justifying the separation from the rest of the mandate territories of a Lebanese state dominated by Maronite Christians – required a system of political organisation which kept them distinct from the rest of the population. Since the main Christian communities were Arabic-speakers, that meant choosing a religiously-ordered organisation. The active contribution of some Syrian Christians influenced this choice. It should be stressed, however, that this policy could be perfectly effective without any reference to the concept of 'minority': it found its justification in religious differences, not number. (In Lebanon, indeed, a similar policy of religious division was effectively put into place, with the active cooperation of some Lebanese, but without anything resembling a 'majority'.) Later, the concepts of majority and minority would be bolted on to those different religious groups by both French and Syrian observers. But they were not there at the outset.

When the French tried to order Syrian society along religious lines, however, the various Syrian communities – religious or other – did not react as planned. Their reactions were conditioned, in a way that French actors often failed to understand, by the transition to a nation-state form. The next part of the chapter considers these communities, grouped into three main categories: non-arabophone Sunni Muslim communities; Arabic-speakers belonging to (broadly) Muslim, but not Sunni, religious communities; and arabophone Christians.[30] References to nationalist sources give 'minorities' the necessary context of a 'majority', showing how a majority in formation both reacted to and acted on the formation of minorities.

Within a Syrian Arab nation-state, Syria's Sunni Muslim community split along ethnolinguistic lines.[31] The various strands of Syrian Arab nationalism were most strongly rooted in, and addressed themselves most directly to, the Sunni Muslim Arabs who dominated Syria's cities and towns: the national 'majority' (though while nationalists may have taken this majority for granted, historians should not: Sunni Muslim Arabs were not an overwhelming majority in the mandate territories as a whole,[32] while the term 'majority' itself glosses over important divisions). Despite the French conception of religion as the main marker of identity, it was probably easier for arabophone religious minorities to join that 'majority' than it was for non-arabophone Sunni

Muslim groups: Circassians, Kurds and Turks. In an editorial written early in the mandate period, the (Christian) newspaper editor Yusuf al-'Issa proposed the adoption of the Prophet's birthday – 'the Arab Prophet's birthday'[33] – as a national holiday which would rally the entire nation: that is, 'all the arabophone communities [*kull al-ṭawā'if al-nāṭiqa bil-ḍād*]'.[34] Moreover, Syria should follow republican Turkey's example by inculcating a national identity through state education – and Syria faced fewer barriers to unity, because 'our country contains only one, Arab, stock'.

Al-'Issa's vision of a nation united by the Arabic language was no doubt partly intended to counter the insistent French claim that religious divisions in Syrian society were irremediable; it shows that majorities are open to multiple definitions. Like any definition of a majority, however, this one creates its own minorities: to find a national identity capable of overcoming religious divisions, al-'Issa adopted an ethnolinguistic definition of nationality that excluded non-Arabic-speakers – indeed, denied their existence on Syrian soil. But such communities did exist. The new nation-state form had created the conditions for them to become 'minorities', a transformation wrought partly by the decision of individuals within those communities to employ a language of 'minorities' in advancing their own political interests. Within the nation-state, such communities had to negotiate their relationship with the national majority, even if the identity of that majority remained vague. One factor governing this relationship was the extent to which minorities were identified with external actors, starting with the League of Nations – a reference point for anyone wishing his or her community to be defined as a 'minority'. To the larger Sunni Muslim ethnolinguistic minorities, other external actors probably mattered more: for the Kurds, the Kurdish minorities of neighbouring states; for the Turkish-speakers of Alexandretta, the Turkish Republic. This situation is comparable with that of minorities (officially recognised or not) in central and eastern Europe at that time. Things were different for the small and dispersed Circassian community, which was not identified with a neighbouring state or with neighbouring populations. Rather, like Syria's Christian communities it was often identified with the French High Commission; for example, because of the latter's heavy recruitment of Circassians into its armed forces, and the willingness of Circassians to be recruited.

Some members of these ethnolinguistic communities made full use of the repertoire of political action opened to them by the growing weight of the concept of 'minority' in international public discourse – not least at the League, since the mandate was a constant reference point for the French authorities. Understanding their changed position, within a decade of the French occupation they were pushing for political representation and international guarantees of their rights as national minorities analogous to those of central and eastern Europe. But 'the High Commission has always refused to consent to the organisation of a Kurdish minority as elsewhere to the organisation of any other ethnic minority'.[35] Some Circassians had requested the recognition of their political rights as a 'minority' by 1928, if not earlier.[36] Such demands troubled the French, who were unwilling to acknowledge ethnolinguistic minorities within the religious majority. One of the High Commissioner's delegates clarified the French position:

> Under the name 'communities' are generally designated groupings of individuals of the same religion and the same rite ... This definition of communities evidently excludes any other grouping whose individuals are united by links other than confessional links (community of religion and of rite).
>
> The Tcherkess [Circassians] are of Sunni Muslim religion (Hanafite rite) and cannot, from the confessional point of view, form a distinct community.[37]

If international law gave them this status and they had specific common interests to defend, he wrote, the Circassians might be considered an 'ethnic minority' – but he preferred to adopt, 'in the political order', a religious classification, as 'resolving without difficulty the problem of representation of the minorities or the distribution of seats in the representative assemblies'.

Such a religious distribution of political power – with a guaranteed proportion of representation reserved for religious minorities – favoured France's Christian clients: this, along with a two-stage electoral system and judicious intimidation, made it easier (though not always easy) to turn supposedly representative institutions into instruments of French domination. Allowing Circassian representation as an ethnic minority, however, would invalidate that religious distribution of power. Syrian identities were in flux at this time, and many French and Christian writers asserted or assumed that religious boundaries implied ethnic, even 'racial', boundaries – stating, for example, that the administrative division of Syria had been 'imposed ... by the populations concerned, who are separated by rivalries of race as well as their religious beliefs'.[38] But such assertions were made to reinforce the religious division of society, not for their own sake. An ethnolinguistic division of society would subsume the mainly Arabic-speaking Christians within a group dominated by Sunni Muslim Arabs, the community perceived by the French – with much generalisation – as being the most 'nationalist'. This would imperil the religious conception of Syrian society that justified both the French presence and the separate status of Lebanon, where France's interests and clients were concentrated. When Kurds requested autonomy for the regions they inhabited, the threat was greater: as a much larger, more concentrated community than the Circassians, their claim to a state menaced not only the religious order France had imposed, but also Syrian Arab nationalism and the nationalisms of neighbouring states. Turkey, especially, put constant pressure on the High Commissioner to ensure that no such autonomy be granted.[39]

Of course, the French reluctance to recognise ethnolinguistic minorities officially did not preclude the exploitation of ethnolinguistic divisions, for example by recruiting Circassian squadrons into the Troupes du Levant.[40] This policy, which extended also to Armenians from the refugee community, had a (deliberately) damaging effect on communal relations. In Ulfat al-Idilbi's semi-autobiographical novel, *Dimashq ya basmat al-huzn*, such recruits are described as 'mercenaries, who had lived by the goodness of this nation then turned against its people and joined the enemy'.[41] The character narrating these words, like the author, belongs to the Damascene Sunni Muslim elite that provided Syrian Arab nationalism with many of its leading figures, and arguably its most responsive audience.

The Arabic-speaking, Muslim, but non-Sunni communities of Syria – notably the Druzes and the ʿAlawis – were in a rather different situation. They had never been officially recognised as millets, since the Ottoman Empire did not recognise divisions within Islam. But, living in areas relatively remote from the urban centres of political life in Syria, they were accustomed to running their own affairs, subject to fluctuating levels of state interference.[42] They can therefore be regarded as 'unofficial' millets: religiously demarcated communities exercising a large measure of autonomy, sometimes with official toleration.[43] These groups are often described as 'compact minorities' because their geographical concentration enabled the French to set them apart in statelets of their own.[44] Because this was done on religious lines, it reinforced the religious conception of Syrian society rather than undermining it. But calling these communities 'minorities' prior to Syria's independence is problematic: the term does not fully explain their relationship with either the French authorities or Syrian Arab nationalism.

At the time of the 1936 treaty negotiations the High Commission received, and forwarded to Paris and the League of Nations, numerous telegrams and statements from inhabitants of the ʿAlawi statelet both for and against its being placed under the authority of Damascus. Petitions arguing against the region's incorporation into Syria generally did not use the language of minorities, instead simply requesting autonomy – sometimes as a community, often without specifying.[45] One of the rare petitions that did use the term 'minority' came from ʿAlawi and Christian members of the region's representative council. It stated that:

> the populations of this government belong to different Communities, each one having its beliefs, traditions, and distinct customs. *Relative to Syria as a whole*, they constitute minorities that cannot and do not wish to be incorporated into Syrian Unity in any way.[46]

They did not consider themselves to be minorities: they were trying to avoid becoming minorities by their incorporation into a larger Syrian state.

This is in marked contrast with the Christian communities, who, as we shall see below, had wholeheartedly adopted the language of minorities by this time. The difference, I think, lies in the geography. The millet system had never had territorial implications and for the Christian communities of Syria (Lebanon apart) it never would. But the Druzes and the ʿAlawis, while considering themselves as separate communities for religious reasons, like millets, were also attached to territorial units. Their geographical concentration had obtained for them separate statelets: an institutional framework within which they could mobilise as a majority, with no more reason to consider themselves a 'minority' than Scots in Scotland. The Syrian judge and politician, Yusuf al-Hakim, who came from the ʿAlawi region and was involved in attempts to re-incorporate it into Syria, frequently refers to the ʿAlawis as a majority, *akthariyya*, in his memoirs.[47] The French, preoccupied with the Christians, might consider Muslim but non-Sunni communities as distinct groups (that is, as millets; hence, the 'officialisation' of ʿAlawi, Ismaʿili or Druze communal law), or recruit them disproportionately into the army,[48] but they rarely considered them as 'minorities'. Nationalist Druzes and ʿAlawis, meanwhile, considered themselves to be not minorities but part of the Syrian Arab majority.

Thus, whether they were motivated by a desire to maintain majority status in an autonomous state (albeit aware of the prospect of becoming a minority in a unified Syria), or asserting membership of a wider national majority, simply describing these communities as minorities is unsatisfactory. It does not explain why individuals belonging to these communities acted as they did, and occludes diverse political opinions within them. It also risks reading history backwards, implying either that a Syrian nation-state with a coherent majority already existed at the beginning of the mandate or that the incorporation of these communities into a Syrian nation-state as minorities was inevitable. The process of state formation that fixed them, as minorities, within a Syrian nation-state was taking place during the mandate, despite the French attempts to separate them. But it was not complete.[49] The fact that in the mandate period they are rarely identified as minorities, either by themselves or by the French, reflects this.

Some communities, though, did have members who described themselves as minorities, and were wholeheartedly claimed as such – unlike the Kurds or Circassians – by the French: the Christian communities which had already had communal legal status as millets in the Ottoman period.[50] Although this chapter contends that minorities are not the same as millets, French officials were most comfortable when that equivalence could be made. So were many Syrian Christians, especially clergymen, who accepted the continuation and rigidification of the millet system. Indeed, they acted perhaps more than ever before according to the ideal of the system: the clergy provided almost the only political leadership of these communities to leave a trace in the French archival sources I have read. This may reveal more about the High Commission's preferences when selecting privileged interlocutors (or which correspondence they took seriously enough to keep) than about the realities of political organisation among Syria's Christians, but it is obvious enough that the French preferred to use religion to structure their relationship with these communities. This also permitted them, and their Christian allies, to marginalise the (many) Christians who were not hostile to nationalism.[51]

This policy suited the historic justification for French involvement in the Ottoman Empire, the protection of the Christian communities; but it sat uneasily with the secular nation-state form and the philosophy of League of Nations. In line with that philosophy, the French, therefore, gradually came to recast both their present purpose and their past involvement in Syria as being the protection of 'minorities'. Pro-French Christians did the same. The concept was in any case becoming increasingly meaningful in Syria, as various institutions of the nation-state took deeper root; now – and only now – it also became an important part of the self-justifying rhetoric of French imperialism. This development was related to the growing pressure on France to put an end to the mandate and sign a treaty granting Syrian independence, especially after Britain had done just this in Iraq. The new nation-states of Europe had had to sign minorities treaties with the League as a condition of their independence: these offered a legal precedent for minorities clauses to be inserted into any treaty with Syria, as a means by which France might retain its right to interfere in Syrian affairs.[52] Unsurprisingly, the 'minorities question' became a crucial and sticky one in successive rounds of treaty negotiations in the 1930s. But behind this terminological shift lay the same preoccupation with Christians: whether it is used by pro-French Syrians, French officials or Syrian nationalists, 'minorities' is frequently a synonym for 'Christian [and sometimes Jewish] communities'.

Thus, Christian clergymen such as Monsignor Ignace Nouri wrote to the High Commissioner, Damien de Martel, to demand continued French protection of the minorities, 'that is to say, the Christians and Jews'.[53] His letter also gives an extremely partial account of the treatment of Syria's (Christian) 'minorities' in history: it is not only modern scholars who project this modern category into the past. Martel's comment to the *New York Times*, meanwhile, that France was in Syria to protect the country's 'Christian elements' elicited protests from Christian nationalists in Aleppo.[54]

The Persistence of 'Millet' Identities?

The controversy about minorities during the 1930s, especially during the 1936 treaty negotiations, raises an intriguing point about the seeming persistence of millet identities in post-Ottoman Syria: that nationalists were just as keen as the French to restrict the term 'minority' to former (non-Muslim) millets. Why?

Externally guaranteed 'protection' for minorities was no more welcome to Syrian nationalists than to the governments of the new states of Europe, whose recognition by the League was conditional on their signing minorities treaties.[55] It represented an infringement of national sovereignty, and in the Syrian case an obvious excuse for permanent French interference. In a 1932 editorial discussing the pretexts for British and French involvement in the Middle East, Najib al-Rayyis summed it up in a few words: 'As for Syria, always minorities'.[56] But if that word might grudgingly be applied to Christians, al-Rayyis had no wish to see its uses extended: this article sets out to rebut the claim, published in *La Syrie*, that France had responsibilities towards a Shi'ite 'minority' in Lebanon. Al-Rayyis points out that '"minorities" had been known as a term for Christians only' and denies that the 'Muslim Arab Shi'a' constitute a minority.[57]

There are several possible reasons for this. The first is the most obvious: that the division of society along religious lines into Muslims (all Muslims), on the one hand, and non-Muslim millets, on the other, was not merely an imperialist construct but had resonance for Syrian writers. We can say this without reproducing French imperialist rhetoric, especially if we take into account the ways in which the nation-state form had altered the relationship between religious groups and the state (something that may not have been clear to contemporary actors). For nationalists as much as for pro-French figures like Nouri, the millet system was a well-established framework within which Syrians could understand their own society – especially when it was taken for granted that that society was an Arab national community.

A second reason has less to do with established structures of thought, and more to do with current political concerns. Admitting the existence of minorities other than the Christian and Jewish communities would have posed difficult new problems to Syrian Arab nationalism – raising the possibility, for example, of Turkish-speakers in the Sanjak of Alexandretta demanding League-backed treaty guarantees with Ankara's support. Extending the term 'minority' to communities other than the former millets was not in the nationalists' interests. Earlier I cited a letter in which a French official mentioned the High Commission's refusal to recognise ethnic (that is, non-religious) minorities; the same letter adds that

> This is also the opinion expressed by Damascene nationalist circles, which intend to hold to respecting the rights already acquired by confessional minorities only. The Kurds being Muslims like the Tcherkesses must in this regard be assimilated to the Syrians [*sic*] of the same religion.[58]

Interestingly, Sunni Muslims (and not only active nationalists) also continued the old assumption that non-Sunni Muslim groups had no right to recognition as separate communal entities – as we saw in the extract from al-Rayyis with respect to the Shi'a. While this can be understood within the 'traditional' framework of the millet system, as a refusal to admit religious divisions within Islam, among nationalists it can also be understood as a convenient means of delegitimising the territorial separation of the Druze and 'Alawi statelets within the new framework of the nation-state.[59]

On the French side, meanwhile, the preference for keeping to a 'millet' understanding of Syrian society has already been explored in some detail above. With regard to the specific question of minorities in the treaty negotiations, we might add that it would suit French interests quite well to retain a right of intervention on behalf of Syrian Christians – a small community, lacking any major external backing from other sources, and with a strong pro-French element. It would be rather less in French interests to take on an obligation to protect, for example, a Kurdish 'minority' whose loyalty to France was far shakier, and whose existence as part of a far larger Kurdish population spreading across regional borders (and far beyond French influence) raised the possibility of France being drawn into conflict not only with an independent Syrian government but with neighbouring states. This did not stop Kurds demanding communal recognition, of course.

The question remains as to why the Christian hierarchies, too, continued to act as millets, despite having adopted a new term – 'minorities' – which fitted the times and qualified them for international protection. The following suggestions are speculative, but I hope plausible. First, as well as legitimating France's presence in the Levant the religious conception of society strengthened the Christian communities as privileged clients of France, in the eyes of some Christians at least. This would also explain why some Christians might prefer that ethnolinguistic minorities were not recognised as such: it would dilute their own claim to special status. Second, the political significance of the religious hierarchies would likely dwindle in a national (as opposed to religious) state. Many clergymen disliked the transition to secular authority within their communities. This process had begun long before, as had their opposition to it: Niyazi Berkes notes that 'the religious leaders of the *millets* were the most strongly opposed to the secularizing provisions of the [1856 Ottoman] Reform Edict'.[60] The French willingness to accept the clergy as the chief legitimate authority within the Christian communities provided an opportunity to arrest the process.

Not all Christians, not even all clergymen, were hostile to nationalism: the Greek Orthodox, especially, seem to have asserted their place within a Syrian Arab nation.[61] (Perhaps because of this, mandate officials often called them 'cousins of Islam'.[62]) At the height of the minorities controversy, in 1936, a senior French official in Damascus complained that the Greek Orthodox Patriarch Alexandros III Tahan had visited nationalist leaders and 'allowed himself to say that he "didn't understand all the noise being made over the question of minorities; we're all Arabs and we don't need any special protection except that of the common laws in an Arab country".'[63] But Tahan was untypical. Many Christian clergymen held onto a religious political order that preserved their own influence, adopting the new term 'minority' for that purpose – at the risk of excluding their communities from the majority in formation.

For Christian nationalists like Yusuf al-ʿIssa, it thus became necessary to transcend millet identities: to insist – to other Christians, to the French, but especially to the wider nationalist movement – that the religious difference did not affect the status of Christians as members of the national community; that they were not, in any politically meaningful sense, a 'minority'. It was not always an easy task, and it was made harder by the cooperation between some other Christians and the French authorities, which reinforced the sense among many Muslim nationalists that Christians were not fully part of the national community.

As we can see, then, it was not only due to simple inertia or the persistence of primordial religious categories that aspects of the millet system remained operative underneath the new terminology of minorities. But the seeming continuity of an older order can mask the current political concerns of those involved; it can also make us forget – as many actors at the time perhaps forgot – that the situation of a minority in a nation-state is riskier than that of a millet. The Ottoman millets had a recognised and accepted place in the Ottoman polity. In the post-Ottoman nation-states of the Middle East, minorities, religious or otherwise, risked a greater degree of exclusion.[64]

High Commissioner Damien de Martel understood that risk. In July 1937 he related to Paris his recent meeting with the apostolic delegate, Monsignor Leprêtre, and the Syrian-Catholic Monsignor Tappouni. They had discussed the relatively light-handed protection of minorities guaranteed by the 1936 treaty:

> these intelligent prelates willingly recognize that the disappearance of the Ottoman Empire has put the question of minorities onto quite new bases. Within an empire composed of heterogeneous nationalities, the Christian communities were able to constitute themselves as 'nations' and benefit from a foreign protection the principle of which was not contested. But on the ruins of the Ottoman Empire states with a national basis have created themselves, whose patriotism risks being all the stormier for being younger ... The traditional mission of protector of minorities [sic] that France has assumed for centuries has become, because of this fact, much more complex. By protecting them too assertively or too strictly, or by seeming to take their presence as a pretext for hindering the development of national sentiment, France would have risked making its protégés into foreign bodies condemned to exodus or massacre on the day when international complications prevented her from defending the threatened minorities effectively.[65]

But even Martel still refers only to religious minorities, despite understanding the 'national' root of the problem. He also lets France off too lightly: although

French humanitarian concern for the minorities was genuine – the refugee communities were a worrying reminder of the fate of national minorities in an era of nation-states[66] – it was inextricably linked with the furthering of French imperial aims. The French had already placed the minorities at risk, not by 'protecting them too assertively' but by using them as a justification for occupation and exploiting them as a political (and military) tool against the formation of an inclusive national community in Syria.

Conclusion

In Chapter 1, I argued that the concept of 'minority' came into widespread usage when it did, after First World War, because it was only in this period that objective conditions made the term meaningful: the term did not exist earlier because 'minorities' did not exist, though the cultural identities by which majorities and minorities would later be defined in some form did. While some of those conditions were falling into place in the late Ottoman period, it was only during the mandate, in the context of a Syrian nation-state, that the term 'minority' was adopted by Syrians and others to describe groups within Syrian society. The 'minorities question' became relevant in Syria at the same time as it did in European states.

It would be an over-statement, though, to say that minorities sprang into existence in 1918, when a Syrian state independent of the Ottoman Empire was established, or 1922, when a Syrian state under French mandate was recognised by the League of Nations. Underlying the quite sudden change in the formal structure of the state in Syria were slower, deeper processes of state formation that had begun in the Ottoman period but continued in the mandate period. By examining here the ways in which the concept of 'minority' was explicitly employed in the mandate period I have tried to give an understanding of some of the changes wrought by the imposition of a new state-form, but also of some of the continuities from earlier times. In a nation-state based on an identity which included the component of the Arabic language, ethnolinguistic divisions – already becoming more salient in the later Ottoman period – gained an added edge. But as we have also seen, that did not necessarily mean that religious divisions became less salient: in some senses, French, Syrian nationalist and pro-French Syrian writers all had an interest in concentrating on religious differences as a means of excluding ethnolinguistic questions from the debate about minorities.

One thing that emerges clearly from this analysis is that the use of the category of 'minority' to describe French policy in Syria has generally been unsatisfactory, largely because it assumes that minorities – and a majority – existed in Syria at the outset of the mandate. If we accept the term as meaningful at all, what made groups as diverse as Syrian ʿAlawis, Greek Orthodox Christians or Kurds into 'minorities' was the emergence and development in this period of a Syrian nation-state with an Arab identity. The same goes for the majority. Even within French rhetoric about Syrian society, the concept of minority only became prominent in the second half of the mandate period.

The rest of this book explores certain specific themes illustrating the different processes that acted to make the concept of minority ever more meaningful in the 1920s and 1930s. In Chapter 1, I noted the importance of a coherent national territory under something approaching a uniform state authority: until these develop there is no reason for members of specific communities to start to see themselves as linked to all other members of the same communities within the state, whether as a majority or minorities. Here, I have noted that describing the Druzes and ʿAlawis as 'compact minorities' implies the prior existence of a Syrian national territory to which the Druze and ʿAlawi statelets – and the Druzes and ʿAlawis themselves – 'belonged'. In Chapter 3, I use the Druze and ʿAlawi cases, and several others, to show how the issue of 'separatism' illustrates both the development of a new conception of the national territory and the spread of state authority. Chapter 4 continues my analysis of the intensification of the state's authority over its territory by examining the causes and effects of the definition of the Syrian–Turkish frontier. It draws out the complex relationship between the definition of frontiers and the emergence of minorities by studying Syria's Kurds.

The final two chapters focus on developments in international and Syrian law. Chapter 5 places the emergence of the language of minorities in Syria in the context of developments in international law between the wars, as the nation-state became the standard state form. The change was not just terminological: the existence of a (novel) body of international law relating to 'minorities' meant that the term had a specific legal content and political implications. But, as I have noted here, it was not until the treaty negotiations of the 1930s that the term became widely used in Syria. Chapter 5 explains why; it also shows what different individuals and groups within the different communities stood to gain, and lose, by adopting this language. The final chapter, meanwhile, uses French attempts to reform personal status law in Syria – part of the effort to structure the religious division of Syrian society described above – to illustrate how the increasing systematisation and 'uniformisation' of the state's relationship to society contributed to the development of a sense of being a minority among certain populations. It also provided an opportunity for certain figures to claim to speak for a majority.

Notes

1. Robert de Beauplan, *Où va la Syrie? Le mandat sous les cèdres* (Paris: J. Tallandier, 1929), p. 53.
2. Beauplan, *Où va la Syrie?*, p. 32.

3. Khoury, *Syria and the French Mandate*; Hourani, *Syria and Lebanon*; Longrigg, *Syria and Lebanon*.
4. Edmund Burke, III, 'A comparative view of French native policy in Morocco and Syria, 1912–1925', *Middle Eastern Studies* (1973), 9(3): 175–86.
5. Khoury, *Syria and the French Mandate*, pp. 80–2; N. E. Bou-Nacklie, 'Les Troupes Spéciales: religious and ethnic recruitment, 1916–46', *International Journal of Middle East Studies* (1993), 25(4): 645–60; Mizrahi, *Genèse de l'État mandataire*, pp. 152–4.
6. Vahé Tachjian, *La France en Cilicie et en Haute-Mésopotamie. Aux confins de la Turquie, de la Syrie et de l'Irak (1919–1933)* (Paris: Karthala, 2004), pp. 32–3 and *passim*.
7. Patrick Seale, *Asad of Syria: The Struggle for the Middle East* (London: I. B. Tauris, 1988), chs 1–2.
8. Khoury, *Syria and the French Mandate*, pp. 628–30; also pp. 133–4 of Eyal Zisser, 'The 'Alawis, lords of Syria: from ethnic minority to ruling sect', in Ofra Bengio and Gabriel Ben-Dor (eds), *Minorities and the State in the Arab World* (Boulder, CO: Lynne Rienner Publishers, 1999), pp. 129–45.
9. Khoury, *Syria and the French Mandate*, pp. 191–2, 196, 206.
10. Provence, *The Great Syrian Revolt*.
11. E.g., in Itamar Rabinovich, 'The compact minorities and the Syrian state, 1918–1945', *Journal of Contemporary History* (1979), 14(4): 693–712, or Birgit Schaebler, 'State(s) power and the Druzes: integration and the struggle for social control (1838–1949)', in Philipp and Schaebler (eds), *The Syrian Land*, pp. 331–67.
12. On French policy towards Armenians, Ellen Marie Lust-Okar, 'Failure of collaboration: Armenian refugees in Syria', *Middle Eastern Studies* (1996), 32(1): 53–68, and Keith D. Watenpaugh, 'Towards a new category of colonial theory: colonial cooperation and the *survivors' bargain* – the case of the post-genocide Armenian community of Syria under French mandate', in Méouchy and Sluglett (eds), *The British and French Mandates*, pp. 597–622. On French policy towards refugee communities more generally: Tachjian, *La France en Cilicie*.
13. Jordi Tejel Gorgas, 'Le mouvement kurde de Turquie en exil. Continuités et discontinuités du nationalisme kurde sous le mandat français en Syrie et au Liban (1925–1946)', doctoral thesis, École des hautes études en sciences sociales/Université de Fribourg; Fuccaro, 'Minorities and ethnic mobilisation'; and McDowall, *A Modern History of the Kurds*, pp. 466–84 on the Kurds.
14. The term comes from Kais M. Firro, 'Ethnicizing the Shi'is in mandatory Lebanon', *Middle Eastern Studies* (2006), 42(5): 741–59.
15. Pierre Fournié, 'La représentation des particularismes ethniques et religieux en Syrie et au Liban', in Blanchard *et al.* (eds), *L'autre et nous: «Scènes et types». Anthropologues et historiens devant les représentations des populations colonisées, des «ethnies», des «tribus» et des «races» depuis les conquêtes coloniales* (Paris: ACHAC, 1995), pp. 137–41 – though note that 'scenes and types' were also

common tropes of urban (especially Parisian) depictions of rural France: Graham Robb, *The Discovery of France* (London: Picador, 2007), p. 313.
16. See introduction, n. 1.
17. Reproduced in Gérard Khoury, *Une tutelle coloniale*, pp. 248–70, quote at 267. In total the word minority is used five times in twenty-three pages; three of those instances come in this one paragraph.
18. Beauplan, *Où va la Syrie?*, p. 50. The term is not entirely absent from Beauplan's book, but it is rare. In his short chapter dismantling 'The myth of Syrian unity' (ch. 3), where we might expect to find it often, it appears only once – a generic reference to the possible 'extinction of the weaker minorities' (p. 33) in the Ottoman Levant.
19. See among others (in a now extensive literature) the articles in Benjamin Braude and Bernard Lewis (eds), *Christians and Jews in the Ottoman Empire: The Functioning of a Plural Society. Vol. 1: The Central Lands* and *Vol. 2: The Arab Lands* (New York: Holmes & Meier, 1982), especially those by Cohen, Karpat and Ma'oz; Fatma Müge Göçek, 'Ethnic segmentation, western education, and political outcomes: nineteenth century Ottoman society', *Poetics Today* (1993), 14(3): 507–38; Lucette Valensi, 'Inter-communal relations and changes in religious affiliation in the Middle East (seventeenth to nineteenth centuries)', *Comparative Studies in Society and History* (1997), 39(2): 251–69; *Encyclopaedia of Islam* 1999: 'Millet'; Bruce Masters, *Christians and Jews in the Ottoman Arab World: The Roots of Sectarianism* (Cambridge: Cambridge University Press, 2001). Makdisi, *The Culture of Sectarianism*, removes sectarian violence in nineteenth-century Ottoman Syria from a narrative of primordial religious (millet) hatreds, seeing it instead as a result of identity formation under the pressure of Ottoman modernising reforms.
20. *Encyclopaedia of Islam* 1999: 'Millet'.
21. Mazower, *Salonica*, pp. 56–7.
22. Benjamin Braude, 'Foundation myths of the *millet* system', in Braude and Lewis (eds), *Christians and Jews in the Ottoman Empire*, vol. 1, pp. 69–88: see pp. 74–7 and following.
23. Haut Commissariat de la République française à Beyrouth, *La Syrie et le Liban en 1922* (Paris: Emile Larose, 1922), p. 53. 'Nation' here is likely a translation of millet – which has become the modern Turkish word for 'nation'.
24. *De facto*, the mandates pre-dated the League, having been granted to Britain and France at San Remo in 1920 by the chief Allied powers: namely, Britain and France.
25. James L. Gelvin, 'The other Arab nationalism: Syrian/Arab populism in its historical and international contexts', in James Jankowski and Israel Gershoni (eds), *Rethinking Nationalism in the Arab Middle East* (New York: Columbia University Press, 1997), pp. 231–48, and Gelvin, *Divided Loyalties: Nationalism and Mass Politics in Syria at the Close of Empire* (London: University of California Press, 1998).

26. Khoury, *Syria and the French Mandate*, pp. 55–7; Burke, 'A comparative view'. Burke states that in the early 1920s the French in Syria sought to administer certain 'minorities' separately; for reasons that will become clear, I would argue that the French did not systematically apply the concept of 'minority' to their Syrian policy until later, and that it is inappropriate for historians to use it in this context. Burke does not use the term 'majority', but is the only historian I have encountered to describe the Bedouin as a 'minority'. The standard English-language work on Lyautey in Morocco is Alan Scham, *Lyautey in Morocco: Protectorate Administration, 1912–1925* (Berkeley, CA: University of California Press, 1970).
27. M. E. Yapp, *The Making of the Modern Near East 1792–1923* (London: Longman, 1987), pp. 112–14.
28. Yusuf al-Hakim, *Sūriyya wal-intidāb al-faransī: dhikriyāt IV* (Beirut: Dār al-Nahār lil-Nashr, 1983), p. 53. See also Firro, 'Ethnicizing the Shi'is'.
29. AD-SL Box 494, dossier *Traité Franco-Syrien – Application – Question des minorités*. Martel to MAE, 19/4/1938.
30. It will be apparent from my laborious terminology that I do not take 'Arab' identity for granted.
31. See Introduction and Chapter 3 for the argument that Syria under the mandate can be taken as a nation-state in formation despite the territorial subdivisions imposed by France.
32. Bou-Nacklie, 'Les Troupes spéciales', p. 645. This useful point is unfortunately undermined by Bou-Nacklie's confused use of statistics.
33. This and following quotation from *Alif Bā'*, 27 October 1923.
34. '*al-nātiqa bil-dād*' literally means 'pronouncing the *dād*', a reference to the emphatic 'd' that is a characteristic sound of Arabic.
35. AD-SL Box 571, dossier *La question des Kurdes en Syrie. Correspondance. Les Comités Kurdes*. HC's assistant delegate for Aleppo vilayet to HC (16/5/1930).
36. AD-SL Box 568, dossier *Tcherkess*, subdossier *Armement des villages tcherkess de Boueidan, Blei, Bourak*. HC's delegate to State of Syria (Veber) to HC's delegate to Contrôle Général des Wakfs (23/2/1928).
37. This and following quotes from AD-SL Box 568, dossier *Tcherkess*, subdossier *Armement des villages tcherkess de Boueidan, Blei, Bourak*. Note (2/3/1928) by HC's delegate to Contrôle Général des Wakfs. NB: The use here of 'ethnic minority' precedes *Le Robert*'s first cited instance.
38. SHAT 4 H Box 122, dossier 1. *Note sur la situation politique dans le Levant* [1924].
39. See Chapter 4.
40. SHAT 4 H Box 261, dossier 1 *Historique du Groupement d'escadrons légers du Levant, 1922–1926*.
41. Ulfat al-Idilbi, *Dimashq ya basmat al-huzn* (Damascus: Dar Tlass, 1989), p. 190.
42. Provided that they caused no trouble. Hanna Batatu notes that, when necessary, the Ottoman state was quite capable of projecting its power into the 'Alawi mountains, for short periods at least: *Syria's Peasantry, the Descendants of its Lesser*

Rural Notability, and their Politics (Princeton, NJ: Princeton University Press, 1999), ch. 8.
43. Schaebler, 'State(s) power and the Druzes', pp. 336–9, gives evidence of such a relationship between the Ottoman state and the Druzes of Syria.
44. Rabinovich, 'The compact minorities'; Khoury, *Syria and the French Mandate*, ch. 20.
45. For reasons explained in Chapter 3, I prefer to avoid the term 'separatist'.
46. AD-SL Box 410, untitled dossier. Schœffler (Governor of Latakia) to Meyrier (Delegate General of HC), 4/4/1936 – copy of statement accompanying letter. Emphasis added.
47. Al-Hakim, *Sūriyya wal-intidāb al-faransī*.
48. A report by General Gamelin places the recruitment of Druze and 'Alawi units in the context of the army's political preference for maintaining territorial divisions in Syria: SHAT 4 H Box 134, dossier 2: *1926. Doubles: rapports Gamelin. Correspondances. Situations d'effectifs*. Gamelin to Minister of War and others (21/8/1926).
49. See Chapter 3.
50. Many of the observations made here would likely also apply to Syria's Jewish community in the mandate period, with the proviso that the community was very small and, relative to the Christian communities, unhierarchical.
51. Compare Firro's depiction of French policy towards Shi'i leaders in Lebanon, 'reward[ing] leaders who sided with the Mandate and the Lebanese state, while marginalizing those who remained loyal to Syrian unity': 'Ethnicizing the Shi'is', p. 747.
52. See Chapter 5.
53. AD-SL Box 493, dossier *Traité Franco-Syrien. Minorités. Sous-dossiers*. Nouri to HC, 7/8/1936. A French translation is also included. Nouri was Patriarchal Vicar of the Syrian-Catholics.
54. AD-SL Box 494, dossier *La question des minorités à la suite de l'évolution du problème syrien*. Enclosed with *Information n° 214*, Sûreté générale, Aleppo 3/3/1936.
55. See Chapter 5.
56. Reprinted in al-Rayyis, *Yā dhalām al-sijn*, pp. 225–9; quote at 226.
57. Al-Rayyis, *Yā dhalām al-sijn*, pp. 226–7. Note the incorporation of the Shi'a, whether they like it or not, into an 'Arab Muslim' majority as envisaged by a Sunni.
58. AD-SL Box 571, dossier *La question des Kurdes en Syrie. Correspondance. Les Comités Kurdes*. HC's assistant delegate for Aleppo vilayet to HC, 16/5/1930.
59. See also Chapter 6.
60. Berkes, *The Development of Secularism*, p. 188. See also Masters, *Christians and Jews*.
61. Khoury, *Syria and the French Mandate*, p. 425.
62. Private papers of Albert Zurayq, kindly made available to me by Souheil Chebat.

63. AD-SL Box 493, dossier *Traité Franco-Syrien. Minorités. Sous-dossiers.* Meyrier to MAE, 8/5/1936.
64. See Barkey, *Empire of Difference*, ch. 4 on the 'capacious administration of difference' in the Ottoman Empire, and ch. 8 on the increasingly rigid 'bounded identities' that emerged in the 'struggle from empire to nation-state'.
65. AD-SL Box 494, dossier *Traité Franco-Syrien – Application – Question des Minorités.* Martel to MAE (7/7/1937).
66. Being refugees from elsewhere, in the mandate period at least these groups seem to have been considered by all concerned as separate from Syrian society rather than as minorities within it.

PART II

CHAPTER

3

SEPARATISM AND AUTONOMISM

Introduction

The local governor was worried about 'separatist propaganda' in his border region, far from Damascus. Concerned about the 'state of mind that reigns among the inhabitants', in the spring of 1939 he sent a secret report to the interior ministry.[1] The people of his governorate, he wrote, were 'very close in their characteristics and customs' to the inhabitants of the neighbouring state, a feeling reinforced by 'their close communication with it'. In the main town, a preacher had stated that the district 'does not recognise the [Syrian] government nor the president of the Republic'. Alarmingly, this sentiment resonated with the local population, who manifested 'hostility towards the Syrian government and its employees, especially those who are not local people [*man kān min ghayr ahālī al-mintaqa*]'. The governor feared for the state's ability to control the situation, especially with a tiny police force whose men were all locals, and of suspect loyalty; and the local French colonel was keen to intervene, which would further undermine the National Bloc government's authority in the area.

Separatist mobilisations of the kind that worried this Syrian official were a common feature of life in the new nation-states of the inter-war world, though perhaps less common than exaggerated state fears about them. Both are still with us. From the Polish government's attitude to its German population in the 1920s to the Turkish Republic's fears of its Kurds today, separatism has also commonly been associated with minorities. Political mobilisations among minority populations are often assumed to be separatist in their ultimate, if not their immediate, aims – at least when the population concerned is large and concentrated enough to form a state by itself (Kurds today), or has links with a neighbouring state (Germans in the 1920s).

Our opening example shows, however, that the connection between separatism and minorities is not self-evident. The 'separatist propaganda' that the governor feared was not circulating in the Sanjak of Alexandretta, among Turkish-speakers favouring reunification with Turkey, nor among Kurds in the northeast of Syria hoping to create a Kurdish state with their kinsfolk over the border, at the expense of both existing countries. It was not grounded in a religious identity, like those of the 'Alawis, Druzes or Maronites, which French support had indeed raised to political autonomy (or independence) from Damascus. The governor's district was the Euphrates, its chief town Dayr al-Zur. The inhabitants of both town and governorate were overwhelmingly Arabic-speaking Sunni Muslims: people usually assumed to be part of the majority in Syria, not associated with separatist mobilisations or susceptibility to French divide-and-rule. And yet their nationalist governor, as we will see, viewed them as both culturally other and politically untrustworthy – just like a minority.

This chapter therefore offers a critical analysis of the issue of 'separatism' in French mandate Syria, to illuminate two related processes: the development of a concept of 'national territory', and the expansion of state authority within a new nation-state form. Looking at the issue in this light allows us to question a number of easily-made assumptions – including the assumption that certain mobilisations are 'separatist'. The first part of the chapter argues that the question of separatism, *infisāliyya*, was used in the nationalist press in order to create and diffuse the notion of a national territory (and the nation it belonged to) in the minds of their readers. The second examines a number of separatist or autonomist mobilisations and argues that they were above all a reaction to the increasing presence of the state at regional and local level in Syria. The mobilisations I discuss occurred among both 'minorities' and the 'majority'; the similarities between them allow us to reappraise the relationship between minority identities and separatism.

Nationalism and 'Separatism'

Separatism divides territory. States depend in part on their control of territory, especially in the modern period when a sacralised notion of an indivisible national territory has become central to the ideology of nationalism.[2] By dividing its territory, separatism poses an existential threat to the nation-state. Nation-states and nationalists are therefore particularly fearful of, and ideologically hostile to, separatist movements that threaten 'their' national territory. By the same token, separatist movements – which in the modern period frequently adopt nationalist ideology for themselves – are fearful of and hostile to nationalisms and states that rule or claim the territory that is the object of their own aspirations.

The question of separatism poses two distinct but linked problems for nationalism: how, in relation to the 'nation', to place the populations associated with separatist aspirations; and how to assert that the territory which is the object of those aspirations is in fact part of the national territory as defined by nationalists. When we read nationalist texts about separatism in the mandate period, especially newspaper articles, the development and diversity of nationalist attitudes towards the 'national territory' of Syria, and the relationship between it and the population, are clear to see.

Although the simplest definition of nationalism is the belief that the borders of nations should be congruent with those of states, nationalisms do not necessarily emerge with a fully-formed notion of what the national state should look like, or even with a belief that the only possible vehicle for national aspirations is an independent nation-state. The Arabism to which various modern forms of Arab nationalism trace their origins began, within an Ottoman context, as a movement of cultural reinvigoration to which it would be difficult to ascribe a precise territorial identity: after all, Istanbul was one of its important centres. Even as Arabist aspirations took on a more specific territorial identity (attached to the Arab provinces of the empire), prior to the First World War they did so mostly within the context of the Ottoman decentralisation movement rather than in the context of outright separatism: for the politically active sections of Ottoman Arab society, the empire's institutions continued to provide an acceptable framework for political action.[3] Nor did Arabism necessarily make the exclusive claim to territory that a modern nationalism does, that the Arab provinces of the empire were the rightful home of Arabs only. It would be redundant to outline here the complicated history of the emergence of such exclusive claims within Arab nationalism prior to 1920, and the changing territorial units that were their object; but a brief overview of the concept of the national territory as it existed in nationalist thought immediately prior to the mandate, during Syria's short-lived independence, is useful.[4]

In his work on popular nationalism in Faysali Syria, James Gelvin discusses the steps by which nationalist aspirations came to focus around the slogan 'the complete independence of Syria within its natural frontiers', a call which won much greater popular acceptance in Syria's towns than wider definitions of the state that included the Arabian peninsula or Iraq.[5] Because of its popularity, this fairly specific conception of the territory was adopted and promoted by the Faysali government. Syria's 'natural frontiers' were roughly defined in a number of nationalist texts as running from the Taurus mountains in the north to Madā'in Salih in the south, and from the Mediterranean coast and the line linking Rafah to 'Aqaba in the west to the Euphrates and Khabur rivers in the east.

Gelvin is duly cautious about the notion of 'natural frontiers', showing what material, social and economic (rather than 'natural') developments underlay the popular appeal of this construction of Syrian territory.[6] However, I would suggest that an even greater degree of caution is in order with respect to the popularity of this conception of the national territory. The view of the national territory described here, while not just the view from the top, is certainly the view from the centre. If, by 1919, there was a broad popular consensus in the towns – especially Damascus – around this construction of the Syrian national territory, there is no reason to assume that the same view prevailed in rural areas, particularly where the population did not share the dominant language and religion of the towns. As Peter Sluglett puts it, recent historical work that examines the development of nationalism by focusing mainly on Damascus does not 'give much consideration to the practical, political and ideological difficulties raised by the creation of a state whose constituent parts had not previously considered themselves part of that wider whole'.[7]

Those difficulties are the focus here. An approximate idea of 'natural' frontiers may be sufficient for rallying popular support, particularly under the threat of imperialist aggression and division, but nation-states require precisely-defined frontiers.[8] The nation-state form imposed on Syria under the mandate had such frontiers. Much more cramped than the 'natural' frontiers described above, they nonetheless contained plenty of people who, to put it mildly, had not fully assimilated nationalist goals. Although several currents within Syrian Arab nationalism retained a more expansive vision for the national territory, the discussion here concentrates on attitudes to the actual territory of Syria under mandate: the territory, already recognised internationally as belonging to a Syrian nation-state, which independent Syria would (more or less) inherit.

That inheritance was frequently in doubt, because of French unwillingness to relinquish imperial control and because of the territorial divisions imposed on the mandate territories. The risk that further divisions might be imposed, and that some or all of them would become permanent, was real. A fundamental concern for nationalists was therefore to oppose the *tamzīq* or *tajzi'a* – dismemberment or division – of Syrian territory. It is hardly surprising, therefore, if autonomist or separatist mobilisations of any kind were viewed with great suspicion in Damascus. But we should be wary of making assumptions either about the origins of such mobilisations, or about the nature of nationalist suspicions.

If nationalists opposed the division of Syria, by the same token they promoted the country's territorial unity, or reunification. However, the justifications they gave for that unity vary greatly. Sometimes they made reference to the populations of Syria's divided regions, and to their aspirations, separatist or not. At other times attitudes to territorial unity were expressed in a way which overrode the wishes of, or even ignored, local populations.

One way of countering separatism was to understand and explain it. In a 1923 report in *Alif Bā*, this Damascus newspaper's correspondent in Latakia described competing calls in the Alaouites,[9] then an autonomous part of the Syrian Federation, for the region's complete separation or its full reunification with a unitary Syrian state. The terms he uses to refer to separation are emotive: not just *infiṣāl*, 'separation', but also the somewhat sharper *faskh*, 'severing, sundering' and *insilākh*, which means 'becoming detached' but derives this meaning from the action of flaying. 'Those who demand separation', he said, 'are the Christians *en masse* and a great proportion of the 'Alawis'.[10] The numerical preponderance of the 'Alawis was the justification for the separation of the Latakia statelet; but in political matters, the author stated, the 'Alawis were 'followers of the influential', and their leaders were 'simple folk'. Their calls for separation, it is strongly implied, derived from the 'interference' of the French-controlled government. Partly true, no doubt; but nonetheless, one gets the impression that the author was not writing for an 'Alawi audience.

Separatism among the region's Christians was more sympathetically analysed. According to the writer, they were pro-separatist because, although a (numerical) minority in the Alaouites, they dominated bureaucratic jobs there: the community depended economically on this privileged relationship with the administration, and feared it would lose it in a unified Syria. They were therefore 'temporarily justified' in their separatism, but nevertheless mistaken because 'they do not look to the long term' and see how unification would benefit everyone, for example by the development of the port of Latakia. But 'they do not want to look at all this, and other tangible benefits, in the face of the temporary benefit of individuals among them [*manfaʿat afrād minhum manfaʿatan muʾaqqatatan*]'.

This author acknowledged the existence of widespread separatist feeling and accepted that the reasons for it were real, albeit mistaken. Another response to separatist mobilisations was to claim that they were unrepresentative of the population as a whole: that is, to accept that separatist feeling existed but to deny that it was widespread. Such assertions came not just from the centre, but also from Syrian nationalists in supposedly separatist regions. In the summer of the Franco-Syrian treaty negotiations (1936), the inhabitants of six villages in the Jabal Druze sent a statement of support for Syrian unity to the High Commission's Delegation in Damascus, criticising 'religious chiefs [who] have obtained full liberty to interfere in political affairs by exploiting their traditional influence, and this in the aim of going against the popular movement': that is, against the popular preference for unity.[11] Around the same time, a number of individuals in the Alaouites describing themselves as a 'union of Christian, 'Alawi, and Muslim youth' went even further, saying that:

> The so-called chiefs currently meeting in Tartus under the pressure and surveillance of the intelligence services to repeat what is dictated to them for an audience in [*à l'adresse de*] France and at the League of Nations reproduce the orders of those services, not the true wishes of the people, nor even the private wishes of those in attendance if they were left free and sheltered from all pressure.[12]

(It bears mentioning that the folders in the archives containing each of these documents also contain documents from separatists – and French officers – denouncing nationalists as unrepresentative of the wishes of the population.[13])

Both of the strategies outlined above acknowledge the existence of separatist or autonomist aspirations, while downplaying them either as being mistaken or opportunistic, or as being the choice of a small part of the population. They also justify unity, sometimes on quite concrete material grounds, as being a better deal not just for the 'centre' but for the population of autonomous or separatist regions as well, because it will lead to economic development, or because it is what those populations want. At other times, however, the aspirations of local populations (whether separatist or unionist) are simply overridden from the centre on the grounds of what might be called *raison d'État*, or perhaps *raison de nation*. Whether or not those populations would benefit from unity does not enter into consideration.

Thus, when the abortive Franco-Syrian treaty negotiations of 1933 were being planned, Najib al-Rayyis, editor of the nationalist daily *al-Qabas*, wrote an article demanding not only the incorporation of the 'Alawi and Druze states 'on the basis of decentralization', but also the reversion to Syria of the Lebanese port of Tripoli and the railway leading to it. He made no reference to the wishes of the inhabitants, separatist or otherwise – a startling omission in the case of Tripoli, where the desire for reunification with Syria was strong. Nor did al-Rayyis attempt to explain why unity would benefit these regions as well as the nationalist centre: rather, he simply stated that 'we will not accept that they [the French] enclose us between the desert and the sea'.[14] This begs the question, who are 'we'? Such writings tend to assume that the populations of areas that were the object of nationalist aspirations will simply fall into line once unity is achieved. Again, the issue of the intended audience deserves to be highlighted: the most revealing aspect of nationalist texts is often what they take for granted.

Perhaps even more common are nationalist writings that, instead of countering the arguments for separatism with arguments for unity, simply declare the area concerned to be eternally and non-negotiably a part of the Syrian territory. This almost mystical claim is summed up by the incantatory phrase 'the return of [area] to its mother, Syria'. With variations, Yusuf al-Hakim used it dozens of times in his memoirs, referring to Alexandretta and the Alaouites. (On one occasion, and with no apparent sense of irony, he recorded the phrase as being used by Atatürk about Alexandretta's return to a different mother, Turkey.[15]) He was not alone: this formula was a commonplace of nationalist writings about the regions wholly or partially detached from the 'rump' Syria under French rule. Such claims vanish the population of the territory completely, making no reference to their aspirations – whether separatist or nationalist. Instead, the population is submerged into a mystically unified and eternal territorial entity. Making no argument, such claims are unarguable. If the national territory (*watan*) is sacralised in this way, the nation as a human community (*qawm*, *umma*) disappears – even its properly nationalist elements. It goes without saying that politics, too, is elided. One can see the value of such an approach for a nationalist making a claim to a strategically useful piece of territory.

Nationalism is built on the idea of a specific and three-sided relationship between a particular state, population and territory. State forms other than the nation-state do not attach the same importance to a specific population, dwelling on a specific territory: in pre-modern monarchies, in dynastic empires and even colonial empires into the modern period, the relationship between state and territory is neither so fixed, nor so dependent on the state's claim to represent the population of that territory. Such state forms can, without contradiction, rule a territory and its local population by means of a bureaucracy and coercive forces brought in from elsewhere, with no reference to that population's wishes. When nation-states do the same – as they certainly do[16] – they must at least claim to represent the population of the territory they rule. If parts of the population are unwilling to accept that claim, then they must either be made to do so (by coercion, co-optation or persuasion) or be rejected as part of the national community. This being so, it is ironic that of the nationalist conceptions of territory outlined above, the one which most effectively 'disappears' the population, along with all human agency, is in a sense the most purely nationalist: the one which regards the national territory as an eternal and indissociable unit in and of itself. But in the positions outlined so far there is little sense of either national community or national territory as shared human constructions.

An exception to this trend comes in an article about the far northeast of Syria in the Damascus newspaper *Alif Bā'*, which explicitly addressed the relationship between population, territory and state. It did so in a way which, unusually, emphasised the agency in constructing a national territory not just of the population in general, but of populations remote from the geographical centres, and culturally-defined mainstream, of Syrian Arab nationalism. This account can be usefully compared with another, very different, report on the same situation published a week later by a second Damascus paper, *al-Ayyām*. Although the two texts can both be described as nationalist, the comparison reveals a radically different approach to the events they report – and, more generally, to nationalist conceptions of territory as they are illuminated by the question of (supposed) separatism. Comparing the two texts allows us to examine those conceptions in depth. The purpose is not to give a comprehensive overview of nationalist attitudes to the national territory in Syria: that would be impossible. Rather, my intention is to suggest a way of reading nationalist texts that, rather than taking the existence of a national territory for granted, questions the existence of such a thing – and, I hope, thereby offers a better understanding of how national territories are created.

The two articles date from September 1932, and they both report on confrontations that had occurred in the far northeast of Syria, the Jazira (see Map 2, p. vii), between the local population, on the one hand, and the local branches of the Syrian administration, on the other. The Jazira was largely inhabited by Christians and Kurds, many of whom had fled the nationalism of the early Turkish Republic;[17] while they were generally happy to deal with representatives of the mandatory authorities (which in this region meant military officers), they had a much more tense relationship with the representatives of the Syrian state bureaucracy centred on Damascus. The local French officers were quite happy to play up these tensions in order to undermine the authority of 'Damascus'. This situation had led to the clashes that these two articles reported. The underlying tensions would only grow as the 1930s progressed, as the region's Christian population rapidly increased with the installation of Assyrian refugees from Iraq, and its economic importance within Syria also grew – a not unrelated fact, which also contributed to the growing interest in the region on the part of Syrian Arab nationalists in the urban centres. These articles thus presaged later events in the region. Their different interpretations of this unrest are evident from the start, in the articles' headlines: *Alif Bā'* had 'No separatist movement in the Jazira. The unrest in the Jazira and its causes', while *al-Ayyām* introduced the same events with the title 'Separatist rebels . . . Are they creating a new "sixth" government in Syria[?]'.[18]

The article in *Alif Bā'* began by referring to an earlier piece (in the Aleppo newspaper *al-Ittihād*) which had characterised the local population as Christians who had migrated from Mardin, over the border in Turkey, 'and settled in Syrian territory'. It had also claimed that:

> the French authorities have settled them in Hasaka and Ra's al-'Ayn and Qamishli, made it easy for them to [find] work, and opened commercial markets to them, and that the people had demanded separation from Syria and the creation of a homeland of their own [*watan khāss bihim*].[19]

According to the Aleppo newspaper, a group of these Christians, led by priests, had attacked the local gendarme chief.

Alif Bā' set out to rebut these claims and the assumptions underlying them. Tellingly, it began its rebuttal by describing neither the events nor the people involved, but rather the territory on which these events unfolded:

> In response to this, I say that the territories of Qamishli, Hasaka, 'Amuda, Darbisiyya, Ra's al-'Ayn and Tall Abyad were empty and desolate, the abode of predatory animals, a place of attacks and raids in which lives were lost [*tuzhaq fīhā al-arwāh*, lit. 'ghosts were given up'] and blood was shed . . . And now, by the effort of the sons of the country and with the help of the mandatory state they have become civilized, populated lands.

Separatism and Autonomism [77

From the start, and throughout the article, the author lays out a particular vision of the relationship between territory and population in which it was the efforts of the population – recognised as part of the nation – that made the territory 'national'. The transformation of the Jazira from desolation to civilisation was what made it into part of Syria's national territory. Simply by referring to these territories by name and discussing them in a national public sphere, the author diffused the notion of their belonging to the Syrian 'nation' among a reading public concentrated far away from these border territories in the urban centres. But the article made clear that the agents of the Jazira's transformation into a productive territory, and thus into a part of Syria, were the region's inhabitants, what it called the 'sons of the country [*abnā' al-bilād*]'. This itself is a significant phrase: the early twentieth century saw a shift in attitudes towards the lower classes (especially peasants) in literate discourse, a shift closely associated with the age of mass politics and nationalism. The peasants (and workers) of earlier ages were the object, not the subject, of politics: there to be ruled over. By contrast, the 'son of the country' may be rustic and uneducated, but he is born of the national territory and is part of, indeed, is the foundation of, the national political community. This is the transformation of workers and peasants, as Joel Beinin puts it, 'from rabble to citizens of the nation'.[20]

What, then, of the claim that these 'sons of the country' were recent migrants from over the Turkish border? *Alif Bā'* made no attempt to deny it, but rather demonstrated that this did not make them illegitimate incomers:

These territories are the property of the people of Mardin and the Kurds of Tur al-'Abidin and its dependencies[,] Muslims, Christians and Jews. When the unforeseen political events [*al-tawāri' al-siyāsiyya*] occurred these territories were separated from Mardin and Diyarbakir and their appendages[, and] the owners of the land were obliged by their attachment [*bi-tab'ihim*] to travel to their lands. Therefore these are not, as the respected writer [in *al-Ittihād*] claimed, foreign migrants who have settled in Syria.

The writer firmly attributed right of ownership over this land to the current inhabitants, even though they had previously lived in towns now separated from the region by 'unforeseen political events': the destruction of the Ottoman Empire and establishment of a new border. This implied that these populations had chosen Syria over Turkey. The author did not express an opinion as to whether the new border was in the right place. He did, however, assert that it was a recent creation, and that the inhabitants of the Jazira had every right to be on this side of it even if they used to live on the other. (He also gave a clear impression of religious and linguistic diversity, and was comfortable with it.) Seen from Aleppo or Damascus, Syria's northeastern border might well look like a distant horizon beyond which all was alien. But unlike *al-Ittihād*,

Alif Bā's correspondent – even though his newspaper, too, was published in a distant urban centre – made the effort to look at the border from the perspective of those whose lives were directly affected by it. Seen from up close, the border was a novel political development that had cut land off from its owners and severed towns from their natural hinterland.

Addressing the question of trade, the article expanded on this point. For *Alif Bā'*, it was the people of the Jazira who had developed the region and opened it to trade with Aleppo. Indeed, had they not done so Aleppo 'would have lost its commercial status for good', because, coming back to the question of the border, Aleppo's trade had previously been oriented towards areas now included in the Republic of Turkey: 'Therefore, there remains no trading outlet for Aleppo except the outlet of the Jazira, which was built by the effort and wealth of its [the Jazira's] sons.' The author also acknowledged the French assistance that had made this development possible.

Alif Bā' was a 'moderate' newspaper, hence its acknowledgement of the colonial power's role in developing the Jazira. But there is no doubt that the vision of territory and population put forward here was a nationalist one: the author emphatically did claim the Jazira as part of Syria. He did not base that claim on a mystical, eternal notion of the national territory, though (the Jazira belonging naturally to its 'mother' Syria), nor on the strategic imperatives of the Syrian state (such as access to the region's water resources). Instead, the Jazira became part of Syria by the human agency of its own population: their development of the previously desolate region had provided Aleppo with a new hinterland, saving the city from the loss of the old. The largest city and most remote rural region in the French mandate territories were bound together in a new economic relationship that mutually benefited both. From such human processes, the national territory was made: a relationship built, in this conception, from the periphery to the centre.

Such was the structural foundation of recent events, as described in the article. Only after this lengthy introduction did the writer return to those events: what *al-Ittihād* had apparently described as an assault on the gendarme chief in the town of Qamishli by a group of Christians, led by priests, with separatist ambitions, and the immediate purpose of releasing an imprisoned Christian leader. Not so, said *Alif Bā'*: the protest resulted from 'the chaos and corruption of the qa'immaqam and the justice of the peace, who have planted the spirit of religious, sectarian, racial, and national division in [people's] minds'.

In this reading, then, the Qamishli demonstration was not a separatist mobilisation, but a popular protest against the misdeeds of local representatives of the central state bureaucracy. It was these two bureaucrats who were guilty of sowing division, not the French, who were (justifiably enough) the more usual target of such an accusation. Until the appointment of these officials, the Jazira had been undisturbed by unrest and 'the people, in their different elements [*'anāsir*], had enjoyed their rights and worked together [*yu'āmilūn*] in justice and equality'. Petitions and protests against the two men went unanswered; instead, they

> increased in tyranny, and used every means to divide opinion. They incited the Arab [that is, Bedouin] tribes to attack and destroy Qamishli by claiming that the Christian inhabitants intended to kill the Muslim functionaries; the inhabitants feared the results, so they undertook a peaceful demonstration in which every element participated – Muslims, Christians, and Jews – and demanded that the government send the tribes and the armed Bedouin back to their homes, and deliver them from the corruption of the qa'immaqam . . .

All in all, the article is a sustained elaboration of the position outlined in its title. It is a fascinating example of how a Syrian nation and its territory were imagined through the debate on separatism; and if it almost certainly underestimates the extent of separatist feeling in the Jazira, it nonetheless understands the region, and the state's actions there, unusually well.

The prominent nationalist journalist Nasuh Babil, writing about the same subject in his newspaper *al-Ayyām* a week later, offered a very different understanding of nation, state and territory. This is already clear from the title of the article, which characterised the population of the region as 'separatist rebels'. The subtitle connected the allegedly separatist intentions of the Jazira's population with the administrative divisions imposed on Syria by France: to the five 'governments' into which the mandate territories were already divided (the state of Syria itself, the autonomous statelets of the Alaouites and the Jabal Druze, the Sanjak of Alexandretta and the 'independent' Lebanon), the separatists wanted to add a sixth.

Whereas the article in *Alif Bā'* made explicit references to the diversity of the region's inhabitants, both linguistically (specifically mentioning Kurds and Arabs) and religiously (Muslims, Christians, Jews), the article in *al-Ayyām* made only passing references to the cultural identity of the population. Describing unrest among the inhabitants of 'Ayn Diwar, Babil mentioned that 'most of them are Armenian [*aktharuhum min al-arman*]'.[21] This simplification identified the 'rebels' as non-Syrian, non-Arab, non-Muslim refugees: in every respect outside the nation as he conceived it, and – more to the point – distant from *al-Ayyām*'s target audience of Damascene Muslim Arabs. While Babil did not specifically describe the 'separatists' as Christians, except implicitly by this reference to some of them as Armenians, his article prominently displayed its own Islamic identity: it began with the invocation 'Praise be to God; there is no power and no strength except through God [*subḥān Allāh wa lā ḥawl wa lā quwwa illā billāh*]'.[22] Babil also skipped over the relationship between the population of the Jazira and the territory itself. Whereas *Alif Bā'* carefully established that the people of the region were legitimate owners of the land and had by their own efforts transformed it from desolation to productivity, to the benefit of the Syrian nation, *al-Ayyām* made no attempt here to explain how the population was related to the land.[23]

The author did, however, give an account of the state's relationship to the territory – in some respects vaguer but in others more explicit than that given in *Alif Bā'*. In *Alif Bā*'s version the Jazira had been made a part of Syria by the efforts of its own inhabitants – a process in which the Syrian state seemingly played no role, though the mandatory authorities did. By contrast, Babil simply took for granted that the territory was a part of Syria, making no effort to explain why. He did, though, offer a clear picture of the role in the territory of the central state, or rather government (*hukūma*).[24] He did this largely by outlining the offences committed against the authority of the government (unquestioningly taken as legitimate) by the 'rebels'. These included the rebels' attack on the prison – to release a prisoner who, in Babil's view, had been quite legitimately detained – and expulsion of the qa'immaqam of Qamishli. In 'Ayn Diwar, the ('mostly Armenian') inhabitants had attacked the local doctor along with 'some of the officials of the caza, and lowered the flag of the constitution from Government House and insulted it; they threatened anyone who went against their will with murder'.

There is a clear notion here of the state imposing order, through its officials and symbols, and of the local population as the (criminally resistant) objects of this imposition. Thus, the qa'immaqam of Qamishli had been expelled 'not for a reason, but because his presence in the caza was unsympathetic to those who insulted the government, infringed its laws and attacked its employees, because he was intent on applying the law and punishing the transgressor'. Babil described those who committed this act as 'chaos-causers [*fawdawiyyīn*]', whose actions had 'exacerbated their rebellion and their going against [*khurūjahum 'ala*] the government in a regrettable and quite intolerable way'. Meanwhile, the functionaries who had fled to Aleppo and Damascus refused to go back to their posts until they could be sure of their safety – and sure that the people understood

> that there is in 'Ayn Diwar and Qamishli an authority that can punish rebels, that is capable of curbing their recalcitrance, and that is able to apply the law, raise the flag, and convince everyone [*ilqā' al-qanā'a fil-nufūs*] that there is in the country a government that has respect, honour, standing, and authority.

One thing that stands out in this account is Babil's insistence on respect for the symbols of state authority – the flag, Government House – and the equation of that symbolic authority with real authority. Even more striking is the unidirectional nature of that authority, which emanates from the centre and is applied to the periphery.

This point is worth lingering on. The manifest content of this piece is a protest against infringements of the state's authority in peripheral regions, by populations who are also characterised as peripheral (if not merely alien). But the latent content of the article is the assertion of that state's authority everywhere on its territory, and perhaps particularly in the centre: after all, the primary audience for Babil's writing was in Damascus.[25] At the risk of making the point too crushingly obvious, states typically respond unsympathetically to separatist movements in peripheral zones not (or not only) because maintaining control over a particular a region and its population is necessarily vital to the strategic or economic well-being of the state, but because permitting the state's authority to be challenged at the periphery risks undermining it at the centre. By the same token, asserting the state's authority at the periphery is a means of asserting it at the centre.[26] The political significance of separatism goes far beyond the zones where separatist movements are active.

All of this provides a background to the attitudes expressed here by Nasuh Babil. As a nationalist – a prominent supporter, at this stage, of the National Bloc – Babil wanted the nationalists to have control of the Syrian state; he also wanted that state to have full authority over the population within the largest 'Syrian' borders possible. In this context, therefore, the use of the word government (*hukūma*) is particularly salient. Syria being under French mandate, the state (*dawla*) was in many senses in the hands of the French. The French authorities were referred to as exactly that, the authorities – or rather, the authority (*al-sulta*). But the government was at least nominally in the hands of Syrians. Attacking 'separatists' and demanding proper respect for the government was a way for Babil to demand a greater role in that government for Syrians – meaning nationalists. It also permitted him to attack the French authorities, but indirectly enough to avoid them suspending his newspaper, which happened often. This is all clear enough in the following passage, with its coy reference to the French:

> The government is incapable of spreading its authority in those two cazas, and feels its own weakness, because it does not possess the strength to discipline the rebels, a little or a lot; while those who do possess that power [that is, the French] are unaware or feigning unawareness – we say no more than that – of everything that is happening in those parts!

Al-Ayyām placed events in the Jazira much more directly in the context of the formal relationship between the central state and the mandatory, an articulation missing from the article in *Alif Bā'*. Throughout, Babil emphasised that this 'separatism' undermined the central state and the institutions – parliament, the constitution, the Republic – that were supposed to be the measure of Syria's independence and development under French tutelage. This also allowed him to target the non-nationalist politicians who actually made up the Syrian government at this time, under whom it had 'abandoned [these two cazas], recognized its inability to administer them, and cleared the way for the separatists there to announce their separation and form the sixth government, under the protection of the republic and the constitution!'

If the government did not have the strength to maintain its presence in the Jazira, he wrote, it should request 'those who are responsible' for the government's weakness (the French again) 'to use that strength against the separatists, so that if they refused the responsibility would fall upon them alone' – rather than falling on, and discrediting, the Syrian government. Thus, Babil used the issue of separatism to assert the authority of the Syrian government everywhere on its territory.

Political slogans about 'natural frontiers' aside, there was no self-evident national territory in Syria prior to 1920, no more than any other 'national territory' exists outside of human agency. The link between population, state and territory is a human construction, and the debate about national territory is itself one important means for spreading the idea, in the minds of the population, that such a thing exists. The author of the article in *Alif Bā'* is unusual in explicitly recognising that territory must be made 'national'. More often, nationalist journalists implied that the national territory already existed by framing this debate as being about 'separatism'. This is illustrated by the terms they used, notably the words *infisāl* and *infisāliyya*: 'separation' implied that there already existed a Syrian national territory, from which 'separatists' wished to separate.[27] But the territory to which these writers were referring had only recently been formed itself, by its separation from the Ottoman Empire.

What is more, in much of the territory under mandate – particularly the more remote areas, like the mountainous Alaouites – the presence of permanent state authority was a novelty of the mandate period: that is, of French rule. Describing the late Ottoman period in the region that would become the Alaouites, Patrick Seale notes that away from the urban centres the state was virtually absent and offered no services:

> The only expression of authority was rapacious and oppressive: the tax collector or the mounted gendarme. It was not unknown for a single gendarme to ride into a village, assemble the villagers, take money if they had any, kill a chicken for his lunch, and make off back to civilization.[28]

'Abdallah Hanna, meanwhile, quotes the opinion expressed by rural Syrians in oral history interviews carried out over several decades that 'in Turkish times there was no state; in French times there was a state [*sār fī dawla*]'.[29] A more elegant rendering, and perhaps more accurate, would be 'a state happened'.

In these circumstances, the idea that populations in regions like the Alaouites wanted to secede from a previously existing whole is hardly satisfactory, and if there was such a whole then it was the defunct Ottoman Empire, not 'Syria'. When nationalists used this vocabulary of *infiṣāliyya*, then, they were not reflecting the actual existence of such a whole, but rather attempting to bring it into being. It is a mistake to take these texts at their word, accepting the prior existence of a national territory rather than asking how that territory was created. By this mistake we abstract the nation-state from history, eliding the always complex and never frictionless processes by which states and the political actors who control them come to exert their authority over territory – and in the era of nationalism, over the 'nation' too.[30]

An example of this comes from the opening chapters of Patrick Seale's work quoted above, an authoritative and astute biography of the former Syrian president Hafiz al-Asad, which describe Syria and particularly the Alaouites in the years around Asad's birth in 1930. As Seale recounts the onset of European rule in the former Arab provinces, the term 'natural Syria' – the (imprecise) region called *bilād al-Shām* in Arabic – quickly escapes its quotation marks. Seale describes the fate of this 'natural' unit using precisely the same cutting terms as the nationalist texts cited above: Syria was 'carved up'; the cession to republican Turkey of much of the Ottoman province of Aleppo was an 'amputation'; the special status granted to the region of Alexandretta 'further whittled away' the same province; the Alaouites and the Jabal Druze 'were severed from Damascus'.[31] All of this is assuming a greater degree of territorial coherence in *bilād al-Shām*, a greater degree of separation between it and the rest of the former Ottoman territories, and a greater acceptance of Damascus as a natural centre and capital than is likely to have existed in the aftermath of the First World War. Seale's own comments about the weakness – indeed, absence – of state authority outside the cities tend to confirm this position; and I doubt that many notables in late Ottoman Aleppo would have agreed with his contention that of the cities of *bilād al-Shām*, 'Damascus was acknowledged to be the most important'.[32] European imperialism certainly imposed divisions on the post-Ottoman Middle East, but seeing these as anything other than the division of the Ottoman Empire is problematic. To see them as the division of a 'natural' Syria, meanwhile, is to take as a starting point the ideological endpoint of nationalism.

Alongside the idea of a national territory, nationalist writings of the sort examined here also use the issue of separatism to spread the idea of belonging to a nation. The article in *Alif Bā'* encourages its readers to see the inhabitants of the Jazira as Syrians, while the article in *al-Ayyām* does everything to exclude them from the Syrian nation; both, however, assume that the reader will see himself as part of that nation.[33] Up to a point this was probably correct: nationalist writers were reflecting public opinion as well as trying to influence it. But just as it is wrong to assume that a coherent national territory existed simply because newspapers took its existence for granted when they wrote about 'separatism' in a particular region, so it is wrong to assume that a coherent national community existed simply because newspapers took its existence for granted when they wrote about 'separatism' in a particular population. Such texts reflect the attempt to construct a national territory and community, not their prior existence.[34] This process of construction – which takes place in every nation-state – goes on happening long after the nation-state is well rooted in both population and territory: nations require continuous maintenance, as historians should recognise.

To express this risk in a slightly different way: by concentrating on the nationalist struggle for control of the state, historians may overlook the state's struggle for control of population and territory – a risk that is evidently not restricted to historians of French mandate Syria. 'Separatist' movements do not simply arise from a desire to break away from some larger, supposedly natural unit, and separatist aspirations among one part of a population are not necessarily a function of cultural differences dividing them from the rest of the population (differences that are often understood as a minority–majority dynamic). Such movements do not develop in a void: they arise in response to the presence, actions, and policies of states. The rest of the chapter explains how. Some of the mobilisations it describes wanted full separation from Syria; others, which I will call 'autonomist', shared many of the same characteristics but did not demand formal separation.

Separatism and State Authority

So far my argument about the national territory being constructed through the language used to describe it has been rather idealist, as if just claiming in a Damascus newspaper that a given region belonged to Syria was enough to make it part of the national territory. The importance of such rhetorical constructions should not be understated: if the population in a state's major centres do not regard a peripheral region as being part of a shared national territory, it might be difficult to persuade them to pay taxes and supply conscripts in order for the state to put down a separatist rebellion there. But without a material basis – those taxes and conscripts, as it were – the rhetorical construction of a national territory outlined above is unlikely to be effective. To put it in Benedict Anderson's terms, the apparatus of the state provides the material basis that permits a national territory to be imagined. In the era of nationalism, states (and non-state nationalist movements) claim a permanent, sacred link with their national territories: some examples of this were offered above. But what permits that link to be made – and what is concealed by phrases like 'the return of Alexandretta to its mother, Syria' – is the expansion of state authority, real or potential, across the territory.[35]

We have already seen this in the article by Nasuh Babil. As I mentioned, Babil was most outraged by what he perceived as the disrespect of the 'separatists' towards the authority of the state: in a modern nation-state the government must be able to raise its flag anywhere on its territory and have that flag respected as a symbol of its authority. But that authority is expressed in material form too: the establishment of a government presence – buildings (*dār al-hukūma*, gendarme posts) and functionaries (bureaucrats, policemen) – even in towns and villages which would until the late Ottoman period at the earliest have been off the government's map, sometimes literally.[36] The physical presence of the modern state across its territory is much greater, and by the same token so is the intrusion of the state into the lives of the population, through taxes, conscription, education and the whole array of methods of enumeration and classification that underpin them. This expanded field of state activity becomes a new field for political action, in two respects.

First, the symbolic and real manifestations of state authority immediately become sites for the expression of discontent or opposition. National flags can be lowered, burned, urinated on, or, indeed, first burned then urinated on, as happened to the Syrian flag in Qamishli in 1939 (a story we will hear in the next chapter). If buildings and functionaries now give the state a permanent presence in even quite small, remote settlements, it is hardly surprising if they become the focal point for the expression of political sentiment whether for or against the state. Administrative buildings are a good example. Decrees of the High Commissioner were in at least some cases effective from the moment at which they were posted on the door of Government House (*'ala bāb dār al-hukūma*), where the local bureaucracy was based in any given town or province.[37] The local population interacted with the state at that site and through that bureaucracy: when High Commissioner Gabriel Puaux visited the Jazira in early 1939 it was in the government buildings of Qamishli and Hasaka that he met representatives of the local population.[38] His visit reveals other aspects of the expansion of state authority: the senior French official in the entire mandate territories visited this relative backwater and was able to do so easily, by aeroplane; he spoke to local notables and employees of the local state bureaucracy, and inspected the garrison at Hasaka.

Such visits from on high reinforced the accurate impression of power in residence. This is why political demonstrations in towns large and small would make their way to the local Government House to voice their protests: for the first three months of 1939, a small sample from the Syrian administration's very incomplete records yields references to demonstrations congregating in front of the Government House in Homs, Dayr al-Zur, Dar'a and Hasaka.[39] The demonstration in Dayr al-Zur, and one of those in Homs, began at the local government secondary school, the *Tajhīz*; this was evidently a widespread phenomenon, and further demonstrates the point that new sites of state authority also created new spaces for contestation.[40]

The differing purposes of these demonstrations point to an irony about the presence of state power. In Homs, Dayr al-Zur and Dar'a the demonstrations were, like numerous others at this time, nationalist in orientation: their protests were against the French occupation. But these and similar protests were also directed at the Syrian government of the National Bloc – at times in straightforward hostility towards a by now discredited administration, at others in support of a government held in an impossible position by France.[41] The demonstration in Hasaka, the administrative centre of the Jazira, was different again. Administered until the early 1930s from Dayr al-Zur, by this stage the Jazira was a governorate in its own right. Its upgraded administrative status reflected its rapid demographic and economic growth, but also the French wish to administer its largely (and increasingly) Christian and Kurdish population separately from the rest of Syria. However, after the signature of the 1936 treaty the High Commission agreed to the governorate's administrative subordination to the Syrian bureaucracy, and the appointment of its governor by the new National Bloc government. This change was unwelcome to significant sections of the Jazira's population; the local French military officers, hostile to the treaty, also never accepted it. The demonstration recorded in January 1939 was therefore outspokenly anti-nationalist and carried French flags; but it was not simply pro-French. As well as expressing their opposition to Syrian Arab nationalist rule from Damascus, Syrian-Catholic[42] Christians were demanding the release of several Christians detained in connection with the abduction of the (nationalist-appointed) governor of the Jazira, and protesting against their own local leaders and the French authorities who together had been promising their release for some time.[43] The irony revealed by all this is that the apparatus of state power can be in different hands, sometimes simultaneously. Its expansion provides a space for contestation that may target that power at a number of different, and sometimes contradictory, levels: the Government House was correctly seen as a locus of both French and Syrian power.

The French had developed the state apparatus in Syria as an instrument of their own rule, although it was overwhelmingly staffed by Syrians.[44] For their part, Syrian nationalists wanted the theory of the mandate to be translated into practice: they wanted Syrians – more specifically, themselves – to control the state apparatus. Anti-nationalists, in turn, contested their control. So if the first sense in which the expansion of the state apparatus created a new field for political action was that the new physical manifestations of state authority became focal points for the expression of discontent, opposition or support, the second, more important sense was that the expanded state apparatus itself became the object of contestation.

The expansion of a modern state apparatus in the geographical region of *bilād al-Shām* did not begin in the mandate period: the process was well advanced by the start of the First World War.[45] What distinguishes the mandate period are, first, the ever greater extension of an increasingly effective state's authority to regions beyond the main towns, their hinterlands and major routes of communication; and, second, the new state-form within which that expansion was taking place. Like the other European dynastic empires in the nineteenth century, the Ottoman Empire had, with a greater or lesser degree of success, developed some of the characteristics of a nation-state – characteristics which are closely connected to the development of a modern state apparatus. But its successor state, though under colonial rule, was recognised as a territorial nation-state from the off. Moreover, it comprised a fairly compact territory whose population, though diverse, was much less so than that of the empire. Within this territory, nationalism became a more appealing ideology for political mobilisation: it became more plausible (though not unproblematic) to associate the state with one particular cultural identity. The territory also had a new capital, Damascus. The city's status as such was neither a foregone conclusion nor undisputed, but it was reinforced by the mere fact that the Syrian government and bureaucracy were seated there: for populations across the territory, engaging with the central government, whether in support or in opposition, now meant engaging with Damascus. Although *bilād al-Shām* was now divided into several states, the bureaucracy across the French-controlled territories, Lebanon excepted, was subordinated to Damascus, whereas in the Ottoman period the same territory was divided between the three provincial capitals of Aleppo, Beirut and Damascus. The presence of the High Commission as a 'higher authority' nuances this picture for the areas with autonomous or other special status, but a countervailing force was the presence across the territory – even in those areas – of nationalists who tended increasingly to treat Damascus as the natural capital of Syria.[46]

The same expansion of state authority that, in the context of an increasingly 'national' state, helped to create a national territory in Syria also helps to explain autonomist mobilisations and the shape they took. Populations may resent the greater intrusions of the modern state into their lives, especially when they are faced with that intrusion for the first time rather than being socialised into it from birth: '*Scappa, che arriva la patria*', said the Italian peasant mother to her son – 'Scarper, the fatherland's coming'.[47] But they are not blind to the opportunities that it offers alongside the inconveniences, an eye for opportunity that is not restricted to groups that already have some independent social or political status, though it may be most developed among them.

Thus, a striking aspect of the demands presented by autonomist mobilisations is their preoccupation with concrete issues relating to the interaction between local populations and the state – so much so that these demands give us a good picture, in imprint, of what that material expansion entailed. Here I will argue that the expansion of state authority should be seen as at least as important a spur to autonomist mobilisations as identitarian feeling. The two factors should not necessarily be separated, but it is useful to distinguish between them – and to question the direction of the relationship between them.

Autonomist demands were indeed frequently, though not always, expressed in identitarian terms. One example among countless others is a petition sent to the French authorities by ʿAlawis in the caza of Masyaf in 1933 (another year of treaty negotiations, abortive in this case) which demanded the continued autonomy of the Alaouites.[48] The preamble warned of the threat posed to 'Alawis by Sunnis – it being taken for granted that the nationalist movement was a purely Sunni affair:

> Considering that the exploitation by the Sunnis of every opportunity to destroy the 'Alawis [*li-hadm kiyān al-'alawiyyīn*] indicates that this community [*umma*] imbued with a spirit of religious fanaticism [*rūh al-ta'assub al-dīnī*] ... cannot be entrusted with a people like ours, separated from them by innumerable monstrosities recorded by history from a thousand years ago up to today. It would be unjust to abandon us as victims in the hands of a majority whose nails are still tainted with our blood, and whose religious leaders' decisions – which authorize massacring us [*tuḥallil taqtīlanā*], raping our women, pillaging our possessions – are attested [*muthbata*] in their religious books, read and studied and transmitted from father to son.[49]

The list of demands which follows this, however, is rather more concrete than a mere assertion of communal difference. It protests Sunni mistreatment of 'Alawis and demands the independence of the Alaouites; but it also, more specifically, requests that government jobs be distributed in proportion to the number of 'Alawis, and rejects any court not composed of an 'Alawi majority. Other petitions submitted by 'Alawis in the same period make similar demands for a share of government jobs and an advantageous tax status without troubling to mention the community's precarious situation vis-à-vis the fanatical Sunnis. A 1936 petition to the French foreign minister, meanwhile, demanded autonomy for the Alaouites, 'Alawi participation in public functions, a return to the name *État des Alaouites* (the region then being known as the *Gouvernement de Lattaquié*), and the banning of proselytism in the region.[50]

Such specific demands are interesting. For instance, when 'Alawis requested an end to missionary proselytism in the Alaouites they were not making a protest against Syrian nationalism, but against the status quo under the French: the mandate had seen a substantial Jesuit missionary effort develop among the 'Alawis, causing some perturbation. Influential 'Alawis might have been happy to cooperate with a French presence that limited the dominance of Sunni landlords in Latakia and pulled their region out of the orbit of the large cities of the interior, but they did not surrender themselves entirely to the French will: 'Alawis were quite ready to protest when French policies threatened established authority among them, even in the context of a petition whose other articles are directed against Syrian nationalism. The very long list of signatories to this petition is headed by France's closest ally among the 'Alawis, 'Brahim agha El Kinj, President of the C.R. [*Conseil représentatif*], chief of the Haddadine tribe'.

It is not hard to find other examples, from a number of different sources throughout the mandate period, of autonomist mobilisations making demands that, like these, betray a preoccupation with the expanding modern state. There is much in common between these mobilisations, whether full 'independence' from Syria is one of their demands or not. For example, in January 1926 the deputy for the caza of Salamiyya, where Syria's small Isma'ili community was concentrated, requested that the caza be detached from the muhafaza of Hama and constituted 'as an autonomous Sandjak under the direct authority of the [*relevant directement du*] High Commission'.[51] He also requested the formation of a 200-strong Isma'ili cavalry squadron under a French commanding officer, but also under the authority of an Isma'ili leader. This request was made at the height of the 'Druze' revolt, and justified on the grounds that autonomy and a local military force would both serve to protect the region from the rebels. It would be a mistake, though, to assume that the deputy's prime motive was hostility towards Syrian Arab nationalism. In the early months of the revolt, the movement's status as a nationalist mobilisation was far less clear than it would seem later,[52] and there were opportunistic raids by Bedouin taking advantage of the precarious security situation. The deputy seems to understand the rebellion as mere Bedouin disorder, justifying his request for an Isma'ili squadron by saying that his community 'desires to safeguard ... the security of its regions, ever menaced by the raids of the Bedouin'.

As with the 'Alawi petitioners described above, the demands of this Isma'ili deputy fall in the domain of state authority. They illustrate the ambiguity of the relationship between that authority and the population. Upgrading the caza to an autonomous sanjak would presumably have entailed a larger share of state expenditure, and an expanded local bureaucracy offering more employment opportunities. The request for an Isma'ili squadron, meanwhile, can be seen as residents of a relatively peripheral region[53] simultaneously calling on and seeking to limit state authority: they request that the state impose order on a disorderly situation, but that its locally deployed coercive forces be made up of local men under the authority of a local notable. Autonomism evidently remained significant in Salamiyya: in 1939 a petition circulating among Isma'ilis there made the very similar request that their area become 'an autonomous Muhafaza directly subordinate to French authority', and was said to have gained 1,500 signatures.[54]

A similar demand was presented to the High Commission in 1927 by 'the Tcherkess': that is, by certain Circassians claiming to represent their community, another fairly small community concentrated particularly (but not exclusively) in a single caza, Qunaytra.[55] In that year the High Commission received a request for the caza to become a sanjak, 'with only Tcherkess functionaries'.[56] By 1933, the year of failed Franco-Syrian treaty negotiations, a document signed by Circassian notables, religious leaders and second-degree electors made autonomist demands on the grounds that the Circassians were a national minority and should be officially recognised as such in the treaty. Their ten demands were for: guaranteed representation in parliament; Circassian officials in Circassian areas; recognition of the rights of Circassian civil and military functionaries; Circassian-medium teaching in Circassian primary schools; scholarships for Circassian students at secondary level and above; Circassian control of Circassian schools; freedom to publish in the Circassian language; free association on a minority basis; participation in waqfs; and the right of 'Circassian religious leaders' to conduct marriages following 'Circassian national customs and traditions'.[57] If Circassian identity was emphatically the basis on which these demands were made, their focus was equally emphatically the interaction of population and state. Again, that relationship is ambiguous. The signatories wanted to limit the threat that the state might pose to them by ensuring – through articles in a treaty guaranteed by outside powers – both communal representation in national politics and communal control over the state's intrusions into the community's life (education, civil law, the bureaucracy in general). At the same time they wanted to take advantage of the opportunities a modern state can bring, as is particularly apparent in the demands centred on education. Demanding scholarships for educational advancement is hardly a resounding rejection of the central state; while demanding Circassian-medium education may simply have been a strategy for gaining more and better schools. Noticeably, their demands did not include separation from Syria.

My point here is not to argue that identitarian motivations were irrelevant to questions of autonomism and separatism, but rather to give a more nuanced understanding of their relevance. Cultural identities do not have an *a priori* political content (or political effect): they acquire political salience in particular conditions – and the modern state, with its unprecedented degree of control over territory and intervention in the lives of the population, certainly creates those conditions, as Charles Tilly has noted:

> In the period of movement from tribute to tax, from indirect to direct rule, from subordination to assimilation, states generally worked to homogenize their populations and break down their segmentation by imposing common languages, religions, currencies, and legal systems, as well as promoting the construction of connected systems of trade, transportation, and communication. When those standardizing efforts threatened the very identities on which subordinate populations based their everyday social relations, however, they often stirred massive resistance.[58]

At the same time, this analysis allows for ambiguity: rather than assuming that an expanding state will automatically provoke hostility from minorities, it understands how that expansion may itself spur a sense of minority identity – and also accounts for the range of options that it opens up for the communities that become 'minorities'. In the Syrian case these included outright hostility and a desire for a separate state, with French support offering a means of going over the head of the central state;[59] a desire for autonomy, simultaneously limiting and taking advantage of state authority, with League of Nations guarantees providing a weaker but still significant external source of support; and a desire for full integration into the 'national' community of Syria and the nation-state that claimed to represent it. Similar options were available to the populations of other states during the process of state intensification and expansion – for example, France in the 'long' nineteenth century to 1914. The presence of an imperial power in Syria represents one specific variable within a process that is generally comparable from state to state.

Many factors influenced the popularity of a particular strategy with any given community. The point is, though, that individuals belonging to any given community could adopt any one of these strategies, or change between them according to circumstance. Just as important, identity could be, and was, harnessed to any strategy. Individuals suspicious of the state or of Syrian Arab nationalism emphasised those aspects of their identity which set them apart from 'Damascus', or from a dominant community however defined. But equally, members of 'minority' communities who favoured Syrian Arab nationalism and integration within the state adopted an interpretation of Syrian identity broad enough to include themselves. For example, in February 1933, fifteen Lebanese Shi'is from Nabatiyya wrote in support of the Syrian National Bloc, stating that 'Syrian Unity constitutes the wish of every Syrian Arab. The Djebel Amel, which is purely Arab, unceasingly demands it with all its strength.'[60] This strategy sometimes involved a broader interpretation of Syrian national identity than members of the linguistic or religious mainstream might have offered, but that interpretation is no less 'authentic'. Examples exist of nationalists belonging to more or less every 'minority' community; the case cited here is particularly telling since, coming from outside Syria, it is the precise opposite of a separatist mobilisation.

These points about the relationship between autonomism, state authority and 'minority' identity can also be demonstrated in reverse, as it were, by considering separatist mobilisations among communities that formed part of the mainstream on both linguistic and religious criteria – that is, Sunni Muslim Arabic-speakers. What we might call regionalist mobilisations were not unknown in French mandate Syria: there is evidence of such mobilisations in Hawran and Qalamun, south and north of Damascus, respectively. If these were not taken seriously even by the French when they emerged in the 1920s (and the nationalist press vilified them), things were different a decade later: under the National Bloc government of 1936–9, Hawran once again saw 'a move for local autonomy, with all-Hawrani officials', which the government sought not to repress but to accommodate by traditional methods: 'postponement of taxes due, remissions of sentences, and the removal of the unpopular Muhafidh'.[61]

An even better example opened this chapter, and we return to it in more detail now. It should be stressed that the case comes not from the archives of the French High Commission, which had every reason to overstate the importance of autonomist mobilisations, but from the archives of the Syrian administration at a time when it was under nationalist control and had every reason to understate them.

When the governor of the Euphrates wrote in concern to the Syrian interior ministry, in the spring of 1939, the National Bloc government was discredited and vulnerable, and the political situation across the country was tense. The 'separatist propaganda' [*da'wa infisāliyya*][62] in Dayr al-Zur was therefore worrying. What the official feared was a campaign for the governorate to become, not a separate state, but part of Iraq. As he pointed out, the local people were culturally close to their Iraqi neighbours; their 'particular inclination [*mayl khāss*]' towards the country was reinforced by 'their close communication with it' – and their sense of both 'the spread of civilisation there' and 'evidence of [its] independence'. This feeling of closeness had inspired widespread mourning upon the death of Iraq's King Ghazi I: on the Friday after the monarch's death the preachers in the town's great mosque had all called for the city's 'attachment to Iraq'. One of them had 'gone so far ... as to say that the Euphrates considers itself part of Iraq' – this was the man who said that the region did not recognise the Syrian government or president. It was on such propaganda that the governor blamed growing hostility towards the Syrian government and its employees, especially those from outside the region.

As we have already seen, the population of Dayr al-Zur was almost wholly Arabic-speaking and Sunni Muslim – part of the 'majority'. Yet the similarity with autonomist mobilisations among 'minority' populations is marked, even looking at the situation there through the eyes of a nationalist functionary. The hostility towards the central government, and the preference for local people in the local bureaucracy, is the same; the governor himself raised the question of cultural identity, in the reference to 'characteristics and customs'. There are also clearly underlying material and political causes: Iraq seemed prosperous and independent relative to a Syria whose subordination to French rule was only increasing, while it was hardly unreasonable for inhabitants of the Euphrates valley to feel a closer connection to cities downriver than to Damascus, hundreds of kilometres away across the desert. Their attitude at this stage shows that neither a national territory nor a coherent majority can be taken for granted as simply having existed in Syria under the mandate (just as these things cannot be taken for granted anywhere else). Like other separatist mobilisations, this one instead draws our attention to the historical processes that made a national territory and allowed a coherent majority to form within it – developments that are always contingent. The governor's suggestions for curing the problem of 'separatism', meanwhile, shed a revealing light on the relationship between the expanding state bureaucracy of which he was a part and the populations of Syria beyond the main cities. He conceived of his governorate as unquestionably part of a Syrian national territory – but this is taken for granted, not explicitly stated. His conception of the national community was vaguer still, and we will see in a moment that the place within it of the people under his administration was uncertain too. His attitudes bear comparison with those of the nationalist journalists we encountered in the first part of the chapter. What comes through most clearly is neither a conception of a national territory nor an imagined national community, but a concern for state power.

It is noteworthy that the governor made no positive case, on either material or ideological grounds, for the Euphrates region to remain a part of Syria. He did not choose to argue for a connection with Damascus, or against one with Iraq. Instead, he concentrated on the practical business of shoring up the Syrian state's authority over a population that he did not describe as fellow members of a Syrian nation (however defined), but rather in terms that closely resemble those of French officials describing the colonised population. 'Although the people as a whole remain primitive', he wrote, 'and the tribal inclination (in which there is something of the roughness of the Bedouin) prevails over them, nevertheless they are quick to yield [sarī'ū al-inqiyād] before strength'. The High Commissioner's delegate in Dayr al-Zur was apparently keen for the French army to take responsibility for maintaining order, which, as the governor noted, would further undermine the Syrian government's authority there. He therefore suggested increasing the local police force by at least ten men, a significant increase in a force which at the time of writing numbered only twenty-eight. Accounting for men on leave or on duty outside the city, at any one time there were only twenty policemen in a town of 60,000 inhabitants, 'and this is a very weak proportion'.[63] He recommended replacing the police chief, on whom he could no longer rely; he also pointed out that many members of the force were from the local population and linked to it by bonds of family and tribe. He evidently viewed this as a problem for the stability of state control, and argued that the new police chief should be free to replace them as necessary.

Of the various nationalist conceptions of the state's relationship to population and territory outlined in the first part of this chapter, this vision is closest to that of Nasuh Babil writing in *al-Ayyām*. It is striking that as far as the governor was concerned, the only way to ensure the state's authority was to reinforce its coercive power: more policemen, more firmly subordinated to the central state. He suggested no non-coercive ways of countering the separatist current, for example by bringing local people into the state apparatus; indeed, he saw the latter as a problem, not a solution. In this understanding, the only thing linking the state to the region and its population was the state's ability to impose its coercive power. As responses to such coercion, autonomism and separatism no doubt had their attractions – just as nationalism did in response to imperialist coercion.

Conclusion

This chapter has used a discussion of separatist and autonomist mobilisations to investigate the relationship between state, population and territory in the era of nation-states. If examined critically, the question of separatism enables us to see how authority over territory was established both in rhetoric and in practice, without confusing the two. In rhetoric, it becomes apparent that the notion of separatism served as a tool for persuading a nationalist audience that a national territory existed, and at times for marking out the bounds of a national community within it. In practice, charting the development of separatism helps us understand both the progress and the limits of the expansion of state authority.

Rethinking separatism in this way also undermines any automatic association of the phenomenon with 'minorities'. In Part I of this book I argued that minorities are created by the extension of the state's control over, and claims upon, both population and territory: a phenomenon that is characteristic of the modern period, the age of the nation-state. In the modern period, there is a strong case to be made for this same expansion of state authority as the primary motivation for separatism: the desire to separate from a state can arise only in response to a state. There is, therefore, a connection between minority identities and separatist feeling. But it is not a precise correlation, still less a self-evidently causative connection. Separatism as a political agenda is open to members of minorities only in certain conditions. These might include the existence of a substantial and concentrated minority population (that largely shares both the sense of minority identity and the desire for separation); the existence of a neighbouring state whose national majority belongs to the community that is a minority on this side of the border; substantial minorities sharing the same identity in adjacent areas of a neighbouring state or states; or the presence of another external actor willing to support the separatist minority at the expense of the state and its national majority. Where such conditions do not obtain, any autonomist agenda developed by members of minorities is likely to fall short of full separatism. When the state's institutions are flexible enough to permit the expression of minorities' political aspirations and cultural identity alongside those of the majority, autonomism is likely to be minimal or non-existent; indeed, in such situations, communities objectively definable as 'minorities' may well not consider themselves as such. None of these outcomes is inevitable or permanent: they depend on prevailing conditions, just as a particular community's status as a 'minority' is neither primordial nor unchanging.

Finally, as we saw, neither autonomism nor separatism are limited to minority communities. These agendas can, and do, also appear among populations which objectively form part of the majority, which supports the argument that the expansion of the state is the primary spur to separatism.[64] Minority identity – itself spurred by state expansion – is a secondary cause. Indeed, in some cases separatism creates, or attempts to create, a sense of minority identity rather than vice versa. Separatist and autonomist mobilisations among the majority, often on regionalist or city lines, demonstrate that it is a mistake to assume the existence of national feeling among the community claimed by nationalists as the 'majority'; unionist, nationalist activism among the 'minority' populations of administratively separated areas demonstrate that minorities are not monolithic either.

These observations all refer directly to the foregoing discussion of cases in Syria under the French mandate. More generally, however, they should also serve for comparative purposes in a world that is organised into nation-states, where separatist movements, autonomist movements and minorities are permanent features of state politics.

Notes

1. All quotes from MWT, *wathā'iq al-dawla*, sijill 2; *wizārat al-dākhiliyya*. 44/5409: handwritten letter from governor of al-Furāt to ministry of interior (13/4/1939). The document is discussed in more detail below.
2. See C. A. Bayly, *The Birth of the Modern World, 1780–1914: Global Connections and Comparisons* (Oxford: Blackwell, 2004), ch. 7, especially pp. 247–9, on the rise of the territorialised state.
3. See, e.g., Kayali, *Arabs and Young Turks*.
4. There is a substantial literature on the development of Arab nationalism in the late Ottoman period, (too) much of it influenced by Antonius 1938, which created a paradigm for understanding Arab nationalism that was still evident at the publication of Khalidi *et al.* 1991. This paradigm has tended to concentrate on the ideology of nationalism rather than, e.g., its social origins: see criticisms voiced by James Gelvin (review of Rashid Khalidi *et al.*, *The Origins of Arab Nationalism*, in *British Journal of Middle Eastern Studies* (1993), 20(1): 100–2) and Edmund Burke ('Orientalism and world history: representing Middle Eastern nationalism and Islamism in the twentieth century', *Theory and Society* (1998), 27(4): 489–507). The precise nature of Arab nationalism's territorial claims, and how those claims were circulated, put into practice and contested in relation to local populations (as opposed to imperial powers) form one neglected aspect of the question.
5. Gelvin, *Divided Loyalties*, pp. 150–68.
6. Gelvin, *Divided Loyalties*, pp. 158–9.
7. Peter Sluglett, 'Will the real nationalists stand up? The political activities of the notables of Aleppo, 1918–1946', in Méouchy (ed.), *France, Syrie et Liban*, pp. 273–90, quote at 274, n. 2.

8. See Chapter 4.
9. My use of this term is explained in the Introduction.
10. This and following quotes from *Alif Bā'*, 19 April 1923: *al-ittihād wal-infisāl aydan* (Federation and separation too).
11. AD-SL Box 413, dossier LE DJEBEL DRUZE ET L'UNITE SYRIENNE, sub-dossier UNITE SYRIENNE – *djebel druze* [sic]. Undated translation of statement to Damascus Delegation, forwarded to Meyrier, secretary-general of High Commission (21/7/1936).
12. AD-SL Box 410, untitled dossier, translation of telegram (No. 724) to HC for transmission to French president, League of Nations and other recipients; signed Abboud Ahmed, Ahmed El Kheir, Boulos Dibe and twenty-nine others (25/2/1936). This is a useful reminder of the undoubted significance of French involvement.
13. For one example among many, see AD-SL Box 413, dossier LE DJEBEL DRUZE ET L'UNITE SYRIENNE, subdossier *Requête de chefs religieux druzes en faveur de l'autonomie du Djebel Druze. Requête addressee à Son Excellence Léon Blum* (16/6/1936), signed by the three Druze religious leaders, Ahmed El-Hijri, Ahmed Jarbou and Ali El-Hennaoui (names as in original): 'the crushing majority of chiefs, notables, and peasants agree with separation. There is no reason to take into account the words of certain individuals who demand Syrian unity in a [self-]interested aim'. In box 410, untitled dossier, a duplicate of an intelligence service *Information* (unnumbered and undated, because a duplicate; *a/s Visite de Mgr. Abed*) reports a Maronite monsignor in the Alaouites stating that only 2 out of the 7,000 Maronites there were pro-unity. Abed named them as Faiez Elias and Boulos Dibé – the latter being a signatory to the unitarian petition described above.
14. *Al-wahda al-sūriyya wal-siyāda al-wataniyya. Hal ya'ūdūn fi mufāwadātihim ila al-warā'?!* 12 February 1933. Reprinted in Najib al-Rayyis, *Sūriyyat al-intidāb (1928–1936)* (London: Riad el-Rayyes, 1994), pp. 539–43.
15. Yusuf al-Hakim, *Sūriyya wal-intidāb al-faransī*. See pp. 166–9 for Alexandretta, pp. 250 and 260 for ʿAlawi region, p. 283 for Atatürk.
16. Cf. Robb, *The Discovery of France*, pp. 257–8, on 'Napoléonville' (La-Roche-sur-Yon) in post-revolutionary Vendée.
17. See Chapter 4.
18. *Alif Bā'*, 1 September 1932: *lā haraka infisāliyya fil-Jazīra. fitnat al-Jazīra wa asbābuhā*, and *al-Ayyām*, 8 September 1932: *al-infisāliyyūn al-mutamarridūn ... hal yakhluqūn hukūma jadīda 'sādisa' fi Sūriyya*.
19. This and subsequent quotes from *Alif Bā'*, 1 September 1932.
20. Joel Beinin, *Workers and Peasants in the Modern Middle East* (Cambridge: Cambridge University Press, 2001), pp. 73–7.
21. This and subsequent quotes from *al-Ayyām*, 8 September 1932.
22. This does not imply that Babil's politics were *Islamist*, merely that his frame of reference was explicitly Islamic.
23. In an article on the same subject a few weeks earlier, entitled 'The plot to detach

the Upper Jazira: how the Kurdish-Armenian homeland was devised [*mu'āmarat fasl al-Jazīra al-'Ulyā. kayfa dubbir al-watan al-kurdī al-armanī*]' (29 July 1932), the newspaper had referred to the inhabitants of the region as *dukhalā'*. The word means 'newcomers' or '[incoming] foreigners'.

24. *Hukūma* should be understood in the wider sense of the *apparatus* of government as well as in the narrower sense of the ruling political authority.
25. This is a plausible assumption rather than an established fact: see note on press sources in Introduction. Newspapers were no doubt also a means of addressing the mandatory authorities.
26. The terms 'centre' and 'periphery' can also be understood in a more than merely geographic sense, e.g., to refer to culturally or economically peripheral groups.
27. This idea may be expressed even more clearly by the Arabic term *infisāliyya* than by the English term *separatism*, since the Arabic term derives from the verbal noun *infisāl*, '[act of] separation', while the English derives from the adjective 'separate', which describes a state. A translation capturing this somewhat more 'active' sense might be 'secessionism'.
28. Seale, *Asad*, pp. 4–5
29. 'Abdallah Hanna, 'Pour ou contre le mandat français. Réflexions fondées sur des enquêtes de terrain', Méouchy (ed.), *France, Syrie et Liban*, pp. 181–8, quote at 186. A clumsier but more literal translation of this phrase (*sār fī dawla*) would be that in French times 'there *came to be* a state'.
30. Manu Goswami ascribes this analytical failure to 'methodological nationalism': 'the common practice of presupposing, rather than examining, the sociohistorical production of such categories as a national space and a national economy'. *Producing India. From Colonial Economy to National Space* (Chicago, IL: University of Chicago Press, 2004), p. 4.
31. Seale, *Asad*, pp. 14–16. Such terms are common in the literature.
32. Seale, *Asad*, p. 14. Aleppo's population was substantially larger and its political and economic weight within the empire was greater: see Sluglett, 'Will the real nationalists stand up?'. In earlier periods Aleppo was not considered part of *bilād al-Shām* at all, as Thomas Pierret pointed out to me.
33. I think it is safe to say that these newspapers assumed the reader would be 'himself'.
34. This does not mean that that territory did not exist in the minds of the authors of these texts. Their belief in it was no doubt thoroughly internalised, even sincere.
35. The theoretical and empirical literature on the expansion of the state in the modern period is immense. Works which have influenced my own thinking in this respect include Timothy Mitchell, *Rule of Experts. Egypt, Techno-politics, Modernity* (London: University of California Press, 2002); Scott, *Seeing like a State*; Stone, *Europe Transformed*; Tilly, *Coercion, Capital and European States*.
36. On the symbolic importance for nationalism of maps, see Anderson, *Imagined Communities*, ch. 10. On the physical process of mapping a national territory,

and its significance, see Scott, *Seeing like a State*, and the relevant case study in Mitchell, *Rule of Experts*, introduction and ch. 3.
37. See, e.g., text of Decree 243/LR (18/10/1934) restricting the making and export of cinematographic images in the mandate territories. MWT, *wathā'iq al-dawla,* sijill 1; *qaḍāyā mukhtalifa*, 47/1148.
38. MWT, *wathā'iq al-dawla*, sijill 1, *qaḍāyā mukhtalifa*: for Hasaka, 67/1168 (governor of Jazira to ministry of interior, 3/2/1939 (misdated: in fact 3/3/1939)); for Qamishli, 70/1171 (qa'immaqam of Qamishli to governor of Jazira, 3/3/1939).
39. Three in Homs in January (MWT, *wathā'iq al-dawla*, sijill 1; *idrābāt*, 7/613 and 11/617), one in Dayr al-Zur in January (same sijill; *idrābāt*, 4/610), one in Dar'a in March (same sijill; *ḥawādith*, 14/794), one in Hasaka in January (same sijill; *qaḍāyā mukhtalifa*, 63/1164).
40. Souheil Chebat informed me that demonstrations of students in Damascus often began at the Tajhiz then filed past, and drew support from, schools belonging to religious communities (see Chapter 6). This was the pattern followed by the student demonstration in Homs described in 11/617 above.
41. Around the same time, twelve Bloc members in 'Afrin – another small town – telegraphed the ministry of the interior to protest that local employees of the French authorities had threatened them with prison if they did not raise *only* French flags the next day. 'The nation', they wrote, 'firmly united behind the decisions of the National Bloc, protests strongly against these measures.' MWT, *wathā'iq al-dawla*, sijill 1; *idrābāt*, 12/618 (7/2/1939).
42. The word 'Syrian' here comes from the Arabic *sūriyānī*. 'Syrian Catholic' is one translation for the name of this church; since there were other Catholics in Syria, I have used 'Syrian-Catholic', to specify this church and its members. 'Syriac' is also used.
43. MWT, *wathā'iq al-dawla*, sijill 1; *qaḍāyā mukhtalifa*, 63/1164. Governor of Jazira to ministry of interior (23/1/1939).
44. Khoury, *Syria and the French Mandate*, ch. 3 gives information about the small number of French officers and officials in the mandate territories, who were concentrated in Beirut. The Syrian state they oversaw, however, and information about its functionaries (especially below the upper ranks), are striking absences in this monumental work.
45. See the articles collected in Philipp and Schaebler (eds), *The Syrian Land*.
46. For anti-nationalists it was common to go 'over the head' of Damascus and directly address the High Commission in Beirut, the Ministry of Foreign Affairs in Paris and/or the League of Nations in Geneva. But, on the other hand, nationalists addressed these three institutions in order to *endorse* Damascus's status as capital of Syria.
47. Quoted, from F. Jovine, in E. J. Hobsbawm, *The Age of Empire 1875–1914* (London: Weidenfeld & Nicolson, 1987), p. 142.
48. Autonomist petitions seem to have been addressed to the High Commission or the League of Nations more often than the Syrian government.

49. AD-SL Box 414, dossier *LES ALAOUITES ET L'UNITE SYRIENNE* (handwritten: *1933–1936*), petition from 'Alawis of al-Haffa (in French 'Haffé') caza, 7/2/1933. My translation is based on the original, verified against a French translation also present. An identical text from the caza of Massyaf (Masyāf) with a different list of signatories is present only in French translation.
50. AD-SL Box 410, untitled dossier, petition to MAE (25/2/1936), signed el Kinj *et al.*
51. This and following quote from AD-SL Box 414, dossier MOUVEMENT AUTONOMISTE, subdossier *Menées Separatistes. Généralités. Traduction résumée* of a request to HC, from 'Le Chef de la Communauté des Islamaïliés et député du Caza de Salimié: S./. Tamer . . . (Illisible)'.
52. When it began, nationalist newspapers in Damascus were by no means uniformly favourable to this rural uprising among a backward community. See the *Revues de la Presse de Damas* for July–September 1925 in AD-SL Box 1727, bound volume avril–décembre 1925.
53. If Salamiyya is considerably less 'peripheral' than the Jazira or even the Alaouites in this period, its position away from the large towns towards the edge of the settled agricultural zone of western Syria means the term is still applicable. See Norman Lewis, *Nomads and Settlers in Syria and Jordan, 1800–1980* (Cambridge: Cambridge University Press, 1987), pp. 58–67.
54. AD-SL Box 414, dossier *MOUVEMENT AUTONOMISTE*, subdossier *Mouvement autonomiste Djebel Druze* (evidently misfiled). *Information No 481* (20/1/1939).
55. Both *Circassien* and *Tcherkess* exist in French; I am using 'Circassian' uniformly in my text, but 'Tcherkess' in direct quotes from French sources where that word rather than *Circassien* is used.
56. AD-SL Box 568, dossier *Tcherkess*, 'Demandes présentées au Haut-Commissaire par les Tcherkess' (5/1/1927). These had been received no later than December 1926.
57. AD-SL Box 568, dossier *Tcherkess*, petition from Circassians in Qunaytra, Homs, Hama and Marj Sultan to High Commission for forwarding to League of Nations (1/4/1933). This was probably the petition reported to be circulating in Homs a couple of weeks earlier: AD-SL Box 620, dossier *Mouvement minoritaire Chrétien*, subdossier *La question des minorités en Syrie et en Irak (Généralités – correspondances – informations). Information No 1203* (18/3/1933). See also Chapter 5.
58. Tilly, *Coercion, Capital and European States*, p. 100.
59. While imposing different limits, set by French imperial strategy, which, e.g., had no intention of allowing the Kurds to establish a state on territories under French mandate (see Chapters 2 and 4).
60. Box 410, dossier *B13 (1933) Rattachement des Alaouites à la Syrie*, telegram to Hashim al-Atasi and Ibrahim Hananu (17/2/1933).
61. Longrigg, *Syria and Lebanon*, p. 246. A digest of press reports on the Hawrani separatist movement immediately prior to the great revolt can be found in AD-SL Box 1727, bound volume avril–décembre 1925, *Revue de la presse de Damas du*

15 Juillet 1925 (18?/7/1925). Material on separatism in the Jabal Qalamun can be found in AD-SL Box 414, dossier *MOUVEMENT AUTONOMISTE*, subdossier *Mouvement Separatiste Damas*.
62. This and following quotes from MWT, *wathā'iq al-dawla*, sijill 2; *wizārat al-dākhiliyya*. 44/5409: handwritten letter from governor of al-Furāt to ministry of interior (13/4/1939).
63. Khoury, *Syria and the French Mandate*, p. 11, based on several different sources, gives Dayr's population as only 33,716 in 1936, but as 61,139 in 1943.
64. For examples from revolutionary France, see Tilly, *Coercion, Capital and European States*, p. 113.

CHAPTER

4

THE BORDER AND THE KURDS

Introduction

In the spring of 1939, the French High Commissioner planned a visit to the Jazira.[1] So nationalists in Qamishli asked the beleaguered National Bloc government to send them Syrian flags, and flagpoles to hang them on during his visit. They wanted 'to show their sound nationalist feeling', and demonstrate this turbulent region's loyalty to Damascus. But hostility to Damascus was strong there, too, and when the flags arrived at the local railway station a group of anti-nationalists tried to intercept them. The stationmaster at first refused to give the flags to anyone other than the addressee, and with seventy armed nationalist youths guarding them, the anti-nationalists hesitated to press him. It was only when they returned with a detachment of Circassian troops sent by the local French officer that the stationmaster was persuaded to relinquish the packets containing the flags. 'Then', wrote the Minister of the Interior, 'they opened them near the municipal offices [*dā'irat al-baladiyya*] and burned them before a crowd of people, and carried out acts of the basest kind [*a'māl sāfila lil-ghāya*].' The qa'immaqam of Qamishli was more specific. One Dawud 'Aziz Hana 'donated a Syrian pound from his own pocket to whoever would urinate on the Syrian flags after burning them, and indeed paid the Syrian pound to one of the rabble [*shakhs min awbāsh al-nās*]', since the latter did just that.[2]

There are many interesting things about this incident, but one thing is interesting by its absence: the Syrian–Turkish border. Qamishli was a border town, and the recently-drawn border ran just south of the railway line. So the local station was in Nusaybin, less than a mile away on the Turkish side, and the reluctant stationmaster was a Turkish state employee. But the documents relating these events nowhere mention the border, even though they describe two

[101]

mutually antagonistic groups of Syrians, at least some of them armed, strolling onto Turkish territory for a stand-off that involved one of them – backed by French military force – pressurising a Turkish official. If any of those involved faced any hindrance at the border, or indeed surveillance, it is not mentioned.[3] The border might as well not have existed.

Ostensibly, historians of the Middle East have been much preoccupied with borders. The artificiality or otherwise of the region's modern frontiers is a staple of scholarship: how they were drawn by the colonial powers ('Winston's hiccup'); the consequences for state stability and legitimacy.[4] Disputes that affected the route of particular borders are well studied: works on the Alexandretta crisis could fill a bookshelf, works on Israel's wars a library. But the border itself has often been taken for granted, perhaps because – like so many other phenomena related to the development of modern states – borders now have such a strong presence in the collective psyche that they are taken as part of the natural order of things, seeming to need no explanation.[5] Philip Khoury notes, quite accurately, that the Syrian–Turkish border cut Aleppo off from its natural hinterland; but how?[6] Jean Perez states, of the mandate period, that the transhumant pastoralism of the Bedouin of the Syrian desert led them to 'make a mockery of frontiers [*se jouer des frontières*]', as if the frontiers had been there before the Bedouin arrived.[7] It would be truer to say that the region's borders – lines drawn very recently on a map that would itself have been quite useless to the nomads concerned – *se jouaient des Bédouins*. Even scholarship whose professed subject is a border, such as Eliezer Tauber's article on the determination of borders between Syria and Iraq,[8] can offer a perfectly sound and thoughtful account of how a particular border came to follow a particular route without asking either the question of what the border actually was – how it was delineated, both concretely and institutionally – or the rather more difficult question of what it meant: how the border's concrete and institutional existence served to constitute the territory of the states concerned, how borders relate to state authority, how they affect populations whether resident close to or far from them.

In one sense the importance of borders to the subject of this book is quite obvious: it is the delineation of a nation-state's borders that decides who, in that state, is going to be a majority and who a minority. The point is too pessimistic: not all nation-states are condemned to a zero-sum struggle between different groups among the population. More important, it is misleadingly obvious, assuming the existence and coherence of the groups involved from the outset. I will be arguing, instead, that majority and minorities are constituted in relation to the state through the process of its establishment, including the drawing of its borders. And it offers a fairly unproblematic view of the border, concentrating on the effect of different groups arguing over where a particular border should run without examining how the establishment of fixed, nation-state borders is a constitutive process in the making of modern states' authority and 'identity'.

In this chapter I try to draw out the complexities in both areas: how borders define minorities (and a majority), and how borders are related to state authority. The chapter continues my analysis of the relationship between state authority, territory, population and identity. The first part of the chapter asks what material presence Syria's new borders had in the mandate period: that is, how the state's authority was manifested concretely at its boundaries. The second part examines the relationship between the border and state authority across the whole territory and population through the lens of the 'Kurdish question' that arose in the region after the First World War as nation-states replaced the Ottoman Empire. This section concentrates on the Syrian–Turkish border in the mid- to late 1920s, when that border was (gradually) created. The final section shows how the drawing of Syria's borders came to 'minoritise' all Kurds resident in the country.

The Border's Physical Presence (or Absence)

The example that opened this chapter suggests that there was no actual 'border' between Syria and Turkey at Qamishli in 1939, and the point holds for long stretches of Syria's borders throughout the mandate period. Tauber's article shows that the zones under the control of Faysali Syria, on the one hand, and British-occupied Iraq, on the other, were defined not by a contest over a particular line, but by a contest for control of certain towns and villages (and their respective gendarme posts and government buildings[9]) across a swathe of disputed territory. In this situation, the term 'crossing the border' was literally meaningless: the border had no material presence, nor was its location agreed by the two jurisdictions it was supposed to separate. Moreover, insofar as Syria's borders did 'solidify' in this period, it was more as demarcation lines between two mutually recognising jurisdictions than in any material sense of lines marked by a physical barrier or permanent surveillance. The fences and watchtowers that mark the Syrian–Turkish border today are for the most part far more recent (1970s), while Syria's long desert frontier with Iraq was largely unmarked on the ground until the aftermath of the US invasion of 2003.[10]

After the First World War, the border between the two new states of Syria and Turkey remained uncertain for several years, into the 1920s, when the Ankara government in Turkey and the French occupation authorities in Syria fought a war over where it should lie. Neither jurisdiction recognised the other: French troops briefly occupied a large area claimed by the Ankara government, which in turn sent armed bands deep into French territory and supported anti-French activities in Syria.[11] With the Franklin-Bouillon Agreement of 1921, France and the Republic of Turkey stopped fighting and formally recognised each other, agreeing a border between Turkish and French mandate territories that was confirmed by the Treaty of Lausanne in 1923. But the border remained very loosely defined: the Lausanne treaty established a joint border delineation committee to fix its exact route on the ground, but the job took years.[12]

This was partly because it was a large and complex task. But both states were also weak along this particular edge – especially the mandatory state. In northeastern Syria, for example, the French only established a semblance of permanent authority in May 1926, with two posts totalling sixty soldiers established at Darbisiyya and 'Amuda. 'Their presence did not modify the general physiognomy of this region, whose principal feature continued to be a profound anarchy.'[13] The installation of more, larger military posts, notably at Qamishli from 1926, seated French authority more firmly in the western part of the 'Bec de Canard', the panhandle of Syrian territory extending towards the Tigris with Turkey to the north and Iraq to the south; but troop movements further east were limited. When a diplomatic protocol of 1929 agreed the precise border in this zone, there were four French and six Turkish military posts between Nusaybin and the Tigris – but the haziness of the border hitherto can be gauged from the fact that four of the Turkish posts were in Syrian territory, well to the south of the agreed border.[14] (Charles de Gaulle was an officer with the French detachment that finally reached the Tigris in June 1930. 'I went with the general', he wrote to his father, 'and we dipped our hands in the river, not without some emotion.'[15]) Whether the border represented any kind of real barrier even after that, though, is dubious: in August 1930, for example, the exiled Kurdish leader Hajo Agha was able to lead an abortive armed incursion across the border onto Turkish territory.[16]

Nor was it only in the furthest northeastern reaches of Syria that the border was ill-defined and state authority hazy. In April 1934, the qa'immaqam of the Kurd Dagh, Khayri Rida, made an inspection tour of his caza, a region of limestone hills lying between Aleppo and Antioch. His report begins by noting the ease with which armed bands – especially one led by 'the famous 'Ali Karu al-Shiqqi' – were slipping across the border at night 'to carry out acts of robbery, plunder, and murder against the persons and properties of Syrian subjects', then returning with the takings to their safe refuge in a Turkish village.[17] With the caza's gendarme chief, Rida decided to increase patrols 'in this sensitive spot'. But it was not just the border that was sensitive. 'Ali Karu's gang had hiding places in at least four Syrian villages where they could take refuge among the inhabitants. On his tour, Rida summoned forty village chiefs and warned them against harbouring criminals, but the incident is revealing. The Syrian state was now reaching down to village level, but it could not take the population's cooperation – which it needed – for granted. Its control over the territory could be asserted by the deployment of coercive forces, but to keep order in the face of border-crossing bandits, as Rida told his superior in Aleppo, 'we rely on private individuals to observe the criminals and those who dare to harbour them [and] to inform the government immediately'.

As this suggests, the state's ability to secure the border depended on its effective authority within its own territory, and vice versa. But the Syrian state's means in this border region were modest indeed, as the rest of Rida's report shows. He describes the functioning and facilities of the offices of the chief of each nahiya or administrative district in his caza. In the nahiya of Bulbul, Rida reported, this office (the *mudīriyya*) was not even furnished. 'Please', he asked his superior, 'if possible, assign a sofa and two wicker chairs to this office [*arjū idhā kān fil-imkān takhsīs maqʿad wa kursiyyayn khayzurān li-hādhihi al-mudīriyya*].' The link between the state's material presence on the territory and the border would be demonstrated sharply in this very area a few years later. One of the villages Rida visited was al-Hammam, on the Aleppo–Alexandretta road. (He was not impressed by the mudir's disorderly office-keeping.) When the French ceded the sanjak to Turkey, the new border's winding path through the village – which brought certain valuable buildings (a hotel, the eponymous mineral baths) and the municipal gardens into the sanjak and out of Syria – was partly defined by the personal political loyalties of their proprietors and partly by the fact that the pro-Turkish authorities in the sanjak sent out a police unit and installed a police station in the village faster than the Syrian authorities.[18] Such was the importance of the material presence of the state that Rida sought to augment: the line of the border depended on it. But as we saw from the flag-burning incident, even in a place where the apparatus of state authority was present on both sides of the border – the towns of Qamishli and Nusaybin, seat of a Syrian qa'immaqam and Turkish kaymakam respectively, faced each other at a bare kilometre's distance – as late as 1939 the border itself did not necessarily pose much of an obstacle.

The mandate period, then, witnessed a steady accretion of state authority along the border, in the shape of military installations, bureaucratic institutions and even wicker chairs (if they ever arrived). This is in line with my argument in the previous chapter about the spread and 'deepening' of state authority across the territory. Yet the border itself as a physical barrier seems to have remained almost negligible right through the mandate period. Its real development in this period was as a jurisdictional barrier.

The Border as a Jurisdictional Barrier, the 'Kurdish Question', and State Authority on Both Sides

As mentioned above, the Franklin-Bouillon Agreement of 1921 brought mutual recognition between the French authorities in Syria (and thus the Syrian state too) and the new Turkish government in Ankara. Although their common frontier remained to be precisely defined, it would now be done by diplomatic cooperation rather than military contest. This mutual recognition immediately had one important consequence for the border, in that each side's military forces retreated to the agreed frontier: the French left Cilicia and Turkey reduced its support for armed bands on French territory. In other words, the states on either side of the new border no longer transgressed it (or at least did so more discreetly). Both the Ankara government in Turkey and the French High Commission in Syria were newly-established regimes facing many internal and external challenges to their authority; for each government, mutual recognition removed one important challenge and freed up men and resources for dealing with others: war against Greece for Ankara, uprisings in northern and western Syria for France.

These pressing but temporary political reasons that pushed France-in-Syria and Turkey to recognise one another and agree to a common frontier were supplemented by longer-term reasons of statecraft. The state-building project on which each government was engaged involved building a nation-state (albeit with greater conviction on the Turkish side[19]), with a national territory and fixed borders. One effect of the modern transformation of the state – as state authority becomes theoretically uniform across the entire territory, and modern communications permit some practical approximation of this – is that these sharp dividing lines replace the buffer zones and indistinct frontiers of earlier periods. Important state functions, not only related to defence, move to the frontier: notably, monitoring and collection of customs duty moves from strategic points within the territory to a point of entry at the border. The links between the definition of fixed borders, on the one hand, and the development of state authority, on the other, are multiple and complex.[20] My intention here is to concentrate on one particular aspect of this question: how these interlocking developments also contributed to the emergence of 'minorities', with specific reference to the Kurds.

The new Turkish state's policy towards the Syrian border zone in the years after the Treaty of Lausanne (1923) reflects its wider policy towards southern and eastern Anatolia. The republic was seeking to replace Ottoman authority in zones that had been occupied by France after the war; impose permanent state authority across a broad swathe of territory with a culturally diverse population; contain the opposition which this process naturally provoked; and forestall any future challenges, including such as might be launched from outside the national territory by groups claiming sections of it. All of this involved the border, and Syria, because in a number of cases the populations involved spread over (or had previously been expelled) into the mandate territories.[21]

The end of the Ottoman Empire and establishment of the Turkish Republic had seen the almost complete elimination (by massacre, expulsion, flight or arranged transfer) of Anatolia's Christian populations, considered inassimilable to the Turkish 'nation' in construction. Nationalist policy towards non-Turkish Muslim populations, most importantly the Kurds of eastern Anatolia, was rather different. The republic had no intention of expelling the Kurds en masse: the aim was to incorporate them as citizens, preferably as Turks.[22] Opposition among Kurdish elites to Ankara's imposition of authority was rooted in the challenge to their political and economic position in the region, and expressed itself in religious terms (as opposition to secularising reform) and in some cases as incipient Kurdish nationalism. Insofar as it therefore posed an existential challenge to the republican regime, armed opposition was put down violently, those involved liable to execution or internal exile[23] – many fled across the border into Syria. Provided that they could be incorporated, however, the republic was not hostile to the existence of Kurds on 'Turkish' territory.[24] What it feared was any movement which posed the risk of a Kurdish *state* on Turkish territory. This Turkish interest in Kurdish affairs had important implications for Syria and the border.

The archives of the French High Commission contain much evidence of the scale of unrest over the border in Kurdish areas of Turkey. During the first major outbreak of violence, the Shaykh Sa'id revolt of 1925,[25] Turkey received French permission to transport troops by rail from Mersin or Adana to the affected areas (the railway line crossed French territory);[26] for several months the French monitored their numbers, which ran into the hundreds or even thousands per day.[27] Although this was one of the largest revolts, violence remained endemic down to the Dersim repression of 1938[28] – and the French in Syria paid close attention.[29] The major revolts of these years were high points on a continuum of constant unrest, not isolated events.

That unrest was a reaction to the expansion of Turkish state authority. Soner Cagaptay describes how the regional bureaucracy in 1930s Dersim, for example, 'focused on building roads, bridges, and *gendarme* stations throughout the region',[30] strengthening Ankara's authority: local opposition focused precisely, and vocally, on these bureaucratic and infrastructural infringements. But by a process of feedback, opposition also contributed to the expansion of state authority, by bringing the state into the Kurdish regions in force: 25,000 soldiers were deployed in Dersim to repress, brutally, what Ankara viewed as a rebellion.[31] It stimulated the development of a permanent state presence. The extension of state authority in general was tending to harden the frontier, but the need to 'manage' the Kurds impelled this process in particular: partly because this population spread beyond the borders claimed by the new republic, and partly because military repression sent Kurdish refugees – especially insurgents and their families – into Syria. Once there, they remained politically active and interacted with others (Syrian Kurds, other refugees, the French authorities and Syrian Arabs) in ways that heightened the border's significance.

For fleeing insurgents, the border's value was clearly as a barrier beyond which they could shelter from Turkey. Even if it was neither precisely defined nor materially 'there', diplomatic accords meant that Turkey recognised the border as a jurisdictional limit. Thus, soon after the Shaykh Sa'id rebellion began, the French Assistant Delegate for Aleppo wrote to the High Commissioner to 'attract [his] attention to the probable repercussion of current events in Kurdistan on the Syrian zone of the Syro-Turkish frontier, in large part populated ... by Kurdish tribes', anticipating that 'to escape the chastisement that threatens them numerous rebels will seek refuge with their brothers in Syria'.[32] This prediction remained accurate for years to come. But although the border afforded them an opportunity for protection, and even a haven from which to prepare future action against the Turkish state, once they had crossed it the frontier also became a barrier which the republic could use to keep them out. Both of these functions depended on, and simultaneously stimulated, the development of state authority on the French side of the border – not just at the border, but deep within the territory too.

At the outset of the Shaykh Sa'id rebellion, the nearby border was not precisely delineated; on the Syrian side, French authority was extremely tenuous. Insurgents fleeing into this zone were not relying on the protection of French troops, but on the fact that the Turkish state recognised French authority and would not follow them there. In many cases, when insurgents arrived and settled on 'French' territory they were entirely outside meaningful French influence. The High Commissioner Henri Ponsot made this point in September 1927, in one of very many documents produced by French officers rebutting or contesting Turkish claims that the mandatory authorities were permitting or even assisting refugee insurgents to organise for further action on Turkish territory. Two Kurdish leaders who provoked Turkish suspicions, Hajo Agha and Emin Agha, 'were installed in a part of the Syrian territory of which we have only really taken possession since the creation, 7th August last [that is, only weeks earlier], of the posts of KUBUR EL-BID and DEMIR-KAPOU'.[33]

French authority was weak when Kurdish insurgents first started fleeing into this 'French' territory: this example shows how the need to bring the region and the insurgents who arrived there under control stimulated the expansion of state authority. A slightly earlier example can be cited further to the west, where French authority was imposed earlier. In March 1925, soon after the Shaykh Sa'id rebellion began, the High Commission ordered that a Service de Renseignements (SR) post be established at 'Arab Punar, another frontier village. Its mission was to gather information on the Kurdish movement and the military operations of the rebellion; to monitor the state of mind of Kurds on the Turkish side of the frontier; and to 'survey the attitude of the Kurds of Syria and prevent any manifestation of solidarity' between them and the Turkish Kurds. All these aims are clearly linked to the events in Turkey, though the third is equally clearly intended to forestall threats to French authority in Syria. But achieving them, again, implied a strengthening of state authority on the border. The post was staffed by one SR officer, assisted by an interpreter and a platoon of *gendarmerie mobile*, whose tasks included carrying out surveillance missions among local tribes and 'making frequent patrols along the frontier'.[34] The post's personnel – and indeed its office furnishings – were to be seconded from the existing post at Jarablus, but it was to report directly to the SR's regional centre in Aleppo.

At its establishment, this post was intended to be temporary. But although Jarablus was assured that it would get its typewriter back,[35] it probably never did: an intelligence post was still functioning at 'Arab Punar in the late 1930s.[36] The general trend was towards the development of permanent state authority: not just military, but also bureaucratic; and not just on the frontier, but 'behind' it as well. This was necessary not only for monitoring the newcomers, but for tasks such as assessing the customs payments they would have to pay on the flocks they brought across the border with them, if any; granting them Syrian nationality, in some cases; and, more pressingly, disarming them and moving them further away from the frontier.[37]

This brings us back to my earlier point that from the Turkish perspective, while the border might have created inconvenience insofar as insurgents could escape across it, once they had done so it also served as a barrier for keeping them out. This function depended on the development of French authority on the other side of the frontier, without which the border was an ineffective barrier: this explains the concern of the Turkish authorities to keep refugees not only on the French side of the border, but far on the French side – and monitored carefully wherever they were. But it stimulated the development of state authority on the French side, too, because of the constant Turkish pressure on the High Commission (via officials in the border region, Turkish diplomats in Beirut and Paris, or French diplomats in Turkey) to keep a tight reign on Kurds and other groups in Syria who were suspected of threatening the nervous and unstable young republic as it sought to impose state authority on its own side of the border.

Turkey's most pressing concern for border security was to prevent any armed insurgents who had fled beyond it from crossing back with their guns. To address this, in early March 1925 the High Commissioner (at that point General Sarrail) sent instructions to his personnel regarding the refugees. Individual insurgents taking refuge among Syrian Kurdish tribes were to be watched to ensure that they did not 'constitute any centres of anti-Turkish agitation'.[38] To this end, the tribes were to be carefully monitored and gendarme units in the area 'reinforced if necessary'. Groups of insurgents were to be treated differently: they 'should be settled at a distance of at least 30 km from the frontier', and 'once settled, they should be disarmed in order that they constitute a threat neither to our own tribes nor to the Turkish populations north of the border'. Later documents sent to the High Commission by officers on the ground, or by the High Commissioner to Paris, make clear that these guidelines remained operative for years.[39] Indeed, after a Franco-Turkish accord on 'good neighbourliness' (*bon voisinage*) in 1926, the 'exclusion zone' was extended to 50 km from the border.[40] This was still the agreed distance in the early 1930s, when the Kurdish leader Hajo Agha – whose tribal lands spread across the new frontier – could not return to his home village after a failed incursion into Turkey because it was less than 50 km from the frontier.[41] (A few years later, the Turkish chair of a meeting of the League of Nations council on the subject of Assyrian refugees from Iraq expressed his country's preference that these 'victims of the world war', if settled permanently in Syria, be kept 100 km from the border, though 50 km would do.[42])

Sometimes the exclusion zone was not enough, and the French authorities expelled the person concerned from Syria entirely. In June 1925, the French ambassador in Turkey, trying to persuade Ankara that 'without damaging our higher principles of humanity, every measure has been taken to make it impossible for the persons in question to foment new disorders on Turkish territory', noted that another participant in the Shaykh Saʿid revolt, Edhem Bek, had been expelled from Syria – a handwritten note to this letter suggesting that the words 'even before the Turkish request' be added.[43] Edhem Bek ended up in Iraq, where a newspaper recorded his disappointment with Syria: entering it 'thinking that it was a free and independent country', he had found the French authorities – their 'higher principles' notwithstanding – 'ready to cast underfoot every sentiment of humanity', and too willing to believe 'Turkish spies'.[44]

Of course, we may doubt the effectiveness of the exclusion zone: Hajo Agha's incursion is just one example of a Kurdish leader passing beyond French control. The limits of state authority were set by the available resources. Shaykh Saʿid's brother ʿAbd al-Rahim, upon arriving in Syria in December 1927, was placed in obligatory residence at Dayr al-Zur, far from the border, and his followers dispersed in the Syrian interior;[45] but around the same time, another prominent Kurdish notable – Hajo Agha's brother Emin Agha, returning to Syria after an illegal trip into Turkey – was permitted to stay much closer to the border, at Hasaka. As the High Commissioner pointed out in a letter to the Quai d'Orsay, Hasaka was still outside the (then) 30 km exclusion zone, and settling him there meant that

> it is easier for him to find the means of existence through agricultural cooperation with families long since settled in the country, whereas the Budget of the State of Syria would have had to subsidize his needs had he been obliged to settle in the capital of the Sanjak [of Dayr al-Zur].[46]

The letter also mentions that it would have been difficult for the French 'man on the spot', Captain Terrier, to prevent Emin Agha's illegal crossing of the border 'since we did not yet occupy the region of Kubur-el-Bid where he had taken refuge'.

Nonetheless, this letter asserts state authority even while admitting its weakness: Hasaka was considered a suitable place of residence for Emin Agha because an SR officer and mobile garrison were stationed there, 'permitting easy surveillance of the refugees, which must give every guarantee to our neighbours' – namely, the Turks. Such surveillance could mean keeping a close count of how many refugees were in each place, and how many weapons they had surrendered: 'Abd al-Rahim, for instance, was reported to have entered Syria at Ra's al-'Ayn with a group of 195 refugees. When the Turkish authorities requested reassurances about this group from the High Commission, the Assistant Delegate in Dayr al-Zur pointed out that 103 of them had already been moved away from the border, to Hasaka, where the rest 'should join them shortly'. Also in Hasaka were twenty-four members of another group that had entered Syria around the same time; others had briefly been unaccounted for, but again, even before the High Commission's telegram arrived they 'were sought out and redirected by a detachment of *gardes-mobiles*'. Meanwhile, 'the disarmament of these refugees was proceeding as normal; more than 70 combat rifles were already in the hands of the Hassetché [Hasaka] SR officer'. This figure had risen to 124 by the time of writing, albeit 'against the will of certain refugees, who sought to conceal their weapons or make them disappear'.[47]

Again, whether the French could always exert such precise control in these regions is doubtful: we have already encountered several open or tacit admissions of the limits of their authority. When responding to Turkish complaints, the mandatory power had numerous reasons to overstate its own effectiveness, starting with the desire to hush those complaints. But this is beside the point: no state can maintain perfect surveillance and control over its territory and population. What matters is that the state's authority over peripheral areas of the territory increased significantly in this period. The border played a complex role in this process as both a causative factor and a consequence. This role is illustrated by a report written in 1928 by a priest named Father Poidebard, a valuable source of information on the far northeast of the mandate territories for the French in the mid-1920s. He stated that 'the regroupment of the populations of upper Mesopotamia (the Syrian Haute Djézireh and northern Iraq) that is in course will necessarily be to the profit of the territory [that is] most quickly delimited and reorganized'.[48] The arrival of Kurds, like the arrival of Christian refugees, was part of that 'regroupment' – which was a consequence of the division of what was once part of the Ottoman Empire into several different jurisdictions. But it also caused the new borders to be more swiftly and sharply delineated, by inciting the new states to spread their authority into the border zone. As Poidebard put it, 'this establishment of Kurdish and Christian refugees requires the rapid solution of the delimitation of frontiers with Iraq and Turkey – the indispensable condition for the installation of good administration, closely controlled by the Mandatory Power'.

The Border and the 'Minoritisation' of Syria's Kurds

The dynamic of border creation – the delineation of the border itself and the concomitant development of state authority behind it – meant that Kurds who fled to Syria from Turkey got 'stuck' there, so to speak. They found themselves in a state with a largely Arabic-speaking population, a developing bureaucracy centred on Damascus and other state institutions – from the courts to the parliament – whose official language was Arabic. Especially as the development of those institutions gathered momentum in the 1930s, and a Syrian Arab nationalist movement more successfully asserted its claim over them, they created a powerful logic that tended to define all Kurds within the country – not just recent arrivals in the Jazira, but also longstanding residents of Damascus – as a single, minority, community.

This tendency was influenced by several factors. The reader will by now be well aware of the French preference for viewing Syrian society as a mosaic of distinct ethnic and religious groups, and governing accordingly. In the case of the Kurds, that view was further conditioned by the wider regional 'Kurdish question'. This is evident from the structure and content of the French archives: boxes whose titles refers simply to 'Kurds' or 'Kurds of Syria' contain material that overwhelmingly focuses either on events that might have repercussions across the border (such as refugee Kurds organising themselves politically), or on events across the border involving the Kurds that might have repercussions within Syria (such as renewed violence creating more refugees). French officials constantly had the wider region in mind when considering the Kurdish populations: it was quite normal for French intelligence reports coming from peripheral, sparsely populated bits of Syria to cite a 'serious source' in support of the claim that a Kurdish nationalist committee was 'working actively to bring about a new Kurdish insurrection' (plausible), and that 'all the Kurds of Turkey, Iraq, Persia, and even Syria would be in agreement to unleash this movement as of next autumn' (less plausible).[49]

The French fretted that 'the ever more powerful pressure that the Turks are striving to apply to the Kurds of their country' might transfer 'the whole Kurdish question' onto Syria, and thus France.[50] But at the same time, they were not unhappy to accept Kurdish immigration, as long as they could control it – in the 'monitor and disarm' sense outlined above – and draw advantage from it. Weighing up the pros and cons, in the mid-1920s, of creating an autonomous Kurdish zone, the senior French army officer in northern Syria came down against such a measure, citing 'the dangers that could result'. The first, predictably, was 'possible complications with Turkey', but the second was 'the predominance without counterweight of the Arab element in the rest of the State'.[51] It served French policy to keep the Kurds of the northeast within a unitary Syrian state, where they could act as that counterweight – especially if they were considered as one community with Kurds elsewhere in the country.

But it also ensured that they were a minority within it, whereas the Druzes and 'Alawis, for example, were not numerical minorities within their statelets.

Pressure from Turkey to restrict Kurdish activities in Syria reinforced the High Commission's tendency to see all Kurds as forming a single group. Ankara was suspicious of any political activity among Kurds in Syria, tending to assume that such activity would naturally be hostile to Turkey. But some of the measures enacted by France in response to that pressure may, in fact, have worked to increase a sense of shared Kurdish identity between Syria's existing Kurdish population and the newcomers.

Turkey had two great worries about Kurds in Syria. The first was that the Kurdish refugees, in coordination with Syrian Kurds or other groups (including Armenian refugees, but also anti-Kemalist Turkish exiles[52]) might contribute to insurrectional activity in the republic – either through direct participation or by supplying money and weapons. This was a realistic fear. The second was that the French authorities might grant Kurds within Syria some kind of formal territorial autonomy that would create a very uncomfortable precedent, even a direct threat, for Turkey. As we have seen, this was less likely. 'It seems very difficult for France to launch herself on a Kurdish adventure that would encounter the hostility of England [mandatory power in Iraq] and Turkey at the same time.'[53] These fears, though, help to explain Turkish interest in Syria's Kurds. Within a developing framework of diplomatic relations with the French government and the High Commission, Ankara sought reassurance regarding populations it viewed as hostile.

Turkish fears were particularly acute when those populations were in the borderlands. Suspicion of Kurds (or Armenians) animated many a cross-border diplomatic exchange, leading to the border's 'hardening' in a number of ways: for example, when the French agreed to establish three new gendarme posts along the border (Darbisiyya, 'Amuda, Nusaybin) after a somewhat obscure violent incident at Darbisiyya in 1926. Ankara immediately expressed worry, though, about 'the employment of Armenians or Kurdish rebels' at the posts.[54] The French were already aware that the recruitment of Kurds or Armenians into the security services on the frontier posed a problem: during the Shaykh Sa'id revolt the High Commissioner's delegate in Damascus launched an enquiry to find out what proportion of gendarmes on the border were Kurds, planning to transfer them away if necessary.[55]

In the High Commission's records on the Kurds for these years, complaints from Turkey that Kurds in Syria were preparing military action against the republic are a common feature, as are accusations that the mandatory power was assisting such action. Following the Darbisiyya incident, the Turkish Embassy in Paris claimed that the cross-border skirmish there was 'the prelude to a large-scale action directed against Turkish territory'. It accused the local French SR officers of supporting Kurdish requests to the High Commission for arms and ammunition, and claimed there was 'no doubt about the preparation on Syrian territory of a vast Kurdish insurrectional movement'.[56] Similar complaints persisted through the inter-war years: for example, Ankara suspected that the 1937–8 unrest in Dersim might be linked to groups in Syria, perhaps Armenian.[57] These suspicions were not necessarily unfounded: there certainly was Kurdish–Armenian cooperation in Syria in the mandate period, albeit uneasy, and we have already seen that some insurgents who had taken refuge in Syria did return to fight in Turkey. (Others returned to cut deals with the government.) This helps us understand why Turkey concerned itself not only with insurgent refugees near the border, but also with Kurds in the rest of Syria. From the Shaykh Sa'id revolt onwards, there was increasing Kurdish political organisation within Syria, notably with the Khoybun ('Independence') committee founded in Lebanon in 1927.[58] This committee espoused a common Kurdish cause for the region; closely monitored by the French, it claimed that its activities were restricted to 'non-political' activities, such as raising money to support the refugees. The French, worried 'that the Turks might take umbrage' at the committee's existence, always took its claim to be non-political with a pinch of salt, calling its stated aim of 'saving and protecting Kurds abroad' a 'euphemism [which] permits a Kurdish nationalist committee to be called "philanthropic"'.[59] At the same time, to the Turks they frequently argued that French surveillance was tight enough to restrict the committee's activities, an argument that rang rather hollow after it coordinated a major uprising in southeastern Turkey.[60] From 1928, when it was prohibited in Aleppo 'following strong protests from Ankara',[61] the committee was also an instrument of Kurdish–Armenian cooperation, apparently channelling funds from the internationally-active Armenian Dashnak Party to support Kurdish anti-Turkish activism: it was through monitoring this cooperation that the French were able to report, for example, that the Armenian company Matossian was employing Kurdish notables as 'money-collectors and salesmen' in the border zone, allowing them to carry out political activities also.[62] One of these Kurds, Kamran 'Ali Badr Khan, later complained to the Turkish Consul in Beirut – in a surprisingly cordial meeting – that he had lost this job because the French had forbidden him from travelling near the border. He also mentioned that the French had expelled one of his brothers from Syria, and responded favourably to 'all the demands presented by your Government concerning measures to be taken with regard to the Kurds'.[63]

Those 'measures to be taken' covered a wide range of potentially Kurdish nationalist endeavour, from military organisation to cultural affairs, throughout Syria. Partly because of Turkish complaints, and partly because of their own desire to limit any Kurdish activism that might provoke Turkish intervention (or otherwise threaten French authority), the French closely monitored Kurdish activists in Syria. They kept particularly detailed notes on members of the Khoybun and their activities, at one point collecting information sheets (*fiches de renseignements*) on thirty-eight of them from intelligence officers throughout the mandate territories – an example of how securing the border required effective state authority across the territory.[64] But Turkish complaints prompting a French response also touched on what Ankara viewed as Kurdish propaganda activities (such as those of one Hilmi Yildirim, in Beirut[65]), or cultural activities. In 1936, the High Commissioner banned the entry, sale, circulation, usage or publication in Syria 'of the Kurdish phonographic disks no. 507/11 and 508/11 put on sale by the "Société Orientale Sodwa" of Aleppo and sung in Kurdish by Said Agha Jisraoui' at the request of the Turkish Consul General.[66]

Ironically, such measures may have encouraged the integration of border-crossing Kurdish insurgents and the longer established Syrian Kurdish population. Earlier, I discussed the French policy of distancing certain groups and individuals from the Syrian–Turkish frontier. In some cases, Kurdish activists were moved not only outside the 'exclusion zone', but to Damascus or Beirut. At one time or another, most of the prominent leaders of the Kurdish movement in the Jazira – the Badr Khan brothers, Hajo Agha and so on – were in *résidence obligatoire* in one of the major cities. Among them was 'Uthman Sabri, who founded a Kurdish-language school in the (heavily Arabised) Kurdish quarter of Damascus and actively promoted 'Kurdist'[67] politics there: not, one imagines, the neutralisation that Turkey hoped for when it pushed for activists to be removed from the frontier zone.[68] Others settled in Syrian cities voluntarily. Once there, men like Sabri certainly did not refrain from politics, as we will see shortly; but as the example of his school shows, they were also active in the field of cultural production. Jaladat Bey Badr Khan developed the Latin script for writing Kurdish and published a review in the Kirmanji dialect of the language while resident in Damascus.[69] His brother Kamran 'Ali Badr Khan also published a review, and in the 1940s would broadcast in Kurdish on Radio Levant and successfully lobby the High Commission for funding to send Kurdish students to study in France.[70] Earlier, in 1924, a Kurdish writer from Iraq resident in Aleppo had requested a French subsidy towards publishing a history of the Kurds, written in Kurdish (in Arabic script).[71] These activities targeted the Kurdish population not (or not only) of the border zone, but of the cities – just as the Turkish pressure that had put these men in the cities applied to all of Syria's Kurds.

It seems reasonable to suggest that cultural activities of this kind contributed to the development of a greater sense of Kurdish identity among Damascene Kurds. Such a sense of identity should not be taken for granted as politically salient: the inhabitants of the Kurdish quarter of Damascus – *Hayy al-Akrād*, literally 'quarter of the Kurds' – were largely Arabised and well integrated into the social structure of the city.[72] The leading notable families of the quarter, the al-Yusufs and the Shamdins, were among the most prominent in the city: they owned land in the countryside around Damascus, had served the local Ottoman administration at high levels, and in the nineteenth century had like other families of their class left their quarter of origin for more comfortable accommodation in Suq Saruja.[73] (Very comfortable: the Yusuf house covered some 2,070 m². [74]) Like other such families, however, they also retained their patronage networks in their quarter of origin. In these circumstances, it may seem odd that in the 1930s we find 'Umar Agha Shamdin supporting Kurdist claims to autonomy in the far northeast of Syria[75]: the mere fact that activists from that region (or Turkey) were in obligatory residence in Damascus only goes part way to explaining it.

A further explanation lies in the local micropolitics of Damascus under French rule. The High Commission was ever keen to divide Syrians up into ethnically or religiously distinct groups, and promote chosen interlocutors as 'leaders' of those groups at the expense of actors with broader Syrian loyalties. For Syria's Christian communities, clergymen often claimed that role. Similarly, presenting himself as representative of Syria's Kurds (rather than 'just' a Damascene notable) could give a figure like 'Umar Agha privileged access to the resources of the mandatory state. This could be a distinct advantage in the inter-family notable politics of Damascus – especially after 1936, when many of the city's notables were committed to the National Bloc government, and the French were seeking ways to undermine it. (It is not surprising that the French paid particular attention to Kurdist mobilisations in Hayy al-Akrad, and the participation in them of notables like 'Umar Agha, during the Bloc's rule.)

At the same time, promoting a Kurdist variety of politics among the inhabitants of 'their' quarter would give such notables a means of renewing their traditional patronage networks under a new form, in the face of the threat from new social forces and the transformation of politics they heralded in the 1930s – a threat that the notables of the Bloc also faced, and (for the time being) successfully. We see this dynamic at work in the tension between communists in the quarter, including the leader of Syria's Communist Party, Khalid Bakdash, on the one hand, and, on the other, the quarter's notables and Kurdist activists from the northeast in forced residence in the city. Communists in Hayy al-Akrad were hostile to French imperialism and to those who treated with it; they tended to perceive Kurdist activities as serving French ends. Hence, when a club in the quarter produced propaganda in favour of Kurdish autonomy in the northeast, the French intelligence services reported that 'communist members inhabiting this quarter . . . are leading active measures to check the development of this idea, saying that the movement's promoters are in the pay of the French'.[76] But this antagonism worked both ways: when Bakdash attempted to set up a 'so-called Boxing Club [*Club sportif de Boxe*]' he ran into bitter opposition from 'Uthman Sabri, who, 'in agreement with certain notables of this quarter', sought to persuade the French authorities to prevent the Interior Ministry from authorising Bakdash's request. Sabri and Bakdash were already in conflict: Sabri's anti-communist propaganda among young

Kurds had led many to abandon the Communist Party. 'He is thus very violently attacked by Bakdash and his friends who openly accuse him of being a spy in the pay of the "French".'[77]

All this is to say that there was nothing self-evident about the choice of some residents of Hayy al-Akrad to adopt a politics based on Kurdish identity. Nonetheless, the logic of the nation-state form tended to create links between Kurds across the territory of the new state; or rather, to create the potential for shared political action on 'ethnic' grounds. As soon as the new border was drawn, it placed Damascus and other Syrian cities within a single field of political action with the northeast, while cutting that region off from centres that were closer – certainly geographically, perhaps culturally, and in the past politically – such as Mosul or Diyarbakir (not to mention the old imperial centre of Istanbul). Hence two leaders of the first great Kurdish revolt against the Turkish Republic, in exile in the Jazira in the 1920s, receiving permission to visit Damascus 'to collect the subsidies of the local Kurdish community there'.[78] Hence, too, Jaladat Bey Badr Khan travelling to Damascus in late 1931, where the intelligence services reported that he was 'canvassing [*travaille*, literally 'working'] Kurdish circles, in favour of cooperation with the fatherland'.[79]

Even activists from the Jazira whose aspirations lay in that region or over the border in Turkey were drawn to Damascus by the structures of the Syrian state. When Kurds who had left Turkey sought to be integrated in the Syrian security forces in the early 1930s, they requested the help of a Kurdish deputy to the Syrian parliament, Mustafa Shahin Bey.[80] For all Shahin Bey's own Kurdish nationalism, they thus became implicated (like him) in Syrian political structures centred on Damascus. The same dynamic, in which the Jazira had become a peripheral zone of a Syrian nation-state centred on Damascus, is visible in the case of one Yunis Agha, 'Kurdish notable of the Haute-Djézireh'. He hoped to improve his chances of becoming that province's governor by coming to the capital in September 1937 'to make contact with the notables of the Kurdish quarter' and seek their support.[81] Kurdish identity provided him with a means of bolstering his political ambitions on the periphery by creating a potential link between him and figures at the centre who had some leverage there, as influential actors in the city or (particularly) as favoured interlocutors of the French. But it was the new state form of Syria that brought him to Damascus in the first place.

Conclusion

In the summer of 1930, a group of Kurdish notables sent a petition to the High Commission requesting that the Syrian state bureaucracy in the Jazira employ more Kurds. The French, though they viewed it as a manoeuvre of the Badr Khans intended to strengthen Kurdish communal feeling, were sympathetic to this desire insofar as it permitted them to treat the Kurds as a distinct population. But their response shows how Syrian state structures determined the options open to Kurds and French alike.

The Jazira was still part of the Sanjak of Dayr al-Zur at that point, and the French Assistant Delegate there noted that seven of the nineteen signatories to the petition were refugees who had 'not yet lost Turkish nationality': to be considered for employment in the Syrian administration Kurds had to be Syrian nationals. But he did agree with the way of accommodating the petition's wishes that his superior had suggested: in the absence of candidates who were both sufficiently educated and Syrian nationals in the region itself, a Damascene Kurd should be appointed to head the still rudimentary local bureaucracy. 'And when the administration is definitively established, we might investigate if among the Kurdish population of Syrian nationality in the Haute-Djézireh there are a few individuals apt to be admitted to subaltern positions.'[82]

The example shows how the unpredictable dynamics of state construction had brought all Kurds within Syria's borders together, in a not entirely voluntary way. In the context of the new state, a shared identity could be a useful vehicle for individual actors' political ambitions, allowing them to forge links with new allies across the territory. Such an identity-based form of politics gained a boost from the presence of the French, with their preference for structuring divisions into Syrian society – which in some cases forced a politicised 'identity' onto ordinary Syrians from above. But it was made possible by the development of the modern state apparatus.

The border, as we saw, was both an outcome of that development and a spur to it. It played a crucial role in the politics of community in the new state, by working to delimit – literally – the field of political action that was open to individuals within it, even when their aspirations lay across the new border in southern Anatolia. As a cross-border group, the Kurds were particularly affected by the border, but they were not alone: Turks in northern Syria or Arabs in southern Turkey also found themselves transformed into minorities by the region's new borders, and dozens of groups in Europe were in a similar situation in this period. The existence of such cross-border groups could, and in some cases did, cause the embryonic borders of the inter-war world's new nation-states to be redrawn; but it also stimulated the development of those borders, as nervous states perceived such groups as a threat, and sought to manage them. It was not the only factor in the firming-up of frontiers, but it was important, and as the borders hardened they in turn acted to constitute such populations as minorities within each state. Those minorities did not exist as such before the borders were drawn: the border defined them as a numerical minority within the state, and the modern state's developing institutions and policies influenced their political and cultural existence as a coherent community:[83] for example, by bringing a Kurdish nationalist activist from the Jazira to open a Kurdish-language school and make political connections with notables among the Arabised inhabitants of Hayy al-Akrad.

What holds for the communities brought together as minorities within Syria, though, also holds for the community brought together as a majority. The notion of a shared Arab identity allowed urban nationalists in Damascus to counter Kurdist demands for autonomy in the northeast:

> we want them to build their independence in their homeland [*diyārihim*] 'Kurdistan', not in the Arab Jazira, the birthplace [*mawtin*] of Shammar, 'Anaza, Tayy, al-Jabbur, and other great Arab tribes. The Jazira was the cradle of Arabness [*mahd al-'uruba*] before the Islamic conquest ...
>
> That a people should work to amputate an essentially Arab part [*juz' 'arabi samim*] from their fatherland for the sake of a hundred Kurdish villages in the north of the Jazira that were and remain grazing lands for the flocks and horses of the Arabs – this is a grave matter, that all the Arab lands will shake over [*hādhā amr jalāl tahtazz lahu al-aqtār al-'arabiyya jam'ā'a*].[84]

Here, it is a nationalist who is using cultural identity to build a political alliance with actors at the periphery, and claim the territory of the Jazira for an Arab Syria.

This also shows the danger of identity-based politics in the modern nation-state. When the state is conceived of as the expression of the will of one nation, there is a risk that mobilisations on the basis of a different cultural identity will be seen by the state and 'its' nationalists as inherently threatening to the integrity of the state. It does not follow, though, that states are condemned to a zero-sum struggle between majority and minorities. The nationalisms that link states to their populations do not have to be closed and exclusive. In the context of anti-colonial struggle it is not hard to see why Syrian Arab nationalism was suspicious of other mobilisations on ethnic grounds, but hostility was not foreordained: we also saw examples of Syrian Kurds who were not attracted to Kurdist mobilisations. Khalid Bakdash is the most obvious of these: as a communist, Bakdash believed that Syrian Arab nationalism was a historical necessity, and accompanied the National Bloc delegation to Paris in 1936 as an adviser. The documents that relate his clash with 'Uthman Sabri make clear that he was not the only communist in the Kurdish quarter, and Sabri's Kurdist group competed for support among the quarter's politically active youth not only with the communists, but with the League of National Action, an Arab nationalist formation that was younger and more radical than the Bloc.[85]

That young Kurds were involved in these political movements shows that their political identity was not defined by being Kurdish; it also shows that these nationalist groups were not closed to 'Kurds' by definition. When we see actors using cultural identity as the basis for their political claims, it may be more useful to ask how the game of political competition – played out on the terrain of the modern nation-state – encouraged them to make cultural identity the vehicle of their ambitions, rather than assuming that cultural identity automatically inspired and defined those ambitions.[86] After all, in this same period, Kurdish leaders in the highlands of the Kurd Dagh near the western end of the Syrian–Turkish frontier were claiming a Turkish identity, and requesting their region's incorporation into Turkey.[87] The development of the modern nation-state made majority and minority into meaningful categories in Syria, as elsewhere, but it did not determine how those categories would be defined.

Notes

1. Many of the places referred to in this chapter are marked on Map 2. I would like to acknowledge at the outset my debt to Seda Altuğ for several long discussions that directly influenced (and benefited) my thinking in this chapter.
2. All details on this incident are from MWT *wathā'iq al-dawla*, sijill 2; *wizārat al-khārijiyya*. 23 – particularly the interior minister's letter to the foreign minister (27/2/1939) and the handwritten letter from qa'immaqam of Qamishli to minister of interior (21/2/1939) that informs it.
3. Also unclear is whether the flags were defaced on Syrian or Turkish territory: it happened in front of a cafe near the municipal building, but the documents do not say which town.
4. To refer only to standard works, see Cleveland, *A History of the Modern Middle East*, pp. 163–73; J. L. Gelvin, *The Modern Middle East. A History* (Oxford: Oxford University Press, 2005), ch. 11 (p. 183 for 'Winston's hiccup'); Yapp, *The Making of the Modern Near East*, ch. 6, and *The Near East since the First World War. A History to 1995* (London: Longman, 1996), pp. 35–46; David Fromkin, *A Peace to End all Peace. The Fall of the Ottoman Empire and the Creation of the Modern Middle East*, paperback edn (London: Phoenix Press, 2000), pp. 513–14 and ch. 61; Avi Shlaim, *War and Peace in the Middle East. A Concise History*, rev. and updated paperback edn (London: Penguin, 1995), ch. 1.
5. There are exceptions, such as Inga Brandell (ed.), *State Frontiers: Borders and Boundaries in the Middle East* (London: I. B. Tauris, 2006). Like much of the best work on borders, however, this is anthropological rather than historical.
6. Khoury, *Syria and the French Mandate*, pp. 104, 122, 135, 185. This was also evident to commentators at the time: see references to *Alif Bā'* (1 September 1932) in Chapter 3.
7. Jean Perez, 'Les compagnies méharistes au Levant (1921–1941)', *Revue historique des armées*, No. 233, pp. 79–96.
8. Eliezer Tauber, 'The struggle for Dayr al-Zur: the determination of borders between Syria and Iraq', *International Journal of Middle East Studies* (1991), 23(3): 361–85.

9. See Chapter 3 for a discussion of the *dār al-hukūma* and other sites of state authority.
10. The information on the Syrian–Turkish border comes from Seda Altuğ; the information on the Syrian–Iraqi border is familiar to anyone who has followed the news since the invasion.
11. Khoury, *Syria and the French Mandate*, pp. 99–110.
12. Khoury, *Syria and the French Mandate*, p. 102; Mizrahi, *Genèse de l'État mandataire*, p. 172.
13. SHAT 4 H Box 168, dossier 1: *Opérations des troupes du territoire de l'Euphrate dans la Haute-Djézireh (occupation du Bec de Canard) 1927–1930*, subdossier *Organisation des Postes du Bec de Canard et occupation de [ces postes]. Note sur l'action politique menée dans la Région Nord de Djézireh* . . . (1/12/1926).
14. SHAT 4 H Box 168, dossier 1, *Opérations des troupes du territoire de l'Euphrate dans la Haute-Djézireh (occupation du Bec de Canard) 1927–1930*. Printed map, *Abornement de la frontière Turco-Syrienne entre Nissibin et le Tigre d'après le protocole d'Angora du 22 juin 1929*. This infringement could still provoke the indignation of a certain kind of French military historian in the twenty-first century: see Perez, 'Les compagnies méharistes'.
15. Quoted Pierre Fournié and Jean-Louis Riccioli, *La France et le Proche-Orient 1916–1946. Une chronique photographique de la présence française en Syrie et au Liban, en Palestine, au Hedjaz et en Cilicie* (Tournai: Casterman, 1996), p. 153.
16. Details, including Hajo Agha's subsequent interrogation in Damascus, are in AD-SL Box 572, dossier *Passage de Hadjo Agha et des fils de Djemil Pacha en Turquie 1930*. NB: for this and other Kurdish names I have used a rough but consistent transliteration rather than adopt any one of the multiple variants in French sources.
17. All details and quotes from MWT *wathā'iq al-dawla*, sijill 2; *wizārat al-dākhiliyya – al-amn al-cām – taqārīr*. 1: report from Khayrī Ridā, qa'immaqam of Kurd Dagh, to wali of Aleppo (25/4/1934).
18. MWT *wathā'iq al-dawla*, sijill 2; *wizārat al-khārijiyya*. 21: documents dated 27/12/1938–15/1/1939. By this time, incidentally, the name of the caza had been Arabised from the Turkish *Kurd Dāgh* to the Arabic *Jabal al-Akrād*.
19. A brief and relevant overview of Turkish history in this period can be found in Erik J. Zürcher, *Turkey: A Modern History*, 3rd edn (London: I. B. Tauris, 2004), chs 10–11.
20. Seda Altuğ and Benjamin Thomas White, 'Frontières et pouvoir d'État. La frontière turco-syrienne dans les années 1920 et 1930', *Vingtième siècle. Revue d'histoire* (2009), No. 103, pp. 91–104, expands on the following, with more detail on the Turkish side.
21. Tachjian, *La France en Cilicie*, chs 5–8, examines this question from the vantage point of the communities regarded as inassimilable by the republican government.
22. A more detailed account of Turkish policy towards the Kurds in this period can

be found in McDowall, *A Modern History of the Kurds*, ch. 9. Henri J. Barkey and Graham E. Fuller, *Turkey's Kurdish Question* (Lanham, MD: Rowman & Littlefield, 1998), ch. 1, surveys this period as background to the contemporary relationship between the Turkish Republic and its Kurds. An overview of Kurdish relations to the modern state more broadly is Martin van Bruinessen, 'Kurdish society and the modern state: ethnic nationalism versus nation-building', in his *Kurdish Ethno-nationalism versus Nation-building States. Collected Articles* (Istanbul: Isis Press, 2000), pp. 43–65.

23. Robert W. Olson and William F. Tucker, 'The Sheikh Sait rebellion in Turkey (1925)', *Die Welt des Islams* (1978), new series 18(3/4): 195–211; Kemal Kirişçi, 'Migration and Turkey: the dynamics of state, society and politics', in Reşat Kasaba (ed.), *The Cambridge History of Turkey, vol. 4: Turkey in the Modern World* (Cambridge: Cambridge University Press, 2008), ch. 7, p. 180.

24. For a recent discussion of Turkish policy towards the Kurdish regions in this period, see Soner Cagaptay, *Islam, Secularism, and Nationalism in Modern Turkey. Who is a Turk?* (London: Routledge, 2006), ch. 6.

25. An account of this revolt, in historical perspective, is given in Robert W. Olson, 'The Kurdish rebellions of Sheikh Said (1925), Mt. Ararat (1930), and Dersim (1937–8): their impact on the development of the Turkish air force and on Kurdish and Turkish nationalism', *Die Welt des Islams* (2000), new series, 40(1): 67–94.

26. AD-SL Box 1054, dossier *Kurdes 1925*, subdossier *Transports des troupes pour la révolte Kurde 1925. Note pour Monsieur l'Officier de Liaison Britannique* (3/3/1925).

27. AD-SL Box 1054, same dossier and subdossier, *Message téléphone*, Délégué Adjoint (Aleppo) to HC, 19/3/1925 gives figures for mid-March – well over 1,000 troops, plus supplies, carried by several trains on 17th, for example. Such heavy use of the line actually strained the economy of the whole Aleppo region: same location, telegram from SR to Mougin, French ambassador to Turkey (27/3/1925). Some figures for June are in AD-SL Box 1054, same dossier, subdossier *Passage des Troupes à Muslimié*.

28. Cagaptay, *Islam, Secularism, and Nationalism*, p. 106, lists numerous minor and major insurgencies in different parts of Turkish Kurdistan in these years.

29. See, e.g., AD-SL Box 1054, dossiers *Kurdes 1925*, *Kurdes 1926* and *Kurdes 1927*, though more material (up to the early 1930s) is scattered throughout boxes 1054 and 1055. The Service des Renseignements reported in February 1928 on Turkish military preparations intended to pre-empt a spring recurrence of the Kurdish insurgency: AD-SL Box 1055, dossier *Question Kurde – Mouvement Kurde en Syrie – Année 1928. Bulletin de renseignements N° 10* (4/2/1928).

30. Cagaptay, *Islam, Secularism, and Nationalism*, p. 111.

31. Some doubt that an actual rebellion had even occurred prior, rather than subsequent, to Turkish repression: Martin van Bruinessen, 'Genocide in Kurdistan? The suppression of the Dersim rebellion in Turkey (1937–38) and the chemical war against the Iraqi Kurds (1988)', in George J. Andreopoulos (ed.), *Conceptual and*

Historical Dimensions of Genocide (Philadelphia, PA: University of Pennsylvania Press, 1994), pp. 141–70, and especially Nicole Watts, 'Relocating Dersim: Turkish state-building and Kurdish resistance, 1931–1938', *New Perspectives on Turkey* (2000), 23: 5–30.

32. AD-SL Box 1054, dossier *Kurdes 1925*, subdossier *Pièces au sujet du passage en Syrie de populations Kurdes ou chrétiennes ou de déserteurs turcs*. Délégué Adjoint, Aleppo, to HC (1/3/1925).

33. AD-SL Box 1055, dossier *Question Kurde – Mouvement Kurde en Syrie. Années 1926 et 1927*. Ponsot to MAE (this copy intended for French ambassador to Turkey; 29/9/1927).

34. Information in this paragraph from AD-SL Box 1054, dossier *Kurdes 1925*, subdossier *Installation provisoire d'un Officier du S.R. à Arab Pounar. Note de Service* (22/3/1925).

35. Before assuming that this material weakness of the state was restricted to colonial backwaters like Jarablus, consider Eugen Weber's comment on metropolitan France in the 1930s: 'Machines in general were not much in demand. *Inspecteurs des finances* on tour through the provinces remember few or none in banks, post offices, tax bureaus; no typewriters, and no typewritten reports, no calculators': *The Hollow Years*, p. 63.

36. It was the source for several *Informations* produced by the Direction de la Sûreté générale – successor to the SR – included in Box 572, untitled dossier (material released under sixty-year rule), subdossier *Les Kurdes en Syrie – Informations*.

37. On the first two items in this list, see AD-SL Box 1055, dossier *Mouvement Kurde (1928)*, subdossier *Question Kurde – Immigrants – Réfugiés Kurdes*. Principal inspector of customs. Syria and Alaouites, to Ripert, assistant delegate for Sanjak of Dayr al-Zur (dated '24 X^{bre} 1927' but referred to in other correspondence as dated 24/12/1927).

38. This and following quotes from AD-SL Box 572, dossier *Passage en Syrie de populations Kurdes ou chrétiennes ou de déserteurs Turcs. Note N° 868/K.3*, signed Sarrail (5/3/1925). This document also gives instructions regarding potential Assyro-Chaldean immigrants from Iraq, and deserters from the Turkish army. The arrival of the former was considered imminent (a harbinger of events in the 1930s); they too were to be kept away from the *Turkish* border. The latter remind us that the imposition of Turkish state authority on the Kurds also involved asserting it, through conscription, over other citizens – some of whom were evidently unenthusiastic.

39. There are literally dozens, if not hundreds, of such documents in the French records on the Kurds for these years. One, sent by the assistant delegate for the Sanjak of Dayr al-Zur to refute Turkish claims about the activities of Kurds who had settled there, refers to the 1925 note as 'still in force' in 1927. AD-SL Box 1055, dossier *Question Kurde – Mouvement Kurde en Syrie. Années 1926 et 1927*. Ripert to HC, 9/12/1927.

40. Mizrahi, *Genèse de l'État mandataire*, p. 178. Mizrahi discusses these agreements

in some detail (pp. 172–8), and describes (p. 178) the 'difficult extension towards the east of the logics of state'.

41. He spent a year or so in forced residence in Damascus before being permitted to settle in Hasaka in June 1931. Details are in AD-SL Box 572, dossier *Passage de Hadjo Agha et des fils Djemil Pacha en Turquie 1930*.

42. AD-SL Box 620, dossier *Mouvement minoritaire Chrétien*, subdossier *La question des minorités en Syrie et en Irak (Généralités – correspondances, informations)*. Minutes of League Council meeting (entitled *Protection des minorités. Etablissement des Assyriens de l'Irak*), n.d. but internal evidence makes clear the meeting took place on 17/4/1935.

43. AD-SL Box 1054, dossier *Kurdes 1925*, subdossier *III l 01*. Sarraut to MAE (3/6/1925). The ambassador in question, Albert Sarraut, played an important role in French colonial history: see Martin C. Thomas, 'Albert Sarraut, French colonial development, and the communist threat, 1919–1930', *The Journal of Modern History* (2005), 77(4): 917–55.

44. AD-SL Box 1055, dossier *Mouvement Kurde (1928)*, subdossier *Réclamations turques a/s des chefs Kurdes de Hte Djézireh – Hadjo, Emin Agha, Edem Tcherkesse, Mudir d'Amouda, Fils d'Ibrahim Pacha*. Extracts from Essiasa (that is, *al-Siyāsa*), forwarded to Beirut by French Consul in Mesopotamia in letter (27/6/1925).

45. AD-SL Box 1055, dossier *Question Kurde – Mouvement Kurde en Syrie. Années 1926 et 1927*. HC (though signed Maugras) to HC's acting delegate in Damascus (13/12/1927). Other documents refer to 'Abd al-Rahim as Sa'id's son.

46. AD-SL Box 1055, same dossier. HC to MAE (14/12/1927).

47. AD-SL Box 1055, dossier *Question Kurde – Mouvement Kurde en Syrie. Années 1926 et 1927*. Ripert to HC (9/12/1927).

48. This and following quotes from AD-SL Box 1055, dossier *Mouvement Kurde (1928)*, subdossier *Mouvement kurde*. Report: *Situation des réfugiés en Haute-Djezireh. Octobre 1927* (actually dated 6/1/1928). Poidebard's name is misspelled 'Poidebar' on the front page. More information from this very well-informed source can be found in SHAT Box 4 H 168, unenclosed subdossier *Notes sur la Haute Djezireh par le P[ère] Poidebard 1924–1930 – Haute Djezireh, note du SR 1924*.

49. AD-SL Box 572, untitled dossier (material released under sixty-year rule), subdossier *Les Kurdes en Syrie – Informations. Information N° 4196* (14/9/1932). NB: the 'would be' translates an untranslatable French use of the conditional to report alleged or unconfirmed facts.

50. AD-SL Box 572, dossier *Immigration éventuelle de Kurdes en Syrie – exonération[s] taxe douanière pour les [troupeaux]*. HC's delegate to Syria to delegate-general (relations extérieures) (25/8/1932).

51. AD-SL Box 1054, dossier *Kurdes 1925*, subdossier *III l 01*. Billotte to acting HC (26/5/1924).

52. One such was Jalal Qadri [Celal Kadri], who usually figures in French sources

as Djélal Kadri. AD-SL Box 1055, dossier *Mouvement Kurde (1928)*, subdossier *Réclamations turques a/s des chefs Kurdes de Hte Djézireh – Hadjo, Emin Agha, Edem Tcherkesse, Mudir d'Amouda, Fils d'Ibrahim Pacha*. Telegram, HC to 'Ambafrance Constantinople' (13/8/1925), and *Message Téléphone*, Délégué Adjoint for Vilayet of Aleppo to HC (11/8/1925). Later, as alleged Turkish agent: AD-SL Box 1055, dossier *Question Kurde – Mouvement Kurde en Syrie. Années 1926 et 1927.* Extract from *Bulletin de renseignements d'Alep N° 274* (27/12/1927).

53. AD-SL Box 1054, dossier *Kurdes 1919–1922 – 1923*, untitled subdossier. *NOTE au sujet des propositions de R. Bey concernant le Kurdistan* (3/1/1923).
54. AD-SL Box 1055, dossier *Mouvement Kurde (1928)*, subdossier *Incidents de Derbissié – mai 26. Compte-rendu sommaire de l'entrevue franco-turque, du 7 Mai 1926 à Derbessié*. (Different spellings of the same place name are entirely normal.) This document also outlines the conflicting accounts of what had actually happened. The Turks claimed it began when rebel Kurds had crossed the border to attack Turkish soldiers guarding a train; French enquiries suggested that the attack was provoked by Turkish soldiers trying to steal sheep from Kurds south of the border.
55. AD-SL Box 1054, dossier *Kurdes 1925*, subdossier *Pièces au sujet du passage en Syrie de populations Kurdes ou chrétiennes ou de déserteurs turcs*. Letter to Commander-in-Chief of Armée du Levant [that is, HC], 18/3/1925. For a later expression of Turkish worry on this subject, see AD-SL Box 1055, dossier *Mouvement Kurde (1928)*, subdossier *Question Kurde – Immigrants – Réfugiés Kurdes*. Note, MAE to Turkish Embassy (13/4/1927).
56. AD-SL Box 1055, dossier *Mouvement Kurde (1928)*, subdossier *Incidents de Derbissié – mai 26*. Letter from MAE, unaddressed but presumably to HC, regarding *Note de l'Ambassade de Turquie* (12/5/1926).
57. Cagaptay, *Islam, Secularism, and Nationalism*, p. 112.
58. McDowall, *A Modern History of the Kurds*, p. 203. A French *Sûreté générale* document outlining the origins of the Khoybun and its relations with the Dashnak is in AD-SL Box 572, dossier *Demande d'installation de chefs Kurdes en Syrie*, subdossier *Installation de Tribus Kurdes en Hte. Djézireh. Note sur le mouvement Kurde* (4/1/1931).
59. AD-SL Box 1054, dossier *Kurdes 1927*, subdossier *III / 01. Note pour le Lieutenant Colonel Arnaud* (19/11/1927).
60. McDowall, *A Modern History of the Kurds*, pp. 202–7; Michael M. Gunter, *Historical Dictionary of the Kurds* (Oxford: Scarecrow Press, 2004), 'Khoybun'.
61. McDowall, *A Modern History of the Kurds*, p. 203.
62. AD-SL Box 572, dossier *Demande d'installation de chefs Kurdes en Syrie*, subdossier *Installation de Tribus Kurdes en Hte. Djézireh. Note sur le mouvement Kurde* (4/1/1931).
63. AD-SL Box 1055, dossier *Kurdes – 1932*, subdossier *Entrevue du chef kurde Kameran Beder Khan avec le Consul de Turquie à Beyrouth. Information N°*

77 (8/12/1932) – the long account here is evidently based on Badr Khan's own description of the meeting.
64. AD-SL Box 571, dossier *[Relations extérieures] en Syrie*, subdossier *Fiches sur les membres du Comité Kurde* – [+ illegible].
65. AD-SL Box 572, dossier *Requête du Consul général de Turquie a/s des brochures de propagande prokurde publiées par le nommé Hilmi Yildirim*. Turkish Consul General in Beirut to Meyrier (Délégué Général), 24/9/1936. An unattributed French intelligence document headed *Hilmi Yeldurum* (27/10/1936) suggested that he was, rather, a Turkish agent.
66. AD-SL Box 571, dossier *Requête du Consul Général de Turquie a/s disques de propagande prokurde mis en circulation à Alep. Décision du Haut-Commissaire N° 343*. The Consul-General's request is also included in this dossier (in fact, just a slender paper folder).
67. I am using this term to denote political mobilisations around the sense of Kurdish cultural identity, without accepting the nationalist claim that all such mobilisations are Kurdish nationalist. Future instances will be without inverted commas.
68. AD-SL Box 572, untitled dossier (material released under sixty-year rule), subdossier *Les Kurdes en Syrie – Informations. Information N° 404/S* (23/6/1939).
69. McDowall, *A Modern History of the Kurds*, p. 468.
70. AD-SL (Series B) Box 33, dossier 1053: *Docteur Kameran Bey BEDER KHAN. Note: Docteur Kamouran Béder KHAN* (27/4/1944). It seems likely that the review in question was the same as that published by Jaladat Bey. However, this source gives its place of publication as Beirut, while McDowall gives Damascus for Jaladat Bey's.
71. AD-SL Box 1054, dossier *Kurdes 1924. Compte-Rendu*, Aleppo SR (24/9/1924).
72. McDowall estimates that some 40 per cent of its inhabitants were 'entirely Arabicized' by 1920: *A Modern History of the Kurds*, p. 467. Tejel Gorgas ('Le mouvement kurde', p. 112), citing but not referencing a British diplomatic source, states that the quarter was divided into three sections, one largely kurdophone, one largely arabophone and one where neither language predominated. See also Benjamin Thomas White, 'The Kurds of Damascus in the 1930s: development of a politics of ethnicity', *Middle Eastern Studies* (2010), 46(6): 901–17.
73. Philip S. Khoury, *Urban Notables and Arab Nationalism: The Politics of Damascus 1860–1920* (Cambridge: Cambridge University Press, 1983), gives details of the rise to prominence of these two families through Ottoman political structures and local landowning in the nineteenth century, and of relations between them. They dominated the prestigious office of commander of the pilgrimage to Mecca in late Ottoman times: Nelida Fuccaro, 'Ethnicity and the city: the Kurdish quarter of Damascus between Ottoman and French rule, c. 1724–1946', *Urban History* (2003), 30(2): 206–24.
74. 'Abd al-Razzaq Moaz, 'The urban fabric of an extramural quarter in 19th-century Damascus', in Philipp and Schaebler (eds), *The Syrian Land*, pp. 165–83, reference at 169.

The Border and the Kurds [127]

75. AD-SL Box 572, untitled dossier (material released under sixty-year rule), subdossier *Les Kurdes en Syrie – Informations. Information N° 5411* (3/7/1939).
76. AD-SL Box 572, same dossier and subdossier. *Informations N° 110/S* (6/3/1939), 5185 (21/6/1939), 6062 (5/8/1939).
77. This and preceding quotations from AD-SL Box 572, same folder and subdossier, *Damascus Sûreté Information N° 404/S* (23/6/1939). NB: the quotation marks around the word «French» are pencilled-in on this document.
78. AD-SL Box 1055, dossier *Mouvement Kurde (1928)*, subdossier *Question Kurde – Immigrants – Réfugiés Kurdes*. High Commissioner's delegate to State of Syria to HC (27/3/1928). The subsidies were to support destitute refugees (though the Turks suspected, probably not without reason, that they were used to fund military activities too).
79. AD-SL Box 572, dossier *Menées Arméno-Kurdes. Information N° 4401* (24/11/1931). The phrase in French is actually '*la mère patrie*', the 'mother fatherland' (*patrie* being feminine). That Kurdistan was the 'fatherland' of the residents of Hayy al-Akrad in this romantic nationalist sense is itself a nationalist assumption.
80. AD-SL Box 572, same dossier and subdossier. *Information N° 2273* (11/5/1932).
81. This and preceding quotes from AD-SL Box 572, untitled dossier (material released under sixty-year rule), subdossier *Les Kurdes en Syrie – Informations. Information N° 4532* (2/9/1937). In this document his name appears as Younès.
82. This and preceding quote from AD-SL Box 572, dossier *Passage en Syrie de populations Kurdes ou chrétiennes ou de déserteurs Turcs*. Assistant Delegate (*délégué adjoint*) for Sanjak of Dayr al-Zur to Delegate for State of Syria (5/8/1930).
83. This also explains why the border worked to constitute as minorities populations which, unlike the Kurds, did not spread across more than one state.
84. In Arabic, '*al-haraka al-kurdiyya fi Sūriyya. lāji'ū al-kurd yas'ūn li-ta'sīs watan kurdī*'. *Al-Ayyām*, 11/7/1932. This article does not refer to Damascene Kurds, however, and nor do others I found regarding the 'Kurdish question'.
85. On the League see Khoury, *Syria and the French Mandate*, especially pp. 400–34 for its origins and composition.
86. We should also remember that the archives we study were not constructed by neutral observers: French imperial policy in Syria is reflected in the construction of the archive itself, which in its very classifications emphasises the political salience of 'Kurdishness' in Syria. See White, 'The Kurds of Damascus'.
87. E.g., during the Alexandretta crisis (see documents in AD-SL Box 571, dossier *La question des Kurdes en Syrie. Correspondance. Les Comités Kurds*).

PART III

CHAPTER

5

THE FRANCO-SYRIAN TREATY AND THE DEFINITION OF 'MINORITIES'

Introduction

Ignace Nouri thought that the meaning of 'minority' was self-evident when he wrote to the High Commissioner in 1936 about treaty guarantees for 'the minorities, that is to say the Christians and Jews'.[1] A few years earlier, the Aleppo deputy Latif Ghanimé – like Nouri, a Syrian-Catholic – took a different view. He told the French intelligence services that the Syrian parliament would be more likely to ratify a treaty containing minority guarantees if they applied to ethnic minorities as well as religious ones: this would make it possible to 'range among the minoritarians the Kurdish deputies of the North and the Djézireh, the Tcherkess deputy of Kuneitra, even Soubhi Bey Barakat and the deputies of the Sanjak of Alexandretta as representatives of the "Turks"'.[2] His own patriarchate apparently disagreed. Ethnolinguistic minorities, meanwhile, were not only defined from the outside: 'the Tcherkess of Syria', said a petition signed by Circassians from several parts of the country, 'have always claimed their national minority rights as a community having its own race, language and traditions different from those of the Syrian majority'.[3]

So who was a minority? The answer was evidently open to dispute. But there is another question, just as important but perhaps less obvious: why, around 1930, did all of these people start calling themselves – or others – 'minorities'? At the outset of the mandate, few people thought that Syria had 'minorities'; by the 1930s, as French observers seriously entertained the possibility of Syrian independence (of a sort), they were commonly using the term – and Syrians were too. This chapter explores the reasons why the term came into use in Syria when it did, and what different actors sought to gain by using it. The question of minorities was part of a wider contest over the institutional relationship between the population and the state, which was being redefined by Syria's transformation from province of a non-national empire to nation-state.

The Legal Status of Minorities as a Measure of States' Independence in the post-First World War World

After the establishment of the League of Nations, the nation-state became the only internationally legitimate form for independent states. The League itself was the guarantor of this legitimacy: at international level, only the League – as the representative of the international community – could recognise a state as independent. But this recognition was granted in different degrees: the independence of states was measured by their relationship to the League. If this was the gauge of a state's independence, the legal protection accorded to 'minorities' might be seen as the needle.

During the inter-war period different states accorded different measures of legal protection to defined minorities, in a system regulated by the newly established League of Nations. The most independent and least independent states, imperial powers and their colonies, had no minorities as such: that is, no legally-recognised minority communities whose rights they were obliged to protect or on whose behalf the League was competent to intervene. The 'old' nation-states without imperial possessions also had no minorities in this sense. The independence of countries such as Sweden or Argentina was not dependent on the League for its recognition, and their membership of the League was not dependent on their offering guaranteed protection to minorities.

This was not the case for the wholly new nation-states of post-First World War Europe, or the nation-states (such as the Balkan states) which had been established before the war but, during it, had expanded their boundaries and acquired substantial 'non-national' populations. Without using the term 'minority', since the nineteenth century, and especially since the Congress of Berlin in 1878, the international treaties by which the Great Powers recognised new states – notably the Balkan states that seceded from the Ottoman Empire – had included guarantees of the rights of subordinate religious groups. The Supreme Allied Council meeting in Paris in 1919 did adopt the term, sought to include in that category not just religious but also 'racial' and linguistic groups, and attempted to regularise the protection of minorities in such states. A Minority Committee set up this wider definition of the term and a system of supervision, based on minorities treaties with standard articles, to be overseen by the League of Nations and the International Court of Justice – with a policing role for the victorious Allied powers. The new and newly-expanded nation-states were obliged to sign up to these treaties to obtain the recognition of the League, and therefore of the international community. Since these obligations limited the authority and formal independence of the state, the new states (and their new majorities) accepted them grudgingly. They also saw the treaties as an encouragement to separatist or irredentist groups, and as an invitation to other states – either the imperial powers, or neighbouring states with links to one of the minorities so defined – to interfere in their internal affairs.[4]

Next came the states under mandate, like Syria, whose independence the League had provisionally recognised, but which were obliged to accept mandatory tutelage. Like the 'ordinary' protectorates and colonies, they had no minorities treaties and no legally-constituted minorities: the protection of various religious and other groups which enabled France to justify its presence in Syria was not expressed in these terms. The mandate charter obliged the mandatory to favour local autonomies (Article 1); to guarantee the personal status and religious interests of diverse populations (Article 6); to prevent unequal treatment of the inhabitants on the grounds of race, religion or language, and to protect the right of each community to keep its own schools (Article. 8) – though the latter article does not define 'community'; and mentions only the right to instruction in each community's own language, not religion. These and other articles provided legal justifications for France to impose or encourage divisions within Syrian society; but none of them refer to 'minorities'.[5] This highlights the fact that at the outset of the mandate, French actors did not necessarily think of Syrian society in terms of a majority and minorities. The charter had been composed by a partly French commission, with French interests in mind. Yet this commission saw no minorities in Syria, even as minorities treaties were becoming an established part of League-related international law.

Thus, mandates, like colonies, had no legally-constituted minorities.[6] They did, however, have recognition from the League (and therefore its members, mandatory powers included) that they would sooner or later accede to the status of independent nation-states: through a treaty of independence to be signed with the mandatory, in the first instance, then recognised by the League. When negotiations for such a treaty took place, in the 1930s, Syrian nationalists hoped to raise Syria to the rank of the new states that had avoided the indignity of the mandate. But achieving formal independence and membership of the League of Nations would also place Syria under the developing body of international law that had arisen to regulate the accession to membership of new states – which included the minorities treaties. This opened the possibility to France of granting Syria 'independence' while reserving the right to intervene on behalf of the newly specified minorities. For certain political actors belonging to these communities, meanwhile, it offered the possibility of appealing to a higher authority than the Syrian government, be it the League, France, or another power. Both possibilities were unwelcome to nationalists, who opposed any external limit on the authority of the state within its own borders.

This was the international context – of minorities treaties and the League of Nations – in which the negotiations for a Franco-Syrian treaty occurred, and a treaty was (eventually) signed then revised, though never fully ratified. I have discussed that context here to avoid an error easily made in studies in imperial history, especially those focusing on a single colony or a single empire: the assumption that the only international relationship that mattered for the colonial state and its inhabitants was that with metropole.

Previous accounts of the Franco-Syrian treaty negotiations, the treaty itself and its gradual failure, have rightly highlighted the controversial role of minorities clauses. But they have tended to consider the treaty largely as a bilateral affair, with France on one side and Syria on the other.[7] Taken at face value, the title of the treaty suggests this reading. But the treaty was more than simply bilateral. It was meant to take effect at the end of a transition period marked by Syria's admission to the League,[8] and therefore of the international community of nation-states; it built on established precedents for recognising states' independence, including treaties signed directly between the 'new' nation-states and the League, as well as between mandate states and mandatory powers.

Existing accounts have noted some of this: they recognise the relevance of the Iraqi precedent, for example, or mention (however passingly) the link between the treaty and Syria's admission to the League.[9] But minorities clauses only acquired such importance in the treaty negotiations because of this wider context provided by the League of Nations, the global order it represented, and the international public discourse that developed around them – not because Syrian society was already divided into a majority demanding independence and numerous minorities that needed protecting (or not). It was the debate about the treaty that gave meaning to the terms 'minority' and 'majority' in Syria, as actors on all sides referred to the wider context and invoked its precedents and principles to argue their case. There was nothing self-evident about the adoption of this language. Through the debate over the terms of Syria's accession to independence, certain groups in Syrian society came to be constituted, by themselves or others, as minorities and a majority – a reconstitution that was of more than merely terminological significance.

From Mandate to Independence: *L'Asie française* Discovers 'Minorities' in Syria

French officials had been aware from the beginning of the mandate that Syrians would judge them partly according to how Britain governed neighbouring countries. In 1921 High Commissioner Gouraud wrote to Aristide Briand that 'if the countries of the neighbouring English [sic] zones have native governments, subject to a single and relative control by the Mandatory Power, the more evolved Syrian elements will demand an analogous regime at the least'.[10] As Gouraud predicted, the British mandates became a reference point for Syrians protesting against the divisions France had imposed on the territories under its control. Britain granted a nominal independence to Transjordan in 1928 and terminated its mandate for Iraq in 1930; under the provisions of the 1930 Anglo-Iraqi treaty, Iraq joined the League in 1932, putting pressure on France to follow a similar policy in Syria. Against this pressure for a treaty, minorities became one of the principal means by which the French planned to maintain their influence in the country.

This was not because minorities simply existed in Syria, although the conditions for their emergence were much more developed by the early 1930s then they had been a decade earlier. Rather, it was because the category had become important within the developing body of international public law that informed the debate about a Franco-Syrian treaty, and later the treaty itself. This international legal context influenced French thinking about a treaty, and encouraged French officers and officials to apply the term to certain groups within Syrian society, where previously they would have used other concepts. The shift is visible in the coverage given to Syria by *L'Asie française*, the bulletin of the Comité de l'Asie française – one of four related committees set up between 1890 and 1910 to lobby for French colonial expansion.[11] Closely connected with the most influential figures in the large, cross-party colonial lobby in parliament, these committees were the heart of the *parti colonial* in France. They drew in diplomats, colonial officials and military officers serving in the colonies, and received support from a much larger interested public in the metropole; but their officers, financing and policies came largely from French business circles with interests in the colonies.

The Comité de l'Asie française had originally been founded to press for French expansion in southeast Asia, but moved towards a preference for establishing French 'spheres of influence' and indirect rule in the continent, including the Ottoman Empire and Persia[12] – a policy well suited for adaptation to the strictures of the mandatory role. The committee's bulletin was edited until 1919 by Robert de Caix, and thereafter by Henri Froidevaux, a specialist in colonial geography and history and indefatigable publicist for French colonialism.[13] It was read, and frequently written, by colonial officials; in addition, it often reported on the activities of colonial officials and concerned politicians in France, sometimes quoting them at length. The bulletin can therefore be taken as broadly representative of currents of opinion within French colonialist circles more widely; it also offers the historian a continuity of coverage across the whole period that can be hard to assemble from archival data or from one-off publications such as books. Within the limits of the bulletin's editorial policy, it thus gives an insight into the colonial debate as it developed over time. The direct links between the *L'Asie française* and the French mandate are, in any case, many. Robert de Caix, who in 1919 went from being its editor to being Secretary-General of the High Commission in Beirut, and from there became France's (and Syria's) representative to the League's Permanent Mandates Commission, is only the most noteworthy.[14]

L'Asie française's interest in the Levant pre-dated the mandate. During the First World War, the bulletin published many articles on the region and France's interests (even 'rights') there.[15] It paid special attention to the wartime Ottoman government's mistreatment of its own population, particularly Christians. The term 'minority' was not applied to Ottoman Armenians, Greeks and others, however: rather than persecuting 'minorities', the Young Turk government was perceived to 'have decided to settle the questions posed by the existence in the Ottoman Empire of allogenous populations by the suppression, pure and simple, of the latter';[16] or, again, to be planning 'the destruction of the Christian nationalities which, in the minds of the Young Turks and their German advisers were to be suppressed as posing an obstacle to the turkification of the Ottoman Empire'.[17] On the one hand, this makes sense: even at this late stage the empire was not a nation-state and had no 'majority'; 'minority' in the modern meaning was only just coming into use in any context. On the other hand, while we may question whether the Ottoman Christian communities constituted 'nationalities', they certainly were not 'allogenous', or non-native, to the empire.[18]

At the end of the war, the notion of legally protecting (national) minorities in the states created or expanded by the peace settlement, and making international recognition of those states dependent on that protection, became widespread. As it appears in *L'Asie française*, this development is clearly linked to the establishment of the League of Nations – even before the League itself was founded: the Ottoman regime could not be preserved in Anatolia, wrote the bulletin in its first issue after the armistice, because

> it has shown itself to be incompatible with the improvement of the lot of the Turkish peasants themselves, and would be even more so with the loyal play [*jeu loyal*] of the guarantees that the group of Allies, embryo of the future League of Nations, wishes to ensure for the national minorities, Hellenic and others.[19]

This is the first mention of 'minorities' I encountered in my survey of articles about the Ottoman and post-Ottoman Levant in *L'Asie française*, and it refers not to the former Arab provinces but to the contest of nationalisms in Anatolia. It is worth repeating here that the post-war minorities treaties that created the legal category from which the wider (and more indiscriminate) modern usage of the term derives generally restricted themselves to national minorities, most often understood as groups identified with one nation-state but resident in another. In the Anatolian case this applied to the Greeks, identified as a national minority here, because there was an independent Greek state – which, as it happened, was one of the Allies.[20] But Syria was different: 'There, in the Arabic-speaking countries, it is not nationalities but religious groups that a traditional opposition divides in almost as serious a way.'[21] More pertinently, there was no internationally-recognised independent Arab nation-state; the point of this article was to press France's claim for 'our fair share of the mandates that will be conferred on Western tutors'.[22] The bulletin did justify the French claim to Syria by reference to the League, but at this point protecting minorities was not presented as part of the task of the mandate in Syria, though it was recognised as an important function of the League elsewhere. There was no nation in Syria, said the bulletin: the country

> has neither the civic education nor above all the unity required to constitute, in the aftermath of Turkish oppression, a nation governing itself in full independence; there, as elsewhere in the Orient, before calling peoples to exercise the right to self-determination, they must be *constituted*.[23]

Unsurprisingly, therefore, there were no national minorities either.

In the early years of the mandate, the bulletin's articles about Syria continued in this vein: the League context was explicitly taken to enframe the French mission in Syria, but without reference to minorities. Since Syria was not yet a 'nation', nor independent, the newly-established legal category of minority did not apply there. The keynote was rather the dividedness of Syrian society as a justification for the mandate. The divisions could be religious, ethnic, 'racial', regional or any combination of these, but articles usually followed the 1920 assessment of the editor, Henri Froidevaux: while noting 'the multitude and ... the diversity of the races of Syria', and without forgetting that 'languages as well as races must be taken into account', 'how little importance these factors present next to the religious factor!'[24] This was why the 'heavy task of presiding over the raising-up of Syria' was a delicate one.

Against this picture of division, the French presence ('a gentle, benevolent, and educative tutelage ... leading the country gradually to prosperity, to liberty while waiting for independence'[25]) was usually justified by reference to the League and the 'heavy task' that France had accepted from it: it added an appealing new dimension to the older notion of an imperial *mission civilisatrice*. It should be emphasised, though, that invoking the League was not just a rhetorical strategy: the mandate was what made the French occupation of Syria legal under international (and internationally recognised) law. It also provided an external guarantee of Syria's existence as a state. In this context it is significant that these frequent references to the League rarely include mention of minorities, despite the new body of international law that the League was supervising on the protection of minorities in newly-independent states. To labour the point, this was because Syria was not independent. The Minorities Commission was concerned with overseeing the application of the minorities treaties; Syrian questions at the League were dealt with by the Permanent Mandates Commission.

The French depiction of Syrian society as hopelessly divided would remain constant in *L'Asie française* throughout this period, but it was not until the aftermath of the 1925–7 revolt that the bulletin began more systematically to attach the concept of minority to those perceived divisions. Still tightly bound to the League context, the concept could be used to justify French policies such as the territorial division of Syria:

> pretending to impose another method [the creation of a unitary state], wishing to drown the voice of the minorities in an electoral consultation common to the entire territory of the Mandate, is to support a policy that is not in harmony with the obligations that the facts, and the terms of the Mandate, make for the Mandatory Power.[26]

References to Syrian 'minorities' became more frequent in the years after the revolt, usually, though not exclusively, referring to religious communities. But the term by no means displaced other categories ('religious community', 'nationality', 'race'). Rather, it slotted into the existing discourse to complement them, as in a long article on 'Nationalities and Arab nationalism in the Near East': this recognised ethnolinguistic communities such as Turks or Kurds, but only applied the terms minority and majority to religious groups, whether in Syria, Lebanon or Iraq. For the latter two, it used the term 'Arab' more or less explicitly as a synonym for arabophone Sunni Muslim: in Iraq, 'the majority . . . is Shi'ite and there are barely 900,000 Arabs out of a total of over two million arabophones'.[27]

Moreover, the term's application remained scattershot. It only became systematic – if not overnight, then from one year to the next – in 1933: thereafter, *L'Asie française*'s interest in the Levant focused on the question of minorities, so defined. To give a rough, but not entirely unscientific, estimate of the scale of the change: I surveyed twenty-five years' worth of the bulletin's articles on the Levant, from 1915 to the end of 1939, looking for material relevant to the question of minorities – that is, any articles about communities that would today be called minorities.[28] My notes on the period 1915–32 run to seventy pages, and the term itself appears infrequently. For the years 1933–9 – a period barely more than a third as long – they run to just over seventy pages, and the term is extremely common.[29] What had changed?

The difference can be explained quite simply. Once Iraq had been admitted to the League of Nations in autumn 1932, French intentions in Syria came under greater scrutiny in Geneva.[30] In Syria, too, Iraq's admission to the League focused attention on France's plans. Before 1933, the French preference was for its mandate over Syria to continue indefinitely. After 1933, this gave way to a grudging acknowledgement that to ensure the continued stability of French control, France would have to follow – or at least, seem willing to follow – Britain's example by putting an end to the mandate, granting independence,

The Franco-Syrian Treaty and the Definition of 'Minorities' [139

and backing Syrian membership of the League.³¹ The text of a treaty had been drafted in Paris in 1931; in early 1933 the High Commissioner Ponsot sought to resurrect it, unsuccessfully, but a little later his successor, Martel, managed to get it signed by the Syrian government – not without heavy pressure, even though that government was a 'moderate' one.³² Although the 1933 treaty was blocked by the National Bloc in the Syrian parliament (which Martel duly suspended), for the rest of the 1930s the question regarding a treaty leading to Syrian independence was 'when?' rather than 'if . . .'.³³

This meant that the entire body of League-derived law regarding the independence of new nation-states, including the law on 'minorities', did now apply to Syria – or would soon. It would replace the mandate law, under which, as *L'Asie française* had pointed out,

> the rights and duties that result for the Mandatory from the Declaration of the Mandate, instrument of application of article 22 of the Charter, are the common affair of it [that is, the Mandatory] and the League of Nations alone [*ne sont affaire qu'entre lui et la Société des Nations*] and do not depend on the consent of the countries which are entrusted to the Mandate.³⁴

France's 'rights' in Syria would be more limited as a friend and ally than as a mandatory power, but the new body of law provided possibilities for asserting them nonetheless. Particularly as it applied, in theory and in practice, to Iraq, this body of law now formed the framework for the writers of *L'Asie française* to construct their vision of the future French role in Syria. It is important to understand that this framework was more than a handy rhetorical vehicle for French imperialism (though it was certainly used as one): it also gave juridical form to the new categories of the modern period – among them the nation-state, national independence, and minority.

The implications of this were clear to the writers of *L'Asie française*, and at least implicit in their treatment of this newly topical question. Over the next years the bulletin sought to keep its readers informed of 'the precarious situation' of certain 'groups in which France had the duty not to lose interest [*dont la France a le devoir de ne pas se désintéresser*]'.³⁵ On the grounds that they were 'minorities', it lobbied for legal guarantees to be applied to these groups, subject to a higher authority than the Syrian government. This could involve extending the understanding of the term: arguing for communal electoral representation for Circassians, for example, who had not previously been considered a minority: 'Syrian nationalist circles have not been minded to recognize rights particular to the Tcherkess minority, under the pretext that they are Sunni Muslims like the Muslim majority.'³⁶ The anonymous writer of these lines, described as an 'eminent personality', did not mention that a few years earlier the mandatory authorities had used precisely the same 'pretext' to avoid granting such recognition.³⁷ At that time the disadvantages of doing so evidently outweighed the benefits; but the new context of anticipated Syrian independence made it worthwhile to revisit the issue, at least. Interest in the Circassians soon waned, however: while this article lamented that Syria's 1930 organic statute 'only recognizes the right of representation of confessional minorities',[38] *L'Asie française*'s own coverage of minorities remained heavily weighted towards religious groups.

In this question, Iraq during and after the British mandate was important not simply as a point of comparison, but because Iraq's independence set a legal precedent on which the French in Syria were expected to draw. In the mid-1930s *L'Asie française* returned frequently to the situation in Iraq, particularly the situation of those groups now defined as its minorities. It usually did so to draw unsubtle implications for Syria. Whether discussing Iraq directly or referring to it in articles on Syria, *L'Asie française*'s assessment of that precedent was that it had been altogether too hasty. Its readers, the bulletin asserted in June 1933, would remember

> the fine promises made to the national minorities of Iraq, at the time of that kingdom's admission to the League of Nations, and the haste with which, to give satisfaction to England, the [League] assembly declared that admission, without taking account of the wise recommendations of the Mandates Commission.[39]

Fine promises notwithstanding, the Iraqi military was currently 'in the process, with the collaboration of the British air force, of exterminating the Kurds subjected to their domination', because they had asserted 'the safeguarding of rights and the respect of liberties which have been solemnly guaranteed them by international pacts'.[40] The following issue returned to Iraq's national minorities, this time talking about a group who would interest the bulletin more than the Kurds over the coming years because they were Christian: the Assyrians.[41] For *L'Asie française*, their mistreatment by the Baghdad government, enthusiastically applauded by the Muslim population, posed questions: 'is Iraq truly capable of governing itself, and would it not be more suitable to place it back among the A-mandate countries?'[42] The point being drawn for the Syrian treaty was obvious, and explicitly argued:

> It is not fitting ... at the moment when the well-known events have just taken place in Iraq, to deliver Syria's national minorities to the mercy of the Arab majority; instructed by experience, the League of Nations will surely not permit it, and such an action would be contrary to all of our country's traditions.[43]

Between the failure of the 1933 treaty and the initially successful signature of a treaty in 1936 – this time negotiated on the Syrian side by a nationalist delegation rather than a 'moderate' government – *L'Asie française* returned frequently to the Iraqi case. In December 1933 it described the conflict between the Assyrians and Iraqi government forces, 'whose origin is difficult to unravel, but which certainly seems, in one region, to have turned into systematic massacre'; it then reproduced the ten-article declaration on the protection of minorities made to the League by Iraq, but with no external guarantor, upon termination of the mandate in 1932.[44] More articles on the Assyrians, in both Iraq and in Syria, followed.[45] They were joined in November 1935 by the Yazidis:

> The conflict with the Assyrians of Iraq [having] hardly eased, another minority of Mesopotamia in its turn becomes the victim of the haste with which the English had the independence of Iraq proclaimed by the L.O.N., without worrying themselves about the fate of the populations living on the ground and practicing another religion than that of Mahomet.[46]

Conflict had broken out between the Iraqi state and the Yazidis of the Jabal Sinjar region on the Syrian frontier over the latter's refusal 'to have themselves enrolled on the army register, as the law on military service recently voted by the Baghdad Parliament order[ed]'; martial law had been proclaimed and a punitive column sent to crush resistance. The article's subtext is so clear it is virtually a headline:

> One cannot ... not notice that under the British mandate the Yazidis lived very peacefully, and have only become agitated under the Iraqi regime. One thus finds oneself led to wonder if they have enjoyed the same religious tolerance under the Arab kings as under the regime of the mandate.

The next month the point was repeated after a number of Yazidis – and two Assyrians – had received harsh sentences from a military court in Mosul, with the bulletin quoting the French-language newspaper *La Syrie* to ask 'if minorities are really defended in Iraq and if the guarantees of the League are anything other than scraps of paper'.[47]

These articles were supporting evidence in *L'Asie française*'s campaign either to forestall the signing of a Franco-Syrian treaty, or to ensure that such a treaty contained the minorities clauses – permitting continued outside involvement – that the British–Iraqi treaty had lacked. When the decision came, in 1936, to negotiate a treaty with a delegation dominated by the National Bloc, *L'Asie française* stated its position clearly:

> The Iraqi precedent can provide a good basis for examination and we accept it as such; but it must not be forgotten that it consists not only in a text but also in its application, which has rendered certain precautions necessary and legitimate, as much in the eyes of the League of Nations as of France.[48]

This quote comes from an article published in March 1936; its coverage of the French decision to negotiate is a hastily-added afterword to an article about the widespread unrest in Syria – the 'nouvelle crise' of the title – that led to that decision. Two more articles on Syria reinforced the point the following month. If the negotiations had now begun, both sides had already recognised 'the necessity of a comprehensive treaty between France and Syria, [and] also how the principles set out by the L.O.N. must be applied to the minorities of the country'.[49] The bulletin also observed that 'as of now, certain apprehensions are manifesting themselves among the minority groups'.[50]

Despite this seeming clarity, many aspects of the 'minorities question' remained confused in the bulletin's coverage of the negotiations, the treaty's signature and its slow demise over the three years to 1939.[51] These points of confusion are echoed in other primary sources for the period, on both the French and Syrian sides, and in some cases in the historiography of the mandate as well. Earlier, *L'Asie française* had at least sometimes referred to Syrian ethnolinguistic communities as minorities; but by the later 1930s, in its discussions of the actual Franco-Syrian treaty, it only mentioned religious minorities. When the issue of modifying the 1936 treaty came up, as it frequently did, the question of minorities was always cited as the major sticking point, but the groups concerned were always religious groups.[52] (The bulletin's authoritative diagnosis of Syria's needs was slightly undermined by the fact that it consistently misspelt the name of Syria's prime minister, Jamil Mardam, as 'Mardan' throughout this period – and up until January 1939, shortly before his resignation.) When the bulletin explained the need for added guarantees for minorities it always did so with reference to Christians first.[53] More, the frequent references to Christians in its coverage of the situation in Syria in 1936–9 are to the Christians of the Jazira – mostly recent immigrants or refugees from Turkey and Iraq – rather than the various arabophone Christian communities dispersed through the 'Arab' cities and agricultural areas of western Syria, or the Armenians who were mostly settled in the cities (principally Aleppo).[54] The precise place of the 'Alawis and the Druzes in the minorities question, meanwhile, was never quite clear.

Nevertheless, the example of *L'Asie française* demonstrates the development of the language of minorities in French discourse about Syria, showing the links between its development and Syria's status in international law. This language was well established by the time of the 1936 treaty. It was not without its inconsistencies and blind spots, but there is nothing troubling to the historian in these: they are inherent to the category of minority itself, as a subjective rather than an objective category. It would be a great deal more surprising to encounter consistency.

The process outlined above explains why the term was adopted in Syria, as elsewhere. As a body of international public law relating to the independence of new nation-states emerged, a subset of it – the minorities treaties – emerged to address one of the problems posed by the establishment of such states. Since nation-states were developing in other parts of the world too, and posing the same problems, groups not touched by the central and eastern European minorities treaties began to demand similar protections. Syria was one such place, especially once the question of its 'independence' arose. This explains how Syrians, too, came to use the term, but not the specific reasons why they used it. In the next part of the chapter I outline some of the ways in which members of such groups, both 'minoritarianist'[55] and nationalist, chose to use the term – among others – in the debate about a Franco-Syrian treaty, and what motivated them to do so.

Syrian Uses of the Language of Minorities

When Syrians contributed to the debate about minorities clauses – in newspaper articles, petitions to the League of Nations or correspondence with the High Commission – they were doing several different things. First, implicitly or explicitly, they sought to define who was a minority, either saying 'community X is a minority' or 'a minority is community X'. Second, and more interestingly, they argued for communities defined as minorities to be treated in a certain way – defining what the category of minority should mean. By applying that category to the communities they claimed to speak for, they sought to redefine those communities, notably in relation to the state: this was part of a wider debate in Syria over the institutional form that should be given to the relationship between state and population. Third, they put forward a vision of legitimate authority within their own communities. With a little digging, this rich content can be excavated quite easily – provided that we understand that the category of minority was not a neutral, descriptive label.

This section considers several examples in detail to show how they work on these different levels. Illustrating each analytical point with a different example would have been quite possible, but returning to the same examples allows us to understand the 'thickness' of the debate, the many meanings contained in any given mobilisation on the part of one particular group or individual. Most of these examples come from members of communities that were being redefined as minorities, crossing a number of minoritarianist viewpoints with the nationalist counter-arguments made by Edmond Rabbath, a prominent nationalist Christian.

We have already met Ignace Nouri, who wrote to High Commissioner Damien de Martel during the 1936 negotiations expressing his confidence that they would result in a treaty containing 'certain clauses and bonds for the protection of the minorities, that is to say the Christians and Jews'.[56] A group of Catholic bishops, writing to Martel just before the negotiations began, approached the issue from the other direction: whereas Nouri started with the concept of minority and then explicitly took it to mean non-Muslim religious communities, these clerics introduced themselves as 'leaders and representatives of the Christian communities'[57] and then used 'minorities' as an implicit synonym for 'Christian communities'. While they expressed the desire 'of each of us to see his country evolve towards independence and acquire a place in the concert of nations equal to that of other countries', and stated that 'the patriotism of the minorities cannot be doubted', they also asserted that that patriotism must 'square with the measures of protection indispensable so that harmony may always exist between all nationals without distinction of religion'. The purely religious understanding of the term is evident.[58] The nationalist delegation in Paris, they said, could not claim to represent minorities.

Other Christian figures had already pushed the definition of the term beyond the circle of Christian communities. In late 1932, receiving a courtesy visit from a French official, the papal delegate to Syria and Lebanon, Monsignor Giannini, 'addressed spontaneously and in the most precise terms the question of the Christian minorities in Syria'.[59] At issue was the place of minorities in the treaty that was then thought to be forthcoming: Giannini insisted that the Christians should be protected by (French) external guarantee. But 'Lastly, this time in terms lacking in precision, Mgr Giannini indicated that he would wish this guarantee to be extended also to the "other minorities".' Whether he meant non-Christian religious minorities, ethnolinguistic minorities, or both, is unclear.

Two months earlier, in conversation with the French intelligence services, a secular Christian figure had been more specific as he sought to widen the application of the term: 'Latif Ghanimé, Syrian-Catholic deputy for Aleppo, deeming that the principal task of the next government – of which he expects to be a part – will be the conclusion of a treaty, emphasises the importance of the question of minorities.'[60] For Ghanimé as for Giannini, what had given the question of minorities its importance was the prospect of a Franco-Syrian treaty and Syrian independence. As we saw at the start of the chapter, it was with an eye on the future discussion of minorities clauses in the Syrian parliament that he proposed a broader legal application of the term:

> Latif Ghanimé also fears that the numerical weakness of Christian representation in the Syrian Chamber – aggravated by the fact that the Orthodox deputies for Damascus and Hama cannot be counted on in practice – may render very precarious the parliamentary base necessary for the discussion of the problem. He is therefore disposed to understand 'minorities' in the broad sense, ethic [sic – éthique] rather than religious, and range among the minoritarians the Kurdish deputies of the North and the Djézireh, the Tcherkess deputy of Kuneitra, even Soubhi bey Barakat and the deputies of the Sanjak of Alexandretta as representatives of the 'Turks'. Here again, he does not seem to be quite in line with [il ne semble pas rejoindre entièrement] the views of his Patriarchate.

Unlike the Christian clergymen mentioned above, then, Ghanimé stretched the term to cover ethnolinguistic as well as religious minorities.[61]

Ethnolinguistic communities were in fact quite capable of seeing for themselves the advantages that a treaty might bring them if they had official minority status. A few months after Ghanimé made his suggestions, with French policy still focused – unsuccessfully, at this point – on getting a treaty signed, Circassian notables in the predominantly Circassian muhafaza of Qunaytra forwarded a petition to their fellows in Homs. It was addressed to the High Commissioner; the French Sûreté générale reported that it 'demands that the future Treaty guarantee the rights of minorities' and listed what the Circassians considered those rights to be.[62] Although the Sûreté claimed that Circassian notables in Homs 'hesitate to sign this mazbata which they find useless and untimely', it was almost certainly the same petition that was sent to the High Commissioner less than two weeks later signed by prominent Circassians from Qunaytra and the region of Hama as well as Homs.[63] I cited this in Chapter 3, and mentioned in passing that it came in the context of a treaty. In fact, the petition's wording is very clear: 'on the occasion of the forthcoming end of the Syrian mandate, and its replacement by the treaty between the French and Syrian Republics', the signatories wrote that 'the Circassians resident in Syria' had claimed and would continue to claim 'recognition of their national minority rights [*huqūqihim al-aqalliyya al-jinsiyya*] as a community having its own race, language and traditions different from those of the Syrian majority'.[64]

These examples offer a range of definitions of the term 'minority': a purely religious meaning attached to Christians and Jews; an emphasis on Christian communities, but a willingness to apply it to unspecified other minorities; a definition that starts with religious communities, but specifically stretches to include ethnic minorities; and a definition that comes from (and only covers) an ethnolinguistic minority. These different uses hint at the range of groups to which it could be applied. Some other religiously- and linguistically-defined groups, such as Isma'ilis or Kurds, made similar claims.[65] Yet others to which the term could have applied seem not to have used it much. The stream of petitions from 'Alawis and Druzes to the League reached its peak flow during the treaty negotiations of 1933 and 1936, motivated by a desire to fix the status of these communities and their regions relative to an independent Syria. But it focused on whether the statelets attributed to each community should be part of a unitary Syria or not, and neither pro- nor anti-unitarians seem to have used the term 'minority' to describe themselves, for reasons discussed in Chapter 2.

It is unsurprising that there were different and inconsistent applications of the term: in fact, consistency would be more surprising. As I observed in Chapter 1, my concern in this book is not with whether 'minority' is an objectively valid category of analysis nor with defining particular Syrian groups as minorities myself. Rather, I am interested in how and why particular actors used it at the time – as they would not have done only a few years earlier – and what specific historical conditions made the term meaningful for them. Syria's legal redefinition as a nation-state, first under mandate and then (putatively) independent, was partly responsible for creating those conditions, as the term's sudden importance in the debate about the treaty shows.

But for what reasons did Syrians choose to use it? Having stated that such-and-such a community was a minority, what meaning did they seek to give to the term? We have already seen that they thought it should imply a community having certain externally-guaranteed rights, and at need, protection. The rights different groups sought to guarantee for their communities, as minorities, involved a redefinition of those communities' relationship to the state.

Latif Ghanimé, for example, wanted the minorities to have 'not only a [defined legal] status, but guarantees coming from the exterior, and in their absence would prefer an indefinite continuation of the mandate'.[66] He therefore requested that the text of any treaty drawn up by France be passed unofficially to the Christian deputies in the Syrian parliament before reaching the parliament as a whole, so that they could 'make their observations heard, and refine [*perfectionner*] the guarantees offered'. If the text were discussed from the outset by the parliament in plenary session, Ghanimé feared that any minority clauses would be 'taken ... by the extremists as a maximum to be beaten down',[67] making it difficult for him and his Christian colleagues to request stronger protection. If passing the text directly to the Christian deputies were impossible, Ghanimé suggested that it could be communicated to them via the Patriarchs – though his own, Monsignor Tappouni, was apparently unenthusiastic.

As should be clear from the earlier quote about minorities in parliament, meanwhile, Ghanimé was afraid that if only Christians were covered by the proposed clauses, the 'minorities' might be in too much of a minority to make their voices heard. Better, therefore, to widen the definition of the term to ensure that a sufficient number of deputies would feel that they had an interest in defending minority clauses.[68] But this implied redefining a number of communities – Kurds, Circassians, even Turks – as minorities: a redefinition that would change their formal relationship to the state, and by extension to the 'majority'.

The example of the Circassian notables shows that some members of such communities were making similar claims for themselves. The purpose of their petition was 'to demand the following articles in the forthcoming Treaty': a list of ten, which I outlined in the earlier chapter, covering issues like guaranteed representation 'for the Circassian minority' in parliament and in state jobs, access to and control over (Circassian-medium) education, participation in the state Waqf administration, and various other cultural freedoms.[69] More Circassian mobilisations as a minority occurred in the period 1936–9. A petition from March 1936, just after the French had put an end to serious unrest in Syria by agreeing to negotiate a treaty with a nationalist delegation, asserts the Circassians' loyalty to France and alludes to the risks that this has entailed. It does not list specific rights they should be guaranteed in the treaty, but it is specific about both the diplomatic context and its desire for explicit French protection:

> We know very well, Your Excellency, that noble France will never abandon us; but we come, by this request [*bi-'arīdatinā hādhihi*], following recent events and the likelihood of the signing of a treaty between your state and Syria, to ask that Your Excellency work effectively to protect the rights of minorities including our Circassian race [*wa minhā 'unsurunā al-sharkasī*] in the treaty ... and to take them under French protection.[70]

Another petition comes from 1938, by which time the National Bloc government elected under the treaty regime was floundering – in large part because of French obstructiveness. The Bloc was under constant French pressure to revise the 1936 treaty by, among other things, adding greater minority protection. In this context, a group of Circassian notables from Homs[71] sent a long statement to the High Commission, to be communicated to the Quai d'Orsay and to the League of Nations. It started, as such statements commonly did, with a history lesson, stating that 'despite [their] forced exodus, and after long years', the Circassians had maintained their sense of communal cohesion in exile.[72] 'The Tcherkesses still conserve their national customs, their language, their habits, their civilisation; and this thanks to their own schools, their writings, their associations, which prove their attachment to their social existence.' The statement explained the community's previous attempts to have its communal existence formally recognised under the mandate, notably in 1925, 1934 and prior to the signature of the 1936 treaty. 'Despite all these petitions, the Tcherkesses have noted with regret and emotion that the Treaty included no articles safeguarding their rights and recognizing them as those of a national minority in Syria.'

As Syria was supposedly in a transitional period to full independence under the terms of the treaty, they were now lobbying for it to be revised in their favour: the Circassians

> do not want to run the risk of being aggressed by the 'Majority' of their compatriots, which will surely happen since Tcherkess youth has spilled its blood to show its attachment to its national principles and its sympathies towards the mandatory power.

They adduced a number of incidents of tension between 'the Tcherkess minority and the "Majority"' in the Faysali and mandate periods, as well as citing the case of the Assyrians in Iraq, to support their claim for the Circassians to be recognised as an 'ethnic minority' by the treaty and afforded protection accordingly. That protection should take the form of eleven explicitly-stated rights: the first ten were more or less the same as those outlined five years earlier; the eleventh was French oversight ensuring that the others were acted upon.

Whether they were arguing for or against them, when political actors debated the granting of defined minority rights of this kind they were taking part in a wider debate about the relationship of state and population. The discussion over the distribution of seats on representative bodies is only the most obvious example: Circassians requesting a particular kind of relationship between state authority and their community, in which Circassians were represented in the Syrian parliament as members of a Circassian minority rather than Syrian Muslims, or even simply Syrians; Latif Ghanimé seeking to define and represent any number of religious and ethnic minorities in the same way. Such a measure would fix the boundaries of these communities: anyone allotted to the Circassian electoral college would 'be' a Circassian in the state's eyes, regardless of, for example, his or her language of ordinary use, habitual manner of dressing, or place of residence. Likewise, a member of the Syrian-Catholic college would 'be' a Syrian-Catholic regardless of whether or not he or she was religiously observant or even a believer. Without this state 'fixing', the boundaries between communities would be rather more fluid; communities themselves would not have external coherence.

These communal identities would be non-territorial: a Circassian would be a Circassian wherever he or she voted. Other suggestions for parliamentary representation were territorial, but likewise concerned themselves with defining the relationship between population and state. At least in the case of the Jabal Druze and the Alaouites, for example, *L'Asie française* argued for allocating seats to distinct territories (that is, gerrymandering). The aim of guaranteeing representation to particular communities was the same – the justification was that any 'electoral consultation common to the entire territory' would be a deliberate attempt to 'drown the voice of the minorities' – but the effect on the institutional relationship of population and state would be different.[73] Provided they wanted to vote along communal lines, for example, this arrangement might benefit 'Alawi voters within the circumscription of the Alaouites. But that advantage would not stretch to an 'Alawi peasant living just beyond the internal frontier in the muhafaza of Homs. Nationalists, meanwhile, thought that any of these positions meant allowing the amplified voice of the minorities to drown out the majority.

Edmond Rabbath did not discuss the subject of parliamentary representation when, at the end of 1932, he drew up a policy on minorities clauses to guide the National Bloc leadership in treaty negotiations.[74] But in his study of the question, the Christian nationalist intellectual from Aleppo touched on many other controversial topics in the debate about the institutional relationship between population and state. Among them was whether the presidency of the Syrian republic would be open to any citizen or restricted to members of one community: his answer, no doubt controversial, was that as part of the process of guaranteeing the rights of minorities in the treaty of Syrian independence, the article of the constitution stipulating that the president be a Muslim should be abrogated.

Rabbath addressed another question which we have already encountered, and frequently: access to state jobs. The minoritarianist Circassians mentioned above, like other groups discussed in this and earlier chapters, wanted proportionate access to state jobs for their community – especially where those jobs concerned the community's own administration, education or policing. Rabbath, by contrast, argued that recruitment should be 'carried out by means of competitive examination [*par voie de concours*] and with no confessional distinction[s]'.[75] If such French-style exams were marked anonymously one might consider this a laudable aim; but a non-nationalist might point out that Rabbath does not specify what language the exams would be written in, perhaps taking for granted that it would be Arabic. Muslims, meanwhile, might observe that such a 'blind' competition would tend to benefit Christians, who were more likely to be educated and particularly to have received – like the Paris-educated lawyer Rabbath himself – a 'modern' education of the sort that such exams would favour. This is not to accuse Rabbath of acting in bad faith, or slyly seeking advantages for Christians under the cover of nationalism; it is simply to point out that a nationalist position on these issues, too, is an attempt to define the relationship between people and state, and one which would offer advantages and disadvantages to individual citizens.

These are not the artificial quibbles of a picky historian. It was because the debate over access to state jobs was so hot, at a time when the state apparatus was expanding, that Rabbath addressed it.[76] Different ways of defining communities had different implications. As we have seen, some Circassians wanted the right to Circassian-medium education, which would require qualified teachers literate in Circassian rather than Arabic. This would imply official status for the language; and a multilingual state, in turn, would by implication be a different animal than the 'Arab' nation-state proposed by the Syrian nationalists. From the latter's point of view, the dangers of a liberal language policy were pressingly illustrated by Alexandretta, where Turkish had official status. This had contributed to a steady strengthening of 'Turkish' identity; a growing identification, among Turkish speakers, with the Turkish nation-state over the border; and, in the period under discussion, the sanjak's gradual removal from Syria.[77]

Another aspect of this question, which the debate over minorities clauses raised, was the competence of state courts over the entire population. It might seem obvious to us today that states should have exclusive jurisdiction over their territory and any person upon it, but this is a view conditioned by the age of the nation-state. In Syria's recent Ottoman past many local inhabitants had been able to abstract themselves from the Ottoman judicial system by becoming the protégés of foreign consuls and placing themselves under the jurisdiction of the mixed courts set up to try cases involving foreign subjects. A version of these still existed in the mandate period. Rabbath noted that 'certain bishops in Aleppo [had] expressed the desire to see the minorities accorded the right to request to be subject to the tribunals competent in foreign law [*la faculté de demander à être justiciables des tribunaux statuant en matière étrangère*]'. Rabbath believed that 'this demand [was] incompatible with the quality of Syrian citizens and that it would not be in the interest of the minorities [*minoritaires*] themselves to raise it'.[78] The first part of this opinion shows that for Rabbath full citizenship meant full participation in uniform state institutions: a modern understanding of what it means to belong to a state. The mixed courts had been a serious obstacle to Ottoman attempts to establish a common Ottoman citizenship. The second part, meanwhile, suggests that he understood how unpopular Syrian Christians would make themselves if they sought to place themselves under extraterritorial jurisdiction – a major source of tension in the Ottoman period.

This question leads to another: what external authorities had a right of intervention in the relationship between population and state, and which parts of the population could invoke it? For the Catholic bishops of Damascus cited above, 'The question of minorities goes beyond the framework of an internal settlement [*règlement interne*] and appertains to international law'.[79] But the notion that certain citizens of a state could, under international law, be guaranteed access to an external power has profound implications for the authority of the state. For nationalists everywhere in this period, limiting the state's authority in this way was deplorable – not a rare opinion today. When the question is phrased in this way – limiting the authority of the state – it might sound like a good thing, given what states are capable of inflicting on their populations. But as Edmond Rabbath pointed out, the legal protection of minorities would tend to disadvantage the establishment of legal equality for individual citizens.[80]

Thus, the debate over minorities clauses was also a debate about the limits of the authority of the state. In different forms the same debate is a constant of state politics. That it was particularly intense in this period, when state authority was expanding and intensifying rapidly in Syria, is unsurprising. In these circumstances, it is understandable that some Syrians looked beyond the country's borders for guarantees of their status, both to international law and to particular powers. But in doing so they ran a risk, emphasised by Rabbath when he wrote in a Beirut newspaper that such guarantees 'will be more useful to the Powers than to the minorities. The latter will find their real guarantee not on paper but in the creation of an atmosphere of reciprocal comprehension and sympathy.'[81] Rabbath's vision of the citizen's full participation in state institutions, as we have seen, included the constitutional guarantee that a Christian could become president of the republic like any other Syrian. The structured and permanent political separation of Christians from other Syrians sought by minoritarianist Christian clergymen would hardly have permitted such a thing.

It is important to understand that this debate was not mere sectarian or ethnic bickering. Modern states, which claim to represent their populations, must somehow decide how the population is to be represented; likewise they must decide on what grounds the population is to be incorporated into the much expanded structures of the nation-state. These questions give rise to permanent contestation – which is not the same as saying that they make conflict inevitable. What we see in the debate over minorities clauses in the Franco-Syrian treaty is political figures who identified themselves with various groups advancing answers to that question in line with their own political interests and the interests of those groups as they defined them. (The 'majority' was one of those groups.) The questions are so contested because Syrian independence was only a prospect, raised by the treaty negotiations but not yet fully achieved, nor fully defined. The institutional relationship of population and state in post-mandate Syria therefore also remained to be defined.

Finally, the debate over minority guarantees also reveals struggles over leadership, legitimate authority, and representation within the communities being (re)defined as 'minorities'. When certain Circassian notables demanded guaranteed seats in the Syrian parliament for 'two Tcherkess members proposed by the Tcherkesses',[82] for example, what did they mean by 'proposed by the Tcherkesses'? Or rather, who did they mean? One can assume that pro-nationalist Circassians put forward in elections by the National Bloc would not count – that if the community were redefined in this way only minoritarianist Circassians like these notables would be electable to the 'Circassian' seats. But these notables did not represent the only current of opinion among Syria's Circassians: during the 1936 treaty negotiations, for example, 150 Circassians from Manbij – one of the largest Circassian settlements in northern Syria, about fifty miles east of Aleppo – drove to the city to display their adhesion to the nationalist cause. One of their vehicles carried a banner with the slogan 'The struggle for the Fatherland, and obedience to the Bloc'.[83]

This issue is explicitly present in the letter that the six Catholic bishops wrote to Martel. When they stated that 'minorities are not represented' in the nationalist delegation in Paris, this was not on the grounds that nationalists were Muslims and minorities were Christians, but because 'the members composing it, Christians included, [were] linked by engagements, the first towards the Nationalist Bloc to which he belongs, and the second towards the government of which he is a part'.[84] The two Christians mentioned are Faris al-Khoury and Edmond Homsi, respectively. The implication is that a nationalist Christian like al-Khoury could represent nationalists but not Christians.

Homsi, meanwhile, was not even a member of the Bloc: they disqualify him simply because he was a minister in the existing caretaker government. So who could legitimately represent Christians? The answer is categorical: 'It is only fair [*de toute justice*] that these minorities should be represented within the delegation by independent persons duly authorized by the supreme heads of the communities . . .'

At issue, then, is not only the place of 'minorities' in an independent Syria, but also the source of legitimate authority within the Christian communities of Syria. These Catholic archbishops saw themselves as the source of that authority: no-one might represent their communities without their blessing. (We have already seen that they started their letter by calling themselves the 'representatives' of Christian communities.) They were seeking to constitute Syria's Christians as legally-defined 'minorities', within which authority would reside with the church leaders. As I noted in Chapter 2, this was a vision – rooted in the Ottoman millet past – that the French were generally keen to accommodate, but it posed greater problems in the context of a (secular) nation-state form than in a religiously-legitimated empire. Many Christians, particularly younger ones, were comfortable with and supportive of Syrian nationalism. But even a nationalist might envisage a political role for the patriarchs. Edmond Rabbath, outlining the guarantees that a treaty might propose for minorities, suggested that these guarantees be placed under the jurisdiction of the League of Nations and the International Court in the Hague. 'The right to petition these bodies would be recognized to the Patriarchs – and to them alone – each for his own community.'[85]

Conclusion

In the inter-war years, as Syria went from being part of the Ottoman Empire to being a separate nation-state, the institutional relationship between population and state was substantially re-formed. 'Nationalising' reforms in the late Ottoman period had begun this process, but the elaboration of nation-state institutions – and the scale and intensity of their impact on population and territory – now changed up a gear. The institutional form and legitimacy of the state were put on quite new bases, not only internally but also externally. The Ottoman Empire was a dynastic empire whose existence required no external institutional sanction other than God's. Syria under the mandate was a nation-state-in-waiting, provisionally recognised as such by the League of Nations; to become a fully independent state it would also require the external sanction of international law.

For newly independent states that sanction depended partly on the legal protection they gave to 'minorities' within their populations. The question of minorities was a point of articulation between the external institutional form of the state (a nation-state recognised by other nation-states) and its internal structure (how the state related to its population). The importance of this question was only heightened by the fact that Syria was passing to independence from the position of being a mandate under French imperial control: an external power was present on the ground, and already had well-established links with groups within the population – and reasons to support their claims to minority status. Within the debate about a Franco-Syrian treaty, the legally-defined category of minority became a vehicle for the political claims of competing groups and individuals within Syrian society. Different political actors could advance their particular claims by harnessing them to the concept. Syrians could use it, for example, to demand special support from the imperial power (because France, faced with the necessity of a treaty, had adopted the language of minorities to justify its own political claims in Syria), and to attract attention and perhaps political support from other international actors (since the international community and notably the League now expressly concerned themselves with protecting minorities, as defined in international law).

At the same time, the concept also became the terrain on which their competition played out. The debate over how minorities were to be defined and what distinct legal status was to be granted to them, if any – in other words, the debate about what the term meant – was itself an arena in which different groups and individuals could advance their political claims. This was part of the contest over the institutional form of the population's relationship to the state, including the degree of control over it exerted by groups within the population: a contest which naturally involved the majority just as deeply as it did minorities. Within that wider contest, the debate over minority guarantees also reveals struggles over leadership, legitimate authority and representation in the communities being (re)defined as minorities. It would be a serious oversimplification to assume that the debate over minorities was about no more than how to balance correctly the interests of discrete groups – a majority and some minorities – whose own internal coherence and structure was already defined. The suggestions made by participants in the debate as to how minorities should be defined and protected were intended to shape the groups they claimed to represent. The debate itself was one means by which the work of redefinition was carried out.

Writers claiming to speak for particular communities rarely raised the question of how their communities were to be defined: instead, rather like nationalists, they took it for granted that these groups existed and that their members both know who they were and accepted the speaker's right to speak for them. But, just as nationalist claims about a 'nation' should be understood less as evidence for the existence of that nation than as an attempt to persuade such an entity into being, so the claims of a minoritarianist should not be taken as simply reflecting the existence of a coherent and self-conscious 'minority' – still less as reflecting the uniform political opinion of such a group. If successful, though, those claims would enshrine the existence of the minority in state structures, just as nationalist claims would enshrine the existence of the nation. This is what the minoritarianists discussed here hoped to achieve, as should be clear. Granting a distinct legal status to minorities would not just attach neutral legal categories to existing defined communities; it would in itself redefine those communities as political and social entities, both in relation to the state and internally (by fixing structures of political and judicial authority within each of them).

It is easy to see how the treaty diplomacy of the 1930s – itself influenced by a constellation of other factors – defined the territory of the Syrian state: the Alaouites, the Jabal Druze and the Jazira were included; most of the Sanjak of Alexandretta was in the end excluded. Along with the internal development of the state apparatus, treaty diplomacy was part of the process that defined this territory as Syria (or not). It would take an anachronistic, nationalist view of the state to argue that the Jazira simply was a part of 'Syria', or Alexandretta a part of 'Turkey', prior to this period. Because the results cannot be traced on a map, though, it is a little harder to see the ways in which treaty diplomacy and the debate about it also shaped both the Syrian 'nation' and the communities redefined as 'minorities' within the Syrian nation-state. But shape them it surely did. And just as the effect of the treaty diplomacy on territory went beyond mere geographical definition, diffusing a notion of the national territory in the minds of Syrians, so the debate about minorities clauses shaped 'minorities' – and the 'majority' – in ways that went beyond the mere definition of legal status.

Notes

1. D-SL Box 493, dossier *Traité Franco-Syrien. Minorités. Sous-dossiers.* Nouri to HC (7/8/1936).
2. AD-SL Box 572, untitled dossier (material released under sixty-year rule), sub-dossier *Les Kurdes en Syrie – Informations.* Unnumbered *Information* 'a/s Latif Ghanimé et la question des minorités' (17/10/1932).
3. AD-SL Box 568, dossier *Tcherkess*, petition from Circassians in Qunaytra, Homs, Hama, and Marj Sultan to High Commission for forwarding to League of Nations (1/4/1933).
4. Roger Owen kindly provided this information in an unpublished paper (see Bibliography). See also Mark Mazower, 'Minorities and the League of Nations in Interwar Europe', *Daedalus* (1997), 126(2): 47–63, and *No Enchanted Palace: The End of Empire and the Ideological Origins of the United Nations* (Princeton, NJ: Princeton University Press, 2009), p. 108; and Susan Pedersen, 'Back to the League of Nations', review essay, *The American Historical Review* (2007), 112(4) online, paras 16–21.
5. References to the Charter come from Nadine Méouchy (ed.), *France, Syrie et Liban 1918–1946. Les ambiguïtés et les dynamiques de la relation mandataire*

(Damascus: Institut français d'études arabes de Damas, 2002), Annexe. The English text is available in Hourani, *Syria and Lebanon*, Appendix A, No. 1.

6. The closest to such a thing in Syria was the Turcophone community in the Sanjak of Alexandretta, which after the 1921 Ankara agreement had specific guaranteed rights. These included official language status within the sanjak for Turkish, which – Article 8 notwithstanding – no other 'minority' language in Syria had. Unlike the rights assigned to unspecified 'communities' in the mandate charter, Alexandretta Turks' rights were not guaranteed by the mandatory's obligation to the League – which had no real autonomous power of its own – but by a bilateral treaty with a neighbouring state, which did have autonomous power that could be brought to bear to ensure those rights were respected. It is no coincidence that the Alexandretta Turks were the only 'minority' community whose existence led to a major alteration in the shape of the Syrian nation-state constituted by the mandate.

7. See, e.g., David Commins, *Historical Dictionary of Syria* (Lanham, MD: Scarecrow Press, 1996): 'Franco-Syrian Treaty of 1936'; Khoury, *Syria and the French Mandate*, pp. 464–8, 479, and chs 18 and 20; Longrigg, *Syria and Lebanon*, ch. 6 s. 2, ch. 7; Peter Shambrook, *French Imperialism in Syria, 1927–1936* (Reading: Ithaca Press, 1998), pp. 205–28.

8. Hourani, *Syria and Lebanon*, p. 203.

9. Shambrook, *French Imperialism in Syria*, pp. 247–8; Khoury, *Syria and the French Mandate*, p. 467.

10. Briand was both foreign minister and *président du conseil* (prime minister) at the time. AD-SL Box 412, dossier containing material on the question of Syrian unity/the Syrian federation. Extract from *Note N° 138*, HC to Briand (27/3/1921) included in document (dated only 1924) from the Service des Renseignements, service central, section d'études.

11. The Comité de l'Afrique française was founded in 1890, the Comité de l'Asie française in 1901. The Comité du Maroc followed in 1904, and the Comité France-Amérique in 1910. They shared one address and formed 'a single colonial–imperial pressure group' (L. Abrams and D. J. Miller, 'Who were the French colonialists? A reassessment of the parti colonial, 1890–1914', *The Historical Journal* (1976), 19(3): 685–725, quote at 687).

12. Abrams and Miller, 'Who were the French colonialists?', p. 687. This article contains much useful background information on the colonialist committees and their place in the wider milieu of French politics.

13. An idea of his activities can be gained from his author details in the catalogue of the Bibliothèque nationale de France, and the ninety-nine items listed (albeit with much repetition) under his name there.

14. For more on de Caix see Gérard Khoury, *Une tutelle coloniale*.

15. Such as 'L'Opinion française et les intérêts nationaux dans le Levant', *L'Asie française* (henceforward AF) 162 (Apr.–Jul. 1915), pp. 42–5. NB: please see note in Bibliography on authorship of articles in the bulletin.

16. 'La politique turque de suppression des allogènes', *AF* 162 (Apr.–Jul. 1915), pp. 57–60.
17. 'L'extermination des Nestoriens', *AF* 167 (Oct.–Dec. 1916), p. 174.
18. The word is slightly less obscure in French than in English, and has a slightly different meaning. The OED, under the variant spelling *allogeneous*, gives 'Of different nature, diverse in kind'; for *allogène*, the *Trésor de la langue française* first gives it as an anthropological term ('Said of an ethnic group installed since a relatively short time ago on a territory' – hardly the case here – 'and still presenting racial or ethnic characteristics distinguishing it from the autochthonous population') then in other senses as non-native.
19. 'La question de Syrie et la paix', *AF* 174 (Oct. 1918–Jan. 1919), pp. 121–9, quote at 121. The phrase *jeu loyal* implies 'playing-out according to the set rules'.
20. Once again I am glossing over the complexities of Greek identity as 'national' identity, such as the fact that many Anatolian 'Greeks' spoke Turkish as their language of ordinary use. Needless to say, similar complexities apply to other 'national' identities also.
21. 'La question de Syrie et la paix', *AF* 174 (Oct. 1918–Jan. 1919), pp. 121–9, quote at 121.
22. As above, quote at 122.
23. As above, quote at 129. Emphasis added, to render an emphatic tone in the original.
24. This and following quotes from Henri Froidevaux, 'Les difficultés de la France en Syrie – leurs causes', *AF* 179 (Feb. 1920), pp. 43–7; quotes at 43. For the bulletin, if not in reality, the 'religious factor' if anything gained in importance at the end of 1924, when Aleppo and Damascus were reunited in one state of Syria: from then on, only religious divisions affected the territorial division of the mandate territories, so highlighting the regional rivalry between the two main cities became redundant.
25. 'Ce que les Syriens attendent de la France', *AF* 178 (Jan. 1920), pp. 13–16, quote at 16.
26. 'Le programme politique déclaré par le Haut Commissaire en Syrie et au Liban', *AF* 253 (Sep.–Oct. 1927), pp. 283–9, quote at 287.
27. 'Nationalités et Nationalisme arabe dans le Proche Orient', signed F.T. *AF* 277 (Feb. 1930), pp. 52–65, quote at 56.
28. I ended my survey in 1939 because the outbreak of the Second World War marks the end of the period covered in this book. The bulletin ceased publication in May 1940, for obvious reasons.
29. This does not mean that it is ever examined or defined by those who use it, however.
30. Shambrook, *French Imperialism in Syria*, p. 247.
31. Both in France and among the personnel of the High Commission there were many who did not even grudgingly accept this necessity, and sought to torpedo any plan for Syrian independence: 'To the missionaries, Jesuits, and military caste the Treaty was anathema.' (Longrigg, *Syria and Lebanon*, p. 224.)

The Franco-Syrian Treaty and the Definition of 'Minorities'   [157

32. Shambrook, *French Imperialism in Syria*, p. 248.
33. 1933 also saw the worst drought in Syria since the First World War, if not in living memory, with a sharp rise in famine proportionate to a steep decline in wheat production. Major social consequences included banditry in the countryside, an influx of peasants to the cities and the temporary emigration of as many as 30,000 people from the hardest hit region, the Hawran. (Philip S. Khoury, 'The paradoxical in Arab nationalism. Interwar Syria revisited', in Jankowski and Gershoni (eds), *Rethinking Arab Nationalism*, pp. 273–87 at p. 278.) If it seems odd to relegate this catastrophic social backdrop to a footnote, it is because it is nowhere mentioned in any of the Syrian or French sources I have read on the minorities question. Nor do French sources on the treaty negotiations of 1933 and 1936 refer to the effects of the great depression in France. These telling lacunae should be borne in mind.
34. 'Le programme politique déclaré par le Haut Commissaire en Syrie et au Liban, *AF* 253 (Sep.–Oct. 1927), pp. 283–9, quote at 288.
35. '***', 'La situation actuelle des Tcherkesses en Syrie', *AF* 308 (Mar. 1933), pp. 94–5. This quote is from an editor's note at the head of the article.
36. As above, quote at 94. Note the common confusion between religious and ethno-linguistic factors: if the Circassians were demanding communal recognition as a minority it was by distinction from an Arab, not Muslim, 'majority'.
37. See Chapter 2.
38. '***', 'La situation actuelle des Tcherkesses en Syrie', *AF* 308 (Mar. 1933), pp. 94–5, quote at 94.
39. 'Le sort des minorités nationales en Irak', *AF* 311 (Jun. 1933), p. 210. *L'Asie française* later reproduced these 'wise recommendations' from the Commission's 1931 report: *AF* 313 (Sep.–Oct. 1933), pp. 268–71.
40. 'Le sort des minorités nationales en Irak', *AF* 311 (Jun. 1933), p. 210.
41. See Husry, 'The Assyrian Affair'; Zubaida, 'Contested nations'.
42. 'Les minorités nationales en Irak', *AF* 312 (Jul.–Aug. 1933), p. 257. It is worth noting here that prior to Iraqi independence, 'national minorities' had been rare in *L'Asie française*'s coverage of Syria and the wider Arab world: more common were arguments that the 'nationality principle' simply did not apply in the Arab countries.
43. 'Le traité franco-syrien', *AF* 314 (Nov. 1933), p. 328.
44. 'L'Irak et la question assyrienne', *AF* 315 (Dec. 1933), pp. 338–48, quote at 338.
45. E.g., on Iraq, 'La question des Assyro-Chaldéens', *AF* 327 (Feb. 1935), p. 27; 'La question chaldéo-assyrienne', *AF* 328 (Mar. 1935), p. 97; on Syria see below.
46. This and following quotes from 'Les Yézidis du Djebel Sindjar', *AF* 334 (Nov. 1935), p. 307.
47. 'Répression de la révolte des Yézidis', *AF* 335 (Dec. 1935), p. 341, quoting *La Syrie*, 27/11/1935.
48. 'Une nouvelle crise syrienne', *AF* 338 (Mar. 1936), pp. 74–8, quote at 78.
49. 'A la suite de l'accord du 1er mars', *AF* 339 (Apr. 1936), pp. 129–30, quote at 130.

50. 'La question des minorités', *AF* 339 (Apr. 1936), p. 130.
51. In its own right and as a point of comparison, the situation of Iraq's minorities continued to get coverage: e.g., 'Causes des révoltes des minorités nationales en Irak', *AF* 340 (May 1936), pp. 163–4; 'Le traité Franco-Syrien', *AF* 344 (Nov. 1936), pp. 281–92.
52. E.g., three articles all entitled 'Le traité franco-syrien sera-t-il modifié?': *AF* 354 (Nov. 1937), p. 289; *AF* 355 (Dec. 1937), pp. 320–1; *AF* 356 (Jan. 1938), p. 31.
53. This is noticeable from the start of the 1936 negotiations: 'La question des minorités', *AF* 339 (Apr. 1936), p. 130.
54. See, e.g., 'Le traité franco-syrien et les minorités chrétiennes de Syrie', *AF* 359 (Mar. 1938), pp. 94–5.
55. I use this barbarous neologism to distinguish a person seeking to enframe and mobilise a political constituency as a minority (a 'minoritarianist') from a member of a minority (a minoritarian). French officials in Syria used *minoritaire* in the latter sense, though usually when talking about people who might be described as the former.
56. The Arabic phrase, containing a grammatical error, is *'ma'a ba'd al-bunūd wal-rawābit lil-muhāfadhat al-aqalliyyāt ayy al-masīhiyyīn wal-yahūd'*. AD-SL Box 493, dossier *Traité Franco-Syrien. Minorités. Sous-dossiers.* Nouri to HC (7/8/1936). A French translation is included.
57. This and following quotes from AD-SL Box 493, dossier *Traité Franco-Syrien. Minorités. Sous-dossiers.* Letter from six Catholic archbishops to HC, 18/3/1936, forwarded under covering letter from Meyrier to MAE, 27/3/1936. (It is not clear whether this is a translation or if the original document was in French.)
58. This insistence on religion alone is interesting, in a letter from leaders of Catholic denominations using Greek, Syriac and Armenian as their church languages (some of them – especially the Armenians – likely using languages other than Arabic at home).
59. This and the following quote from AD-SL Box 620, dossier *Mouvement minoritaire Chrétien*, subdossier *La question des minorités en Syrie et en Irak (Généralités – correspondances, informations). Information N° 103* (21/12/1932). Giannini might be considered both an internal and external actor in Syrian politics: the representative of the Holy See, he could also claim with some authority to speak on behalf of the Catholic churches of Syria and Lebanon.
60. This and following quotes from AD-SL Box 572, untitled dossier (material released under sixty-year rule), subdossier *Les Kurdes en Syrie – Informations*. Unnumbered *Information* 'a/s Latif Ghanimé et la question des minorités' (17/10/1932).
61. In his brief memoir 'Syrie 1929, itinéraire d'un officier', in Anne-Marie Bianquis (ed.), *Damas. Miroir brisé d'un Orient arabe* (Paris: Autrement, 1993) pp. 95–104, Pierre Rondot reproduces (p. 100) his diary entry of an encounter with Ghanimé, whose forceful personality was evidently quite marked.
62. This and following quote from AD-SL Box 620, dossier *Mouvement minoritaire*

Chrétien, subdossier *La question des minorités en Syrie et en Irak (Généralités – correspondances – informations)*. Information No 1203, 18/3/1933.
63. The petition described by the Sûreté gives the same demands as those received by the High Commission, in the same order. It lists nine rather than ten demands because two items regarding education are conflated.
64. AD-SL Box 568, dossier *Tcherkess*, petition from Circassians in Qunaytra, Homs, Hama and Marj Sultan to High Commission for forwarding to League of Nations (1/4/1933). Although references to minorities, majorities and the treaty are clear in both, checking the original Arabic against the French translation reveals small but significant differences. The translation gives 'the Circassian population of Syria' for the original's 'the Syrian Circassian people [*al-shaʿb al-sharkasī al-sūrī*]' – a warmer assertion of Syrian identity?
65. The Kurds are discussed in Chapter 4. For the Ismaʿilis, see, e.g., contents of AD-SL Box 410, untitled dossier, subdossier *Requête de la communauté Ismailieh a/s sauvegardee [sic] de leurs droits*. Most of these documents are in French translation only; the Arabic originals that are present use the term *tā'ifa* to describe the community, but do refer to 'minority rights [*huqūq al-aqalliyyāt*]'.
66. This and following quotes from AD-SL Box 572, untitled dossier (material released under sixty-year rule), subdossier *Les Kurdes en Syrie – Informations*. Unnumbered *Information* 'a/s Latif Ghanimé et la question des minorités' (Beirut, 17/10/1932).
67. This document being a French report on Ghanimé's views – though clearly one based on discussions with him – the term 'extremist' may not be Ghanimé's own.
68. This explains the aberrant presence of this document in a box otherwise dedicated to the Kurds, in which few documents call them a 'minority': Ghanimé's proposal, although it mentions them only in passing, would recast them as such.
69. AD-SL Box 568, dossier *Tcherkess*, petition from Circassians in Qunaytra, Homs, Hama and Marj Sultan to High Commission (1/4/1933).
70. AD-SL Box 494, dossier *Traité Franco-Syrien – Application – Question des minorités*. Petition from Circassian village chiefs and members of 'councils of elders' addressed to HC via assistant delegate for muhafazas of Homs and Hama, 11/3/1936. A French translation is also enclosed.
71. Not, as far as I can tell, the same ones – though two Daghestanis head the list of signatures, and the earlier mazbata was supposed to be 'sponsored' in Homs by another. However, Daghestani is not a rare name among Circassians in Syria, many of whose families originated in Daghestan.
72. This and following quotes from AD-SL Box 494, dossier *Traité Franco-Syrien – Application – Question des minorités*. Statement to the League of Nations by Khaled Daghestani *et al.*, Homs, March 1938, included with letter to assistant delegate for Homs and Hama muhafazas. French translation (original not present) forwarded by HC to MAE (22/3/1938).
73. 'Le programme politique déclaré par le Haut Commissaire en Syrie et au Liban', *AF* 253 (Sep.–Oct. 1927), pp. 283–9, quotes at 287.

74. I do not know if his study became the Bloc's official policy, but it was at least carried out 'at the demand of Djémil Mardam Bey and with [Ibrahim] Hanano's knowledge'. My knowledge of it is from a High Commission document evidently drawn up after an interview with Rabbath himself: AD-SL Box 620, dossier *Mouvement minoritaire Chrétien*, subdossier *La question des minorités en Syrie et en Irak (Généralités – correspondances, informations). Information N° 101* (21/12/1932).

75. AD-SL Box 620, dossier *Mouvement minoritaire Chrétien*, subdossier *La question des minorités en Syrie et en Irak (Généralités – correspondances, informations). Information N° 101* (21/12/1932).

76. I have already pointed out in Chapter 3 that individuals could also use regionalism as a means of demanding – and getting – guaranteed access to state jobs.

77. This was not 'because' of those linguistic rights themselves, but because of the use to which nationalist Turks had successfully put them. The nationalist assumption that this was a natural expression of Turkish national feeling, whether stated overtly in nationalist historiography or implicitly reproduced by historians who do not question the categories of nationalism, elides the actual history of the process – notably the generational change in the 1930s – as well as the alternative outcomes that not only could have existed but did exist. Many 'Turks' in northern Syria became 'Arabs'. Subhi Bey Barakat, with his poor Arabic and strong Turkish accent, might not have been an Arab nationalist, but he seems to have been content to remain a Syrian politician, and not to become a Turkish one. Satiʿ al-Husri, one of the most influential ideologues of Arab nationalism, also spoke Arabic with a Turkish accent.

78. AD-SL Box 620, dossier *Mouvement minoritaire Chrétien*, subdossier *La question des minorités en Syrie et en Irak (Généralités – correspondances, informations). Information N° 101* (21/12/1932). These words are presented as direct quotes from Rabbath.

79. AD-SL Box 493, dossier *Traité Franco-Syrien. Minorités. Sous-dossiers.* Letter from six Catholic archbishops to HC (18/3/1936), forwarded under covering letter from Meyrier to MAE (27/3/1936).

80. See following note.

81. AD-SL Box 494, dossier *Traité Franco-Syrien – Application – Question des minorités*. Press clippings from *Le Jour* (Beirut): series of articles by Rabbath entitled 'Les problèmes du Traité Franco-Syrien: Les minorités', 6–10/3/1936.

82. As cited above.

83. AD-SL Box 568, untitled dossier (material declassified 1998), *Information No 2092* (15/6/1936). Such a display of loyalty should not, of course, be taken simply at face value.

84. This and following from AD-SL Box 493, dossier *Traité Franco-Syrien. Minorités. Sous-dossiers.* Letter from six Catholic archbishops to HC (18/3/1936), forwarded under covering letter from Meyrier to MAE (27/3/1936). As noted above, it is not clear whether this is a copy of a French original or a translation from Arabic – the

latter might explain the odd grammar of the sentence. NB: *al-Kutla al-Wataniyya* can be translated as both National and Nationalist Bloc. I have used the former; this source uses the latter.

85. AD-SL Box 620, dossier *Mouvement minoritaire Chrétien*, subdossier *La question des minorités en Syrie et en Irak (Généralités – correspondances, informations). Information N° 101 (21/12/1932)*.

CHAPTER

6

PERSONAL STATUS LAW REFORM

Introduction

In February 1939, a French attempt to reform personal status law in Syria provided an opportunity for Jamil Mardam Bek's discredited National Bloc government to leave office honourably after a succession of failures. A High Commissioner's decree on the issue dated back to March 1936, but had not been enacted. When a new decree, modifying but also resurrecting the original, was promulgated in November 1938, it provoked widespread opposition because it 'treated the Moslems as one sect among many, and thus struck at the root of the traditional Moslem conception of the State'.[1] As opposition grew over the next months, the Mardam Bek government was able to make the issue a point of honour: instructing the Syrian courts not to apply the new law; asserting the Syrian parliament's authority as sole legitimate source of legislation in Syria, and thereby denying the authority of the High Commission; and, when ordered to back down, resigning instead. This allowed Mardam Bek to regain some of the political legitimacy lost during the Bloc's years in government because of its failure – to name only the gravest issues – to get the treaty ratified by France, to prevent the gradual loss of the Sanjak of Alexandretta, and to impose its own authority on the newly incorporated regions of the Jabal Druze, the Alaouites and the Jazira. With little left to lose, Mardam Bek used the personal status reform issue to regain some of his political standing and resigned 'on a large wave of public enthusiasm'.[2]

This, roughly, is the account of personal status law reform given in existing political histories of the mandate. The issue is mentioned briefly insofar as it affects the historian's account of nationalist politics, but it is not discussed in or for itself.[3] Two studies omit to mention that having precipitated the fall of the Mardam government and its short-lived successor over the issue, the

French were eventually forced to suspend both reform decrees – at least for 'Muslims'.[4] Another does mention this suspension, but not its implications.[5] The relative lack of interest in the question of personal status law reform may be understandable in the context of political and diplomatic histories. But the issue deserves more attention than it has been given: its implications are far-reaching and profound.[6]

This chapter gives a detailed account of French attempts to enact legal reform in this area, their failure, and what the controversy reveals about much larger issues of state transformation. The first part explains the function of personal status law in general terms, showing how it raised questions going far beyond the merely personal. The rest of the chapter approaches the issue from three different angles. First, it outlines French attempts to reform personal status law in Syria during the mandate – attempts which failed in the mid-1920s and the later 1930s, in each case leading the High Commission to decide (for the time being) that the question should be left to the legislation of local governments. It also identifies the moment at which the question of personal status began to be understood as part of the question of minorities. Next, it turns to the Syrian communities affected by the reform, whether because they were defined as 'personal status communities' or because they were not, and places those effects in the wider context of the development the nation-state. Rather than involving 'minorities' from the outset, this was one of the areas where the changing nature of the state (and of its relationship with the population) made the concept of minority meaningful. Finally, the chapter considers opposition to the reform among Sunni Muslim 'ulama', and shows how minority's paired concept, majority, fitted into that opposition. The controversy illustrates the process by which both of these categories became meaningful, but at the same time it highlights the dangers of taking them as objective categories for analysis.

Questions of Personal Status

The mandatory authorities had inherited from the Ottoman Empire what they considered to be a confusing mixture of legal jurisdictions, despite the considerable reforms of the late Ottoman era (reforms for which French writers gave the Ottomans little credit).[7] The first confusion was the unclear distinction between the jurisdiction of common law – derived from Islamic legal principles but exercised by civil courts – and the jurisdiction of the shariah courts, which had the force of state law in matters of personal status. The second confusion arose from the state's official recognition of multiple non-Muslim communities: these had their own communal authorities which, for their own members, also had jurisdiction in personal status matters.[8]

The relationship between these different jurisdictions was not clear.

Religious authorities responsible for personal status carried out all sorts of acts relevant to civil law, such as recording births on the civil register. When personal status cases involved members of different communities there was competition – sometimes bitter – over which legal authority was competent to try them. Christian leaders felt that they were at a permanent disadvantage to Muslims in this respect, since the general rule was that if a Muslim was involved then the case was heard by the shariah courts, while cases tried under common law were *de facto* under Muslim law. Even more galling to non-Muslim religious authorities was when members of their own communities preferred to use the shariah or civil courts in matters the communal authorities were competent to try. Frequently, it was not so much that non-Sunni communal authorities wanted to assert their own jurisdiction in order to apply different laws and reach different verdicts than the shariah or civil courts, as that they wanted the right to reach the same verdicts for themselves.[9] I say 'communal authorities' rather than 'communities' because there is no reason to assume that lay Jews or Christians, for example, shared the enthusiasm of bishops and rabbis for new legislation that would increase the religious authorities' power over ordinary members of each community. At one point in the reform debate, for example, a French official noted that while rabbis were keen to expand the authority of rabbinical courts over the Jewish community and limit as far as possible the range of cases that Jews could bring under other jurisdictions (shariah or civil courts), ordinary Jews were no more keen on being subjected to rabbinical jurisdiction than to the jurisdiction of the shariah courts. General feeling in this community favoured a 'maximal' civil law.[10]

Legal recognition from the state as a personal status community, meanwhile, was not uniform; some had greater privileges than others. Another issue was that the Ottoman state had not recognised divisions within Islam, so what the French called dissident and heretical Muslim communities had no communal autonomy in the matter of personal status – at least, not in theory. In practice, one such community, the Druzes, did (exceptionally) have a degree of official recognition in the form of Ottoman *berats* and *firmans*, while unofficial recognition was extended to communities such as 'Alawis, Isma'ilis, and Yazidis.[11]

Underlying these many confusions was a greater one: what exactly was personal? Ostensibly, personal status law is just that: law governing the personal status of the individual – marriage and divorce, testament and inheritance, guardianship, religious belonging. In recognised personal status communities (in French, *communautés à statut personnel*), the community's own religious authorities had jurisdiction over their own members in these matters. Certain specified legal powers – not necessarily the same ones in each case – thereby devolved from the state to the communal authorities: a marriage celebrated by a Greek Orthodox priest would be recognised by the state as legitimate; a child's birth to Jewish parents could be recorded on the civil register by a rabbi.

And where communal law differed from shariah law or civil law, it could be applied to members of the community with the force of state law. Thus, one effect of the official recognition granted to the Druzes was that a Druze couple could bequeath most of their estate to one son rather than distributing it among all their inheritors in the proportion that common law, following the shariah, defined – though, as we shall see, the lucky son's sisters might contest the will, and the principle.

Personal status communities were differentiated from other communities which, despite distinct religious beliefs, were not recognised as having their own personal status. Where communities of the latter sort had a sufficiently coherent communal existence, the French referred to them as common-law communities (*communautés de droit commun*), but they lacked the privileges of personal status communities: this applied mostly to Muslim communities other than Sunnis, but not exclusively to them. Among Christian communities during the mandate era, Protestants at one point found themselves reduced (as they argued) to this status; it also applied to a schismatic church founded by the Greek Orthodox Bishop of Latakia, Epiphanios, over a disciplinary dispute with the Patriarch.[12] I will discuss the disadvantages faced by common law communities relative to personal status communities in more detail below; to understand the difference between them it might be useful to consider the advantages accorded by states to official marriages (whether civil or religious) in comparison with the status of common law unions. Sunni Muslims, meanwhile, were not constituted as a personal status community because Syrian common law was based on Sunni interpretations of the shariah: Sunnis did not need a distinct personal status regime. This situation was viewed as increasingly anomalous by the High Commission, however:

> the Muslim community in general complains of having lost, since the occupation, and without compensation, the major part of its privileges. Above all it complains of being subjected to a regime of exception, which places it in a state of manifest inferiority vis-à-vis the other communities.[13]

The High Commission took the view that 'the laicisation of the States, and the transformation of the principle of sovereignty', had left the Muslim community – alone among Syria's religious communities – without a legal personality or 'proper organization'.

Because personal status was governed by religious law, the religion to which the individual belonged was also considered a matter for personal status law: conversion was one of the most controversial aspects of the topic. Personal status law also covered the possessions of the personal status communities – not the private possessions of their members (whose sale and purchase, if not inheritance, would be regulated by common law), but the possessions of the religious community itself. In the case of a Christian Church this might include church buildings and cemeteries, but also communal schools or other real estate, not to mention their contents.[14] In this and other areas, personal status usually also defined certain privileges for members of those hierarchies: patriarchs might not pay customs duties on luxuries imported for church use, for example; but also, senior clerics might have the right not to appear in court in person.[15] This was an important and controversial point of variance between the different personal status communities, since the privileges accorded to each by precedent differed – one of the many areas where the French hoped to bring a new uniformity to the law. Lastly, personal status law was also meant to decide where any legal disputes involving such matters would be heard: another important point, especially when the dispute involved members of more than one community, since it effectively placed the jurisdictions in a hierarchy.

Two things should be apparent from this brief discussion. First, the area of personal status law constituted a virtually unbounded field for legal (and political) argument, especially as the limits of the 'personal' were – like any such legal constructs – debatable. If such substantial concerns as education or (much of) property law were placed under the purview of personal status law, and therefore of the communal authorities, the state would be little more than the guarantor of those authorities: its own direct interaction with the population would be much reduced. One French official felt that a draft communal statute for the Catholic communities, presented by the Apostolic Delegate in Syria and Lebanon, set the bounds of Catholic personal status so far to the advantage of the Church, and correspondingly to the disadvantage of the state, that the latter would be transformed – at least, where Syria's Catholics were concerned – into the 'secular arm [*bras séculier*]'of the Church.[16] This leads on to the second point: that in Syria, personal status law was an important structuring element of the institutional relationship between population and state. French attempts to reform the law wholesale therefore implied major changes to that relationship.

French Attempts to Reform Personal Status Law: Aims, Stakes, Results

On 1 April 1939, the High Commissioner Gabriel Puaux wearily informed a colleague in Iraq that the question of personal status law reform in Syria '[had] been under study at the High Commission for long years'.[17] The previous day he had definitively abandoned the most recent attempt in the face of violent unrest and governmental crisis in Damascus. This section gives a chronological overview of French reform efforts, and examines French motivations in the light of the broader development of the nation-state form in Syria. A detailed discussion of what the question meant to Syrians is left to the following sections.

Puaux's predecessors had indeed been studying the question for years. Requests for legal reform in this area had been coming from religious leaders themselves 'since the military occupation'.[18] The early High Commissioners took the view that:

> One of the missions anticipated by the mandate that has been confided to FRANCE concerns the reorganisation of [the system of] justice ...
>
> The absence of unity in the administration of justice and the unfortunately rather arbitrary character of that justice had already, long before the war, been the object of complaints from all fractions of the population, Muslims as much as Christians.[19]

That is, they considered it necessary to overcome the confusions and inconsistencies outlined above. This note pointed out that in Turkey, the distinction between shariah courts and civil courts had been overcome by the simple abolition of the former: 'one of the most striking acts of the Ottoman [sic] Republic'.[20] The French in Syria, similarly, wanted to limit the jurisdiction of the religious courts, especially the shariah courts. The High Commission's early studies of the question concluded that:

> it was necessary to reduce the jurisdiction of the Cadi [*al-qāḍī*, the shariah court judge] to just proportions – which is to say, to leave to him only certain matters closely pertaining to religious law [*tenant de très près au droit religieux*], like marriage, other matters that were formerly part of Personal Status being confided to the jurisdiction of the common law courts ...[21]

Limiting the authority of the shariah courts, one of the most powerful social institutions in Syria – a vast tree rooted in the Sunni Muslim population, but either sheltering or (depending on one's point of view) overshadowing the whole of society – would have obvious political benefits for France, especially as the civil courts would 'also receive the guarantee of the presence of one or two French magistrates'. But abolishing them completely, feasible for an indigenous nationalist government in Turkey that had just fought a successful war for independence (and whose secularising aims were not yet widely understood), was much more problematic in mandate Syria, where France was a foreign occupier viewed as illegitimate by much of the population.

The situation was also different in Turkey in that the near elimination of the Christian population of Anatolia in the decade 1914–24 meant that the existence of multiple personal status jurisdictions posed little practical obstacle to a secularising nationalist government intent on imposing uniform state authority. In Syria, by contrast, the Christian population remained proportionately much larger, and its diverse communal authorities were determined to maintain their legal privileges – partly, no doubt, because events in Anatolia had convinced them more than ever of the need for solid legal defences against the 'Muslim' state. Under French rule there was also more scope – and more incentive – for Muslim but non-Sunni groups to mobilise as distinct political communities. The French preference for standardisation and desacralisation of the legal system was thus offset by a tacit understanding that maintaining and, in some senses, extending the legal autonomy of religious communities might be politically useful for France. First, it would at least partially satisfy the lobbying of the church hierarchies – a key political client – which tended towards the maximum possible extension of that autonomy (though different patriarchs had different conceptions of what was possible). Second, it would reinforce the authority of the church hierarchies relative to both the Syrian state and the Christian population. Similar effects would be created in the Muslim 'dissident sects', though here the margin for action was reduced by the absence of legal precedents justifying communal autonomy.

Such were the concerns of the mandatory authorities in the early 1920s. But although the question was studied, new legislation was slow to emerge. A High Commissioner's decree was prepared under General Weygand, which

> brought about jurisdictional equality by reducing the competence of the confessional tribunals, including the Shariah tribunals, to cases relative to the matrimonial statute while still leaving them a right of voluntary jurisdiction [*droit de juridiction gracieuse*] in matters of succession and testament.[22]

Since the shariah courts had a wider range of competence than other religious jurisdictions, this measure would have involved a proportionally greater reduction of their authority. But the project 'satisfied no-one [and] was rejected unanimously by the representatives of the communities'; when Weygand was replaced at the end of 1924 it was shelved. His successor, General Sarrail, revisited the question but was also recalled before a decree could be promulgated.

The first actual legislation came in 1926, with the civilian High Commissioner Henry de Jouvenel. He promulgated a decree – Decree 261/ LR of 28 April 1926, to come into effect on 1 June – giving the civil courts competence over all personal status matters previously heard by communal courts except a very limited range pertaining directly to marriage and divorce. Since the civil court officials had pointed out the difficulty they would have 'in applying laws and usages which were nowhere codified'[23] in the matters newly transferred to their jurisdiction, it was to be supplemented by the codification of the existing canon laws and the institution of a civil personal status legislation, including a civil marriage regime.[24]

However, this decree fell victim to the combination of local opposition and the rapid turnover of High Commissioners in the early years of the mandate. Everywhere outside the Alaouites the decree provoked such protests that the High Commission decided to 'leave to the States [that is, the local governments] the care of assessing whether the new legislation should be put into effect immediately or, on the contrary, deferred'.[25] The political vocabulary of a later era would describe this solution as a 'fudge'. Jouvenel having returned to France to seek election to the Senate, the decree was simply suspended – initially until the end of October 1926, but then, it seems, indefinitely. A document written in Paris in the middle of that month ringingly asserted that 'no important reason can now prevent the reform from being executed' and argued that 'this initiative indisputably falls to the High Commission' – not the local governments – since it affected all the states under French mandate. But Jouvenel's successor, Henri Ponsot, evidently took a different view.[26] During Ponsot's seven years in Beirut – as long as his four predecessors combined – the High Commission continued to study the subject, but no further action was taken.[27] 'Having considered until 1926 that the accomplishment of this reform was a mandate task [œuvre de mandat]', another official later wrote of this period, 'we seem to have decided since this time to leave to the States the care of legislating in this matter.'[28] It was not until after the arrival as High Commissioner of Count Damien de Martel, in 1933, that the earlier line reappeared.

Martel believed that 'the settlement of this important question is a mandate obligation'.[29]

> This reform having a general character must be applied to all the confessional minorities, including the Shi'ites, the Druzes, the 'Alawis and the Isma'ilis. Moreover, it must permit every community to obtain its legal recognition, under conditions to be determined, and every individual to withdraw from confessional law in matters relative to his Personal Status.

Two points deserve to be drawn out here. First is the introduction into this debate of the language of minorities, hitherto absent. Documents in the High Commission archives on this subject dating from the later 1920s much prefer the term 'communities'. It was only in the 1930s that the term 'minority' was also attached to existing or prospective personal status communities, both by the French and by Syrians claiming to speak for those communities. This emphasises the point made in the previous chapter, that it was only as the prospect of a Franco-Syrian treaty and Syrian independence arose that the term really took root in Syria. Indeed, in the debate on personal status law, 'minority' crops up most often in documents that address the vexed question of whether that law should be the object of an externally guaranteed treaty obligation.[30] But 'community' remained by far the preferred term in this context, perhaps partly because the set expression 'personal status community' was so well established. (I have nowhere encountered the term 'personal status minority'.) If it was hard for the French to discuss a treaty without talking about minorities, the same was not true of personal status law. This highlights the dangers of assuming that personal status law was a minority issue, or that personal status communities can unproblematically be described as minorities.

The second point to underline is the forthright restatement of a secularising intent. The legal competence of religious communities in personal status matters was to be set out in any reform, but so too was the right of any individual to have his (or her) personal status dealt with in the civil courts rather than the personal status courts of the community to which he or she 'belonged'. However useful the legal segregation of Syrians by religion might have been to French imperialism, a more fundamental aim was to assert the place of the state as the arbiter of religious authority, rather than religion as the arbiter of state authority – the state in question being the Syrian state, not the mandatory authorities that oversaw it.[31] Although the High Commissioner's note concluded that a Turkish-style secularisation of the law – outright abolition of religious courts, and the establishment of an exclusively civil law of personal status – was impracticable in the mandate territories, it set out a crucial principle for the 'amelioration, consolidation and regulation of the existing system':

> in the last instance, in the fixing of relations between the States and the Churches, the supremacy of the civil powers must be admitted as a fundamental rule; in this aim, any provisions of the communal laws liable to harm [that supremacy] must be prohibited [on devra admettre comme règle fondamentale, la suprématie du pouvoir civil et dans ce but, interdire toutes dispositions des règlements communaux de nature à y porter atteinte].[32]

Christian patriarchs would prove willing to accept this bargain as being less disadvantageous to them than that offered by a 'Muslim' state, especially as it would reinforce their own political authority. Muslim 'ulama', however, would reject it.

This concern to establish state authority over religion echoes the Turkish case, but is observable in modern states at large. Two examples might be Tunisia or Italy. In Tunisia, under French protectorate, religious marriage had been brought within the ambit of the state by granting religious ministers the status of officers of the civil register – combining religious and civil functions under state authority. Italy passed a law on the same subject in 1929: it did not grant civil powers to religious ministers, but rather insisted that religious marriages submit to state authority. Among its provisions were that 'the nomination of ministers of religion must be submitted to the Ministry of Justice for approval', and that ministers officiating at a marriage must read Articles 130, 131 and 132 of the Italian civil code to the bride and groom and receive their 'express declaration ... that they intend to take each other respectively for husband and wife, observing the dispositions of article 95 of the civil code'. These two examples are not chosen at random: the French Ministry of

Foreign Affairs, discussing Martel's proposals for reform, cited them as possible examples for similar legislation in Syria.[33] For modern states the world over, 'husband and wife in the eyes of God' is all very well, but God must duly genuflect to the state. If French officials wanted to introduce legislation to this effect in Syria it may have been less out of a specific desire to reduce Islam to the status of 'one sect among many' than because this was simply how they felt a modern state should act – which is not to say that any consequent reduction of the institutional power of Muslim religious authorities would have been unwelcome to them.

Tunisia and Italy were not the only countries to which the mandatory authorities turned to gather information on existing legislation and legal practice. They sought information from the neighbouring states under British mandate, other countries in the region, and further afield. I encountered references to more than a dozen countries, from Palestine to the Dutch East Indies, Egypt to France,[34] not to mention the single most important reference point: the Ottoman Empire. Such references could be brief, as in the claim that a draft reform had borrowed from earlier legislation (much of it specified by title or name of drafter) in the Ottoman Empire, Egypt, France, the Dutch East Indies, Algeria, 'the Indies' and Russian Turkestan.[35] Just as often, though, they were rather detailed. The Contrôle des Wakfs reached the conclusion that outright secularisation would not succeed in Syria and Lebanon after a comparison of reforms in Turkey, Palestine, Iraq, Egypt and Persia.[36] In specific cases foreign legislation could be cited at length (as with Italy, above), or the legal practice of other countries studied in detail. French officials used the example of Palestine to decide how Russian refugees in Syria – some stateless since the civil war, some still holding Russian nationality – should fit into Syrian personal status law.[37] They also took note of British practices relating to the election of Christian patriarchs.[38]

With these concerns in mind the High Commission under Martel patiently prepared new legislation, discussed over months and years with local religious authorities (especially the Christian patriarchs), the Syrian government, and the ministry in Paris. Given the great care that the French took in drawing up the reform legislation, it may seem surprising that it failed so completely.

Martel's first decree on the subject was Decree 60/LR of 13 March 1936, 'fixing the status of the religious communities'.[39] The timing was important: the decree, in preparation for well over a year, was finally issued just after France reluctantly agreed to negotiate a treaty with a nationalist delegation, but before the delegation's departure for Paris. This reflects a concern of the High Commission that went back to Ponsot's attempts to negotiate a treaty in 1933:

> if the Syrian constitution clearly states the [comporte bien l'exposé des] permanent guarantees of public law conferred on individuals and communities, the status of the

communities itself and the personal status of minoritarians belonging to the different confessions is not defined by any organic text. These texts, of secondary interest for as long as the mandate lasts, would become crucially important under the Treaty regime. They must necessarily be drawn up before the Treaty comes into effect.[40]

If the treaty were to include guarantees for minorities, the High Commission felt, there had to be legislation in place for France to guarantee: considering the *communautés à statut personnel* as minorities would allow personal status law, once it was settled, to fill that role. Ponsot had believed that because of 'the difficulty and complexity of the definitions to come [*à intervenir*] in these matters' it was unrealistic to make France's signing a treaty conditional on the establishment of such legislation: that is, he was guided by his sense that personal status reform was, for political reasons, best left to the local governments. He therefore proposed that the treaty include an annexe obliging the Syrian government to draw up and enact its own personal status legislation in the four-year transitional period between the treaty's signature and Syrian independence. As we have seen, however, his successor Martel believed that the reform was a task for the mandatory. He was motivated by the same concern to get personal status legislation onto the statute books before a treaty came into effect, but decided to do it by High Commissioner's decree before the treaty was even negotiated, let alone signed.

Decree 60/LR set out to fix the status of the religious communities, and the choice of verb is important.[41] The decree certainly did, for what it is worth, consider Sunni Muslims as one religious community among others.[42] But here it is more important to note the 'regularising' intent of this decree, and its assertion of the state's authority over religion. By the terms of this decree, the state sought to fix religious communities in several ways. First, in a regular relationship to the state, as either personal status or common law communities,[43] all communities within each of these categories having the same status vis-à-vis the state as the others. Second, the decree also fixed the internal structure of each recognised community: although each community was to produce its own statute of personal status, also outlining communal organisation, the state would approve it (Article 4). Once approved, it would have the force of law for members of that community, falling 'under the protection of the law and the control of the public powers' (Article 2): it could be changed only by a legislative act of the state (Article 6). Communities could no longer evolve according to their own internal dynamics, but must do so by reference to – and permission of – the state. The same would go for individuals, who would be permitted to change community but must declare this to the state (Article 11).

Authority within the communities was also established relative to (and by devolution from) the state: the decree stipulated that communities and autonomous groupings within them would be represented by their religious leader in financial and legal matters, for example (Article 8), and 'in their relations with the public powers by their highest religious leader' (Article 9). Whereas authority within the Ottoman millets had, owing to developments internal to them, become increasingly secularised since the mid-nineteenth century or earlier,[44] clerical authority was now reasserted from the outside, by the state. Even common-law communities, with their much more limited rights and privileges, would be subject to many of the same obligations towards the state: a communal statute must be approved by government authority, and then it too could be changed only by legislative act of the state (Article 16); the state must be notified of the nomination of ministers of religion wishing to celebrate marriage (Article 18); since the ministers of common-law communities were not themselves empowered to record marriages officially, the marriages they celebrated must be authorised and recorded by an 'agent of the civil register' (Articles 19–21).[45] And the status granted by the state, whether that of personal status community or common-law community, could also be revoked by the state (Article 23). All in all, the text of this decree attempted a vast extension of the state's formal authority over religion – and through it over whole sectors of Syrian social life. This was especially the case because Sunni Islam was treated as one such community, to be defined according to norms set by the state, rather than as the true religion that set the norms that the state must implement.

It was not only the opposition of Sunni Muslim clerics that made Decree 60 a dead letter when it was first promulgated, however. Religious figures from other communities also found much to object to, and the Syrian government privately warned the High Commission that it would be unable to put the decree into effect.[46] There was also disagreement over how, exactly, each communal statute was to be drawn up: who were the legitimate authorities, and on what would they base their text? The High Commission received no less than three competing draft statutes from different groups within the Lebanese Druze community alone.[47] The archives suggest that the church hierarchies maintained a monopoly over the drafting of statutes for the different Christian communities, but it is safer to take this as evidence that the High Commission accepted their authority than as proof that all Christians did.

These are some of the reasons why Decree 60 remained unimplemented. When Martel invited the religious communities to comment on the text of the decree, and set up a Franco-Syrian commission to study their remarks,[48] it seems to have been taken as a virtual abrogation by religious leaders. None held back from suggesting revisions. One Christian clergyman's comments referred to the decree as a 'draft [*avant-projet*]', as though a decree already promulgated by the High Commission were merely a planning document – a salutary reminder that when the state sets out to impose its authority over other institutions within society, they can offer effective resistance.[49]

In the meantime, the political situation in Syria changed dramatically with the signature of the treaty and the election of a nationalist government.

Between this and the succession of crises that quickly soured the elation of late 1936, the question of personal status reform was eclipsed for a while. But the commission continued its work, and in secret negotiations with the High Commissioner in February 1938 the nationalist prime minister Jamil Mardam Bek agreed to the text of a new decree; his justice minister ʿAbd al-Rahman al-Kayyali also accepted its terms.[50] The decree was not issued until the following November, however, after further guarantees had been extracted in Paris from Mardam Bek – among them a promise to respect Christian personal status.[51] With the issuing of Decree 146/LR of 18 November 1938, 'modifying and completing decree N° 60/LR',[52] we rejoin the political narrative of the end of the National Bloc government.

The first four of Decree 146's six articles each abrogated and replaced individual articles of the earlier decree. These modifications introduced the possibility, for Syrian or Lebanese nationals, of not belonging to any recognised community for personal status matters, in which case civil law would apply (Article 1, revising Article 10 of Decree 60); ensured that in case of death or separation ending a marriage the children would always follow the father's community, even if the mother had care of the children (Article 2, revising Article 12); and stipulated that in case of collective secession from a community, the seceding group could take its property with it – except waqf properties ('*biens dédiés*') (Article 3, revising Article 13). Since these would include much of a community's immovable property, this small qualification would make it considerably harder for any group secession to take place, thus 'fixing' the community even more. The new decree also abrogated the earlier article granting a halfway status of Protestants in Lebanon (Article 4, revising Article 22). Article 5, meanwhile, replaced – and expanded – the entire third section of the original decree, with three articles of 'general provisions [*dispositions générales*]' being replaced by eight.[53] It included an article adding the Protestant community of the mandate territories as a whole to the list of fully recognised communities (new Article 28). It also removed the state's right to revoke a community's recognition as a personal status community, as included in the original Article 23 – the biggest single surrender of state authority in the modifications.

The other revisions mostly applied to marriage and conversion; the most important for our purposes are the new Articles 25 and 27. The former recognised marriages contracted abroad by Syrian and Lebanese nationals, whether with another Syrian or Lebanese national or with a foreigner, provided that such a marriage followed the legal forms in the country where it took place. It also stated that if those forms were contrary to the provisions of either spouse's personal status regime in the mandate territories, then the marriage would there be considered subject to civil personal status law. This is significant, as it raised the possibility of Syrians and Lebanese of different communities escaping religious jurisdiction by going abroad to marry. As the 'ulama' would forcefully observe, the marriage of a Muslim woman to a non-Muslim man could thereby become legitimate under Syrian state law. The new Article 27, meanwhile, set up a higher jurisdiction to rule in cases of conflict between personal status jurisdictions or between them and the civil courts. It would also decide if the judgements of personal status jurisdictions passed over to the state for execution had 'been rendered competently and must be executed'; rule on contraventions and infractions of personal status law; and give an authoritative opinion on the interpretation and application of Decrees 60 and 146 to the Syrian and Lebanese governments and to community leaders. Notwithstanding a paragraph stipulating that in cases regarding conflict or competence, the jurisdiction would include 'alongside the President and members composing it' a representative named by the head of each community concerned, this article maintained the ultimate authority of the state over religious jurisdictions – as the 'ulama' would also point out.

Signing Decree 146 was one of Martel's last acts before retiring as High Commissioner. He was replaced by Gabriel Puaux, who arrived in Syria at the beginning of January 1939. According to Puaux, opposition to Decree 146 was muted until February:

> It was only at the beginning of that month that the Nationalist Bloc, desirous of creating difficulties for the mandatory power, and of setting its agitation on a religious base in the Muslim world, provoked a petition from a group of Uléma.[54]

The 'petition' in question was actually a letter, sent to the Syrian interior ministry by the president of the recently founded Damascus Association of 'Ulama' (*Jam'iyyat al-'ulamā' bi-Dimashq*), Shaykh Kamil al-Qassab. Reserving judgement for now on Puaux's assessment of its origins, it is enough to note here that the opposition triggered by this letter quickly spiralled beyond the French capacity to control it – certainly beyond the capacity of the Syrian government to control it. Hence Mardam Bek's decision to ride the opposition instead, making a stand against a legal text he had himself accepted. The Bloc government responded to al-Qassab's letter by instructing the courts not to apply the revised decree since it was 'not drawn up by the Syrian parliament, unique source of legislation in the country'.[55]

This qualification should be noted, for two reasons. First, it raised the stakes by directly challenging French authority in the country; and second, even if the Bloc was now running to keep up with the religious opposition, by extension it nonetheless attempted to assert parliament's authority over the 'ulama'. While this may have been an empty gesture at the time on both counts, it is worth noting that the attempt to assert the civil state's authority over religion did not only come from the French: nationalist politicians could try to do the same even while trying to capitalise on, and channel, religious opposition to a French reform. On the same day – 13 February 1939 – the Syrian Ministry of Justice set up a commission to study the reform decrees, consisting of Mustafa Barmada and Yusuf al-Hakim (respectively president and counsellor of the High Court of Cassation) and the acting Mufti-General Shukri al-Ustuwani.[56]

Contrary to Puaux's claim that the Bloc had stirred up religious feeling to its own ends, the *Jamʿiyyat al-ʿulama'* had issued its declaration not only in opposition to the French for having issued the text, but to the Bloc for having agreed to it. Ordering the courts not to apply the decree, and setting up a commission to study it, allowed the Bloc to regain the political initiative. The measures temporarily succeeded in this aim – a delegation of Damascene nationalist merchants came to thank Mardam Bek the next day, when the press published the news[57] – but exacerbated the situation beyond the Bloc's ability to control it; which may have been the intention. Puaux, faced with an unacceptable challenge to French authority, responded by ordering his delegate in Damascus to demand the withdrawal of the Syrian government's memo to the courts. He also published a communiqué in the Syrian press which noted that Decree 146 had been drawn up 'in agreement with the Syrian government and taking into account the observations presented by the religious communities, and notably the Uléma, following the promulgation of decree 60'.[58]

The communiqué emphasised that 'only a decree of the High Commissioner can annul or suspend the execution of a decree emanating from that same authority'. Alongside this robust-sounding assertion of French authority, however, Puaux also invited the religious communities to present 'the new objections they believed they should formulate'. Over the next weeks, as Mardam Bek's government fell, its short-lived successor came and went, and unrest spread across Syria, Puaux set up a commission of his own to study Syrian objections[59] – and accepted that 'while waiting for this commission to finish its work, the decree would not in practice be applied to the Sunni community'.[60] He also brought his oratorical skills to a calming radio broadcast to the Syrian people.[61] But in the meantime, angry demonstrations continued on the streets of towns and villages across Syria: in Damascus they exceeded the abilities of the police or gendarmes to maintain order, and French troops were called out on 20 March. With no government able to replace the Bloc, the French delegate in Damascus implemented direct rule. In the meantime, the Syrian government's commission on the question had undergone a change in personnel: Shukri al-Ustuwani had been replaced, due to ill-health, by ʿAbd al-Muhsin al-Ustuwani – and Kamil al-Qassab had been appointed as a fourth member. By a majority of three to one it issued a statement comprehensively rejecting Decrees 146 and 60 on religious grounds; Yusuf al-Hakim was left to write a minority report arguing for them to be accepted.[62] Faced with a legal opinion so evidently in line with popular feeling against the reform, the French commission in its turn observed that the objections made in the name of Islamic law bore on such a large number of article [*sic*] that, to take them into account, a general rewriting of the legislation would be necessary. Moreover, these objections could not be taken into account as they are presented without leading to solutions irreconcilable with the rights and interests of the other communities.[63]

Puaux therefore accepted that he was cornered, and on 30 March issued a new decree stating that Decrees 60 and 146 'are and remain without application as regards the Muslims'.[64] His earlier, temporary suspension of the reforms had only specified Sunni Muslims. The use of the vaguer term 'Muslims' in the permanent suspension had important implications; so did the maintenance of the reforms for Christians and Jews.

When Puaux notified the Quai d'Orsay of his intention to suspend the reform decrees, his superiors asked if this measure could not be 'put off until later'.[65] Only after he had issued his suspension did Puaux reply that his staff had judged it 'impossible to defer any longer an impatiently-awaited measure. The adjournment would have been exploited against us, and the repression of a movement of a religious character would have been perillous.'[66] The ministry evidently did not realise quite how serious the situation in Syria had become, or the extent to which – in Puaux's opinion – the French had brought it on themselves:

> I remind you that already, in 1926, a decree on personal status could not be implemented. The new experiment that has just been tried demonstrates the impossibility for the mandatory power of legislating in matters that directly touch on a religious legislation – which she is, besides, bound to respect by the very terms of the mandate. The only way to assure freedom of conscience in practice would be the institution of a civil status by the Syrian state.

In other words, Puaux was renouncing the task of reforming personal status law in Syria. Once again, an attempt to make it a 'mandate task' had failed; once again, a new High Commissioner accepted that this was a job for the local states. At the end of the period covered by this book, that was where the matter stood. Although they remained operative for non-Muslims, at least on paper, the reforms had been thwarted. But as we shall see, their story – both the attempt to enact them, and the opposition they provoked – illustrates how the development of the nation-state form in Syria made the categories of minority and majority increasingly meaningful.

Personal Status Law Reform and the Minorities

In Chapter 4, I showed how the establishment of fixed borders, of the sort that define modern nation-states, has the effect of fixing certain communities into a nation-state structure where they are a minority. Since the nation-states that replaced the Ottoman Empire, like those that replaced the other European dynastic empires, were each dominated by one particular 'national' community, this effect was even felt by communities that were wholly or mostly concentrated within one new state – communities that had previously been one community among many others, large and small, in a polity that was not dominated by any single 'national' group. The question of personal status law reform offers more examples of the same phenomenon at work, because the legal institutions involved were now national institutions: they stopped at the newly defined borders, and they were increasingly defined by norms set by the largest community – on the grounds, precisely, that it was the largest. Here, though, the lines of definition were religious rather than ethnolinguistic. Communities redefined by personal status legislation were cut off from their members outside the new borders; they had to relate to the local state as a community limited by the state's own borders. Within those borders, personal status legislation imposed a new uniformity on the relationship all members of any given community had with the state – part of the expansion and intensification of the state's intervention in the lives of the population, as the preparation and enactment of this reform demonstrate.

While nation-states may recognise the spiritual authority of an external figure over a part of their own population, they explicitly deny the temporal authority of such figures. This applies to the religion of both majority and minorities: the national church must be national first, and even other churches must establish their national credentials. This was the model that the mandatory powers sought to apply in the post-Ottoman Levant. In Palestine, as French officials in Syria noted, Britain asserted new 'national' rules for the selection of a new Armenian Orthodox Patriarch of Jerusalem. Previously, this patriarch had been nominated by the Ottoman Sultan from a list drawn up by a gathering of senior clerics from 'all the territories ... belonging to the Ottoman Empire'. But during the mandate, the British authorities insisted that the patriarch must be nominated (by King George V of England, *in loco sultani*) from a list drawn up by senior Armenian Orthodox clerics from within the borders of mandate Palestine only. Moreover, he must himself belong to the Armenian Orthodox community of Palestine – that is, he must be a Palestinian national.[67]

A similar concern to 'nationalise' religious authority is evident in French mandate Syria. Article 9 of Decree 60, which appointed each community's 'highest religious chief' as its representative 'in their relations with the public powers', also stipulated that in any community where the relevant spiritual authority resided outside the French mandate territories, in this quasi-temporal dimension of his authority he must 'delegate his powers to a local representative'.[68] In this case, the careful wording – resident outside the French mandate territories (*hors des territoires des États du Levant sous mandat français*)

– allowed the Christians of Syria to be represented by a patriarch resident in Lebanon. The patriarchs could thus serve as a channel for political authority between the High Commission and Christian Syrians, bypassing the intermediary of the Syrian government: an arrangement that was to the mutual advantage of the High Commission and the patriarchs, if not of ordinary Christian Syrians. We see here the tension between French attempts to 'nationalise' religion in Syria (as part of the mandatory's state-building project) and the French concern to undermine the development of national, and especially nationalist, politics in the country. But as the development of the Syrian state's national institutions gathered momentum, it proved impossible to justify the attribution of temporal authority over Syrian communities to religious authorities resident over the border in Lebanon. The logic of state development made it impossible for the French to have their cake and eat it, as the example of the Druze community demonstrates.

Earlier, I mentioned that the Druzes, uniquely among the 'dissident' or 'heretical' Muslim communities of the Levant, had enjoyed a degree of formal recognition in the late Ottoman Empire that allowed them to maintain a distinct personal status regime, notably with regard to inheritance and succession: Druze parents could leave most of their estate to one child rather than following the strict proportions set down in both Islamic law and Syrian civil law. One such case was that of Husayn and Asma Kanafani, of the village of Jaramana outside Damascus, who left all their immovable property to their son Fakhri – half directly, half in the form of an endowment to his and his descendants' benefit. Fakhri's sisters received only 'a few gold pounds'. In 1933 Fakhri had the property entered on the land register (*livre foncier*) in conformance with the will. Perhaps understandably, his sisters, 'Atiyya and Fawziyya, were unhappy with this arrangement. By 1935 the family was engaged in two internecine legal actions.[69]

The first was launched by Fakhri, to justify and affirm his inheritance. It passed to the Druze qadi of Hasbaya-Rashaya ('sitting, as we know, in Lebanese territory'), who in successive judgements of 10 February and 6 April 1935 affirmed his own competence, *ratione loci*, to hear the case, and found in Fakhri's favour. The judgement was confirmed on appeal (17 May 1936) by the Druze shaykhs of Baakline, the highest Druze religious authorities. In the meantime, however, 'Atiyya and Fawziyya had contested the will in the Syrian civil courts – whose inheritance law would guarantee them a fixed proportion of their parents' entire estate. The Syrian courts duly found, and confirmed on appeal, that the parents' wills were invalid, and ordered 'that the properties [*immeubles*] be registered in the names of all the living children of the late Hussein Kanafani, according to the rules of devolution *ab intestat* applicable to alienable state land [*terres amirié*]'. The tribunal of first instance had argued its competence on the grounds that 'the disputed land, being in Syrian territory, could not come under a judge sitting outwith this territory'; the court of appeal added that in Syria, Druzes were subject in personal status matters 'not to jurisdictions proper to the Druze community, but, like all Muslims, to the shariah tribunals'.[70] In the face of these conflicting judgements, by the end of 1936 the case – now 'combined' into one – had passed to the *tribunal des conflits*: a body created by the High Commission in 1924 to rule in such matters.[71]

The jurisdictional dispute at issue here is complex. The Syrian courts were asserting the 'nationalisation' of justice: the competence of the Druze legal authorities was initially dismissed because they were not Syrian: they lay over the new border in Lebanon.[72] This meant that the Syrian courts were also recognising the border as the limit of their own jurisdiction: such institutional recognition is one of the ways in which borders become more than mere lines on maps. By extension, though, the case also provided an opportunity for the Syrian civil courts to challenge the existence of multiple personal status regimes within Syria – but not, as it turned out, to the benefit of the civil courts themselves. The court of appeal, as well as accepting the 'national' argument, made its own argument against the very right of the Druzes to exist as a community separate from the Sunni Muslims. They countered the late-Ottoman legal precedents cited by the High Commission that seemed to enshrine a separate status for the Druzes with a more recent one, a letter from the Ottoman *shaykh al-islām* from shortly before the First World War stating that Druzes, 'Nusayris' ('Alawis) and Isma'ilis were to be considered as Muslims, recorded as such on the civil register, and governed by the shariah courts.[73] The general principles of this argument had already been put to the French by the Syrian interior and justice ministries, probably as a result of the Kanafani case, in 1934 – at which point the Syrian government was not exactly nationalist in complexion.[74] This suggests that legal institutions which the French had hoped would permit them to institutionalise divisions within Syrian society buckled under pressure from the community with the greatest weight – of numbers, of existing influence – in Syrian society: the Sunni Muslims. The state would be made in their image, and they did not accept the separate communal existence of the Druzes. The opinion of the Druzes became irrelevant, and the French were in the end forced to go along with political realities in Syria. Ironically, it was the new borders that had given Sunni Muslims that numerical advantage: in the mandate territories as a whole they were a rather less overwhelming majority.

One might see this as a majority imposing its will within the nation-state form, against the wishes of the imperial power and the minorities alike. Several other points need to be made to nuance this argument, however. This judgement of the Syrian courts was not imposed spontaneously from above but solicited by members of the Druze community, 'Atiyya and Fawziyya Kanafani: it was in their interest for the Druzes to be governed (whether through the civil or the shariah courts) by Islamic personal status law. The 'pro-Druze' argument was made by their brother Fakhri; his cause was backed by other influential Druzes who had an interest in Druze communal separateness. It would be wrong to see the Druzes as a coherent minority uniformly disadvantaged in this question. Neither they, nor by extension any other community, were monolithic and univocal in their relations with the state and wider society in the mandate territories: as we have already seen, when Decree 60 called for the existing authorities within each personal status community to produce a communal statute, at least three different Druze groups produced competing versions for theirs. This illustrates two further points. First, Syrians who sought a degree of cooperation with the High Commission were by no means passive tools of the French; and, second, within each community, different groups and individuals sought to use legislative reform in this area in order to redefine that community to their own advantage – as we also saw in the debate about treaty guarantees.

These points hold, *a fortiori*, for the Sunni Muslims too: whether a coherent majority mobilised around this issue, rather than a coalition of socially and politically influential Muslim actors, is doubtful. But although this term, like minority, should always be used with caution, the conditions were developing in which both were becoming increasingly meaningful: the jurisdictional hardening of Syria's borders was a part of that development. In the Kanafani case, no-one seems to have defended the 'Sunni' point of view on the grounds that Sunnis were the majority. Just a few years later, during the protests over Decree 146, they would. In the meantime, the development of Syria's national legal institutions made 'minority' an increasingly meaningful concept.

At the end of 1935, the French delegation in Damascus sent a letter to its senior regional officials across Syria requesting information on the 'personal status of sects dissident from Islam: Yazidis, ʻAlawis, Ismaʻilis and Shiʻites'[75] in their region. The High Commission was minded to grant recognition to at least some of these communities under the personal status law reform, and wished to inform itself of current legal practices.[76] As a model to guide their answers, the officials were sent a copy of an earlier letter on the subject from the assistant delegate in the autonomous Sanjak of Alexandretta, which discussed local practice in a range of personal status matters.

The first was marriage. Under existing law, the letter noted – the Ottoman Family Law, enacted as recently as 25 October 1917 – only the Sunni cadi was legally qualified to celebrate the marriage of Muslims, Sunni or otherwise. However, 'it is normal practice for him in fact to delegate all his powers to the imams of the different sects to proceed to nuptial ceremonies'.[77] Doing so had the aim of not only 'dispensing him from a personal inconvenience', but also of 'respecting the liturgical precepts of certain sects deriving from Islam', since not all non-Sunni Muslims accepted the cadi's officiation as valid. The cadi issued a marriage authorisation for the couple to the relevant imam; in turn, 'the latter draws up a marriage certificate which is returned to the Cadi for registration, then transmission to the civil register' – a neat interlocking of state and local practices. In matters of succession, the cadi apparently always acted as notary for all communities, Christians included; but 'he writes out the acts of devolution upon sight of documents addressed by the mukhtars in conformance with the customs of each sect'.

Officially or unofficially, certain other privileges had been accorded to different communities within the sanjak. The 'Alawis, by French decree, had a commission overseeing their own pious endowments; they were also recorded as 'Alawis on the civil register. The handful of Isma'ilis in the sanjak – seventy, resident in the village of Jandaliyya – also seem to have managed their own waqfs, but they were listed on the civil register 'under the generic heading of "Muslims"'. The officer attributed to 'a sentiment of fear' their failure to request a more specific designation. 'However', he continued, 'in statistics and on the electoral roll, the Sanjak authorities never fail to mention them under the name of their sect.'

When the other French regional officials sent in their own letters following this model, many similar examples of tacit understandings and rule-bending emerged. In the governorate of Homs, the Sunni cadi had sole competence over the civil register, pious endowments and succession – in principle. In practice, though, 'the ['Alawi] Imams by tacit delegation from the Cadi take responsibility for all operations, regularized thereafter by the Cadi'.[78] Each 'Alawi village had such an imam. In the rural caza of Salamiyya, 'Alawis were listed as such on the civil register; in Homs itself, the formula "'Alawi Muslims' had replaced 'Muslims' to designate them. The Isma'ilis, meanwhile – more numerous here than in Alexandretta – had since 1920 also been listed specifically on the civil register; they possessed waqfs, and, again by delegation from the cadi, their imams could officiate at weddings. In matters of succession, 'everything is settled amicably [*réglé à l'amiable*] before the shaykhs. In case of litigation, the affair is brought before the Cadi who judges according to the Mufti's opinion.'

The assistant delegate in Aleppo forwarded reports from sub-officers in the countryside to the north and south of the city. In the cazas of A'zaz and the Kurd Dagh, only the Yazidis were concerned. The French intelligence officer responsible wrote that they 'have no specific status and follow in all circumstances the general rule imposed on Muslims by the existing laws' – but added that 'in matters of marriage and succession, the decisions taken by the Cadi and local shariah tribunals are always ratified unofficially by the head of the Yazidi community representing the high religious leader of the Djebel Sindjar'.[79] He thought, though, that this was a mere 'formality' whose main purpose was to 'swell the coffers' of these local community heads. Perhaps more significantly, 'in all acts concerning the members of this sect', the local civil registry had started to mention Yazidis' communal belonging, unofficial though it was.

A greater degree of practical autonomy in personal status matters extended to Shi'is in the caza of Idlib, south of Aleppo. A Shi'i shaykh designated by the contracting parties officiated at marriages, by delegation from the Sunni cadi – though the French officer there noted that 'if this procedure is strictly observed among the Shi'is of the villages Faoua and Kéféria (Idlib caza) it is rarely so among those of Maaret Mesrine (same caza) who tolerate the celebration of marriage by a Sunni Sheikh'.[80] Divorce, meanwhile, 'is pronounced by the Sunni Cadi but only takes effect, from the religious point of view, when the Shi'i Imam has proceeded to the separation of the bodies'. The Sunni cadi notarised succession for 'all Muslims', but Shi'i waqfs were overseen 'by a Shi'i commission officially designated by the government'. Shi'is in the caza were also entered as such in the civil register.

Closer to the centre of gravity of 'mainstream' Sunni Islam in Syria, and of Syrian Arab nationalism, however, French officials turned up less evidence that non-Sunni Muslim communities lived with such tacit recognition on the part of local state officials, civil and religious. Scattered among an overwhelmingly Sunni population, the small Shi'i and 'Alawi communities of the Damascus and Hawran regions, each numbering around 1,650, lived with no personal status recognition: 'Shi'is and 'Alawis depend directly from the [Sunni] Cadi of their caza, for questions of marriage as much as for questions of succession. The Cadi only delegates his powers to the Imams to proceed to the nuptial ceremonies.'[81] Some 1,200 of the Shi'is were listed as Sunnis on the civil register.

This difference in practices from region to region, caza to caza, village to village, is significant. Divergent local practices existed, many of them involving greater or lesser degrees of recognition – especially unofficial recognition – of different religious communities that lacked such recognition at the state level. This demonstrates the relative weakness of the state's interventions in the social life of the population, as well as the relative freedom of action afforded to the state's local officials – here, the cadis – to bend the rules in the interests of communal harmony, or even an easy life ('dispensing with a personal inconvenience'). But the High Commission was collecting this information for a reason. Informed by a knowledge of current practices as well as current legal 'theory', the mandatory authorities were planning a legal reform that was intended to bring standardisation and 'officialisation' in both theory and practice. By standardisation I mean that the relationship between state and religious jurisdictions was to be legally defined by the state, with all religious communities being recognised as either personal status communities or common law communities. All communities within each of these categories would be accorded the same rights and privileges, uniformly across the territory; all individuals within each community would be governed, everywhere within Syria's borders, by one standard legal status. By 'officialisation', I mean that communities derived from Islam that had previously been recognised only unofficially, and patchily across the territory, by local state functionaries or the French, would now be officially recognised by the Syrian state.

To an extent, both standardisation and officialisation served French aims. The former, because it would extend to Sunni Islam on the same basis as any other community, would circumscribe the social and political power of the shariah courts in particular and the Sunni Muslim community in general. The latter, by granting a state-guaranteed institutional existence to communities once legally subsumed within (and politically and socially subordinate to) the Sunni Muslim community, would have a similar effect, and – it was hoped – gain France the loyalty and goodwill of these communities. However, while the importance of these political considerations should obviously not be discounted, it would be a mistake to think that they were the only motivation for reform. If the French had little enthusiasm for building a nation in Syria, they were nonetheless committed to the task of building a state: colonial rule no less than national(ist) rule requires a state apparatus. Reform of the legal system would bring about a new uniformity in the state's relationship with religion that was in line with modern conceptions of the state – a uniformity given order from above, rather than a flexible *modus operandi* established at the level of society by local authority figures and local state officials. The modern French conception of the state prizes uniformity particularly highly,[82] but the diversity and number of precedents sought by the High Commission show that this breed of reform is characteristic of modern states more generally.

In other words, personal status law reform should not be seen merely as an imperialist design, but also as part of the modern expansion of the state: in this case, through its greater regulation of, and implication in, religious affairs at both macro and micro levels. Once again, it is from this expansion and intensification of state activity that 'minorities' emerge. The creation of a codified legal status, applied uniformly across the territory to govern all members of a given community in their relationship to the state, on the one hand; on the other, a centrally-propelled tendency towards greater uniformity of legal practice in their relationship with the state at local and national levels, including the creation of state-ordered, state-wide communal institutions: both of these developments, I would argue, would act to increase the feeling within that community of being a coherent group within the state as a whole.[83] The scope for divergent practices and unofficial rule-bending of the sort described above would be reduced. This process, naturally, should not be separated from those described in earlier chapters: the increase of the state's authority across the whole territory, or the development of new forms of political institutionalisation for the communities during the treaty negotiations. Other examples could be suggested, too: for example, that of language, as certain languages were formally made official state languages. The expansion of an education system teaching, and a bureaucracy using, the official language puts speakers of non-official languages at an increasing disadvantage relative to speakers of the official language; at the same time it increases their sense of being a coherent linguistic community. Where the state opposes or even represses the use of non-official languages, that sense is only increased.[84]

However, although it surely produced communities with a greater sense of coherence than the Ottoman millets – with all their local variations in status – had known, this 'uniformisation' within the religious communities did not by itself produce the sense of being a minority. In the Syrian case, at least, two further elements were required. The first of these has already been mentioned: the application to the common law and personal status communities of the term itself, as it spread in Syria in the 1930s with all its legal and political implications. But the other was even more important: the existence of another community which, while the state was imposing itself more forcefully on the population, was able through weight of numbers – by mobilising itself as a numerical majority within the nation-state – to impose itself as the definer of the state 'norms' from which other communities were seen to diverge, even where that divergence was legally accepted. This was not part of French plans: the French preference was clearly for a religiously 'neutral' state and a civil law (albeit both serving as tools of French imperial policy), to which all religious communities would be equally subordinated. The religious community which, against French wishes, imposed itself as the 'majority' in this controversy was the Sunni Muslim community.

How the Reform was Blocked: the 'Majority' View?

High Commissioner Puaux's description of a 'petition' against Decrees 60 and 146 sent in February 1939 by a group of 'ulama', cited above, is misleading. The document in question was not a text signed or stamped by a number of individuals, like countless petitions contained in the French archives, but a letter signed by one individual – Kamil al-Qassab – in his capacity as president of the Damascus Association of 'Ulama' (Figure 1). Sent to the Syrian interior ministry on 8 February 1939, it set out the association's objections to the decrees and 'the provisions they contain that contradict the book of God most high to which all Muslims adhere':

> The Association considers it a religious duty to set out what is contrary to the provisions of Islamic legislation in these two decrees, and the dissolution of the ties of harmony and brotherhood between the Muslims and the other communities [tawā'if] that is intended by them.[85]

The association identified seven problems with Decree 60, as amended by Decree 146. First, Article 1 'considered Muslims in their abode [fī dārihim][86] to be a religious community like the other communities in the Syrian land':

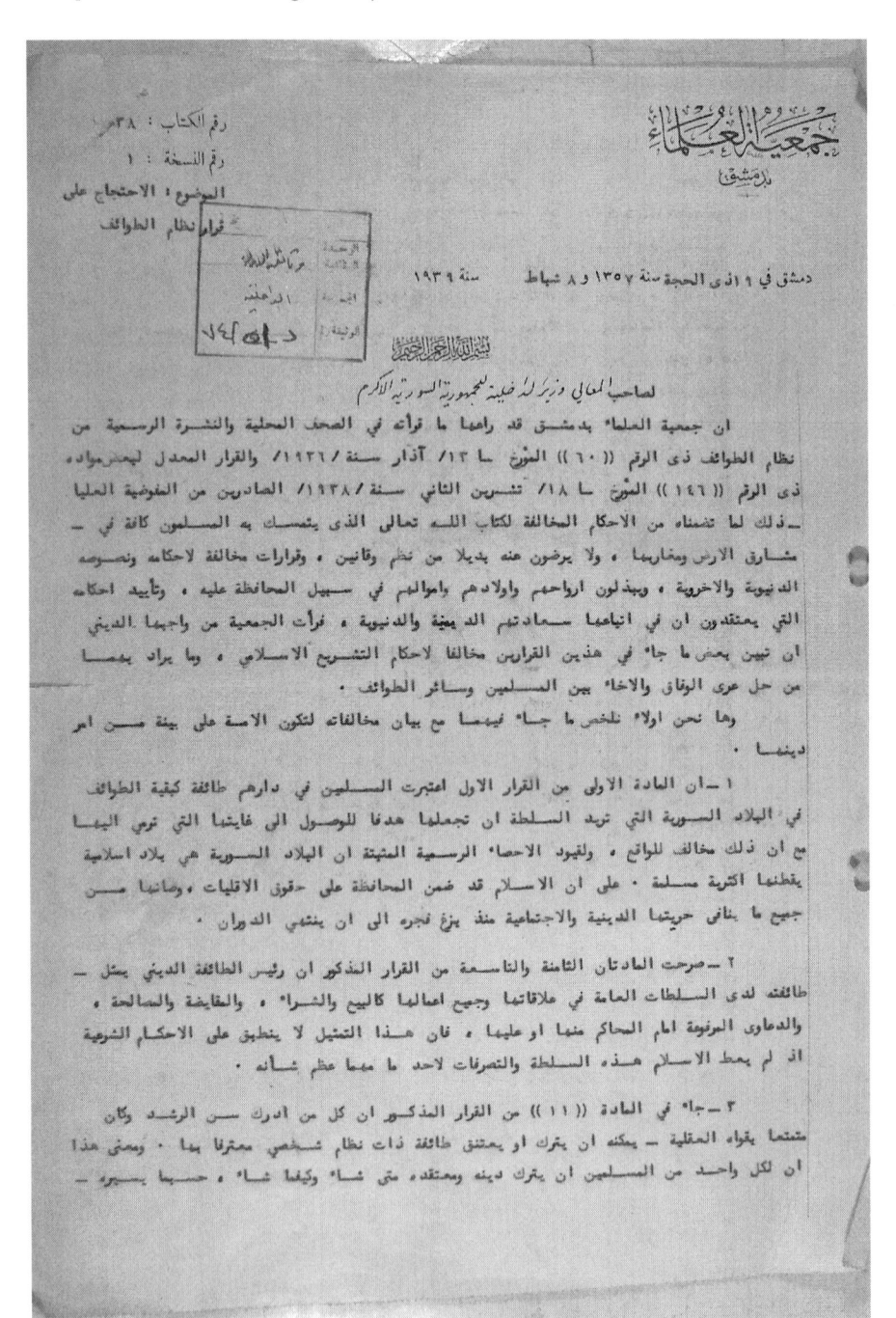

Figure 1 First page of al-Qassāb's letter to the interior ministry (8 February 1939). *Courtesy of the Historical Documents Centre, Damascus.*

But this is contrary to the reality, and to the verified, official records of the census, that the Syrian land is an Islamic land inhabited by a Muslim majority [*bilād islāmiyya yaqtunuhā akthariyya muslima*], though Islam has guaranteed the preservation of the rights of minorities and defended them from everything incompatible with their religious and social freedom since its very beginning [*mundhu bazagh fajrihi*: literally 'since its dawn broke'] and until the [world's] turning stops.

Second, Articles 8 and 9 granted authority to the highest religious chief of each community to carry out various acts on the community's behalf and to represent it to the public powers. 'Such representation is not in accordance with shariah provisions: Islam does not give this authority or these rights of disposal [*hādhihi al-sulta wal-tasarrufāt*] to anyone, however senior.' Third, Article 11 permitted anyone of sound mind having attained the age of reason – Muslims included – to join or leave any recognised personal status community. 'This is something that the true Islamic religion has never in any way permitted: it punishes the apostate from his religion by death in this world, and eternal fire in the hereafter.' All that was meant by the Syrian constitution's guarantee of absolute freedom of conscience, al-Qassab continued, was that all communities were free to practise their existing religion unmolested.

Fourth, the amended Article 12 stated that in the case of a marriage ending, for whatever reason, children would follow the father's religion; but Islam states that children must follow the Muslim parent. Therefore, the children must follow the mother if she converted to Islam, whether after her husband's death or during the marriage. (The latter would under Islamic law imply the annulment of the marriage – indeed, a fair proportion of conversions involved Christian women using this means to obtain a divorce.[87]) Fifth, the amended Article 23 stated that if one spouse changed religion, rather than both, the marriage would remain valid and subject to the personal status regime under which it had been contracted; any children would remain legitimate. But Islam could not permit a woman who converted to Islam to remain under the custody of a non-Muslim husband, or allow non-Muslim children to inherit legitimately from a Muslim parent. Sixth, the new Article 25 allowed marriages contracted abroad by Syrians and Lebanese to be considered legitimate in Syria, under civil law if they contravened the personal status of either contracting party: 'it thereby permitted the marriage of a Muslim woman to a stranger to her religion, even though the shariah does not consent to it'. Seventh, the new Article 27 established a higher jurisdiction to judge on conflicts between different personal status jurisdictions or between them and the civil courts, and to decide the validity of judgements issued by the personal status jurisdictions:

> This means the creation of a new legislation for Muslims' personal status, changing their laws, which they have adhered to since the dawn of Islam until now; the granting to the higher jurisdiction of competence to execute, replace, or abolish [those laws]; and rule by other than what God most high sent down in his noble book . . .

Such a thing could not be countenanced; indeed, it had already – continued the letter – provoked the opposition of Muslims in the rest of the Islamic world. In sum, 'the personal status decree cannot be applied in this country'. It was contrary to the shariah, which 'guarantees the rights of minorities and others, and the ensuring of their personal status'; indeed, as it stood the decree would 'cause division between the majority and the minority'.

> Because of all this, the Damascus Association of 'Ulama' and the Muslims as a whole protest against this decree which is contrary to the laws of their true religion and in violation of articles six and nine of the Mandate charter, to which the French Republic adheres in claiming its mandate over this Syrian land.

The association rejected its promulgation and application, and demanded that the Syrian government send it back to the High Commission – and order the courts not to consider it as law until such time as the High Commission abrogated it.

The religious grounds on which the decrees were rejected are clear enough, though it is instructive to note, with Puaux, the long delay between the promulgation of Decree 146 and the onset of protests against it. To understand this document's wider significance to the argument of this book, however, it is useful to compare it with another document received by the Syrian interior ministry a couple of days after Kamil al-Qassab sent his letter. This document really was a petition, written by hand in Homs' Nuri mosque, signed by over two hundred people, and presented to the governor by 'a large delegation of the city's senior 'ulama' and the cream of its notables' (Figure 2).[88]

They voiced similar objections to the decrees, though with a less clear grasp of the texts. First, that 'Article 1' (in fact, Article 11 of Decree 60, as al-Qassab correctly stated) permitted individuals to leave Islam.[89] 'This is evidently contrary to the text of the venerated Qur'an. Anyone who dared to do such a thing would be sentenced to death, as is well known and established.' Second, they objected to 'amending article 2' – that is, Article 2 of Decree 146 – but for a slightly different reason to the Damascus association. This article stipulated that in case of a marriage ending, the children should follow the father's religion. Al-Qassab had noted that according to Islamic law the children must follow the Muslim parent, so if a Christian mother converted to Islam, either after her husband's death or during the marriage (thereby annulling it), her children must convert too. For the Homs petitioners, the problem was that if a Muslim apostatised from his religion ('God forbid'), his children would follow him into apostasy.

The petition's third and fourth objections also related to marriage; al-Qassab had also made them. The amended Article 23, stating that if only one spouse changed religion the marriage remained valid and subject to the personal status regime it had been contracted under, would mean that if a

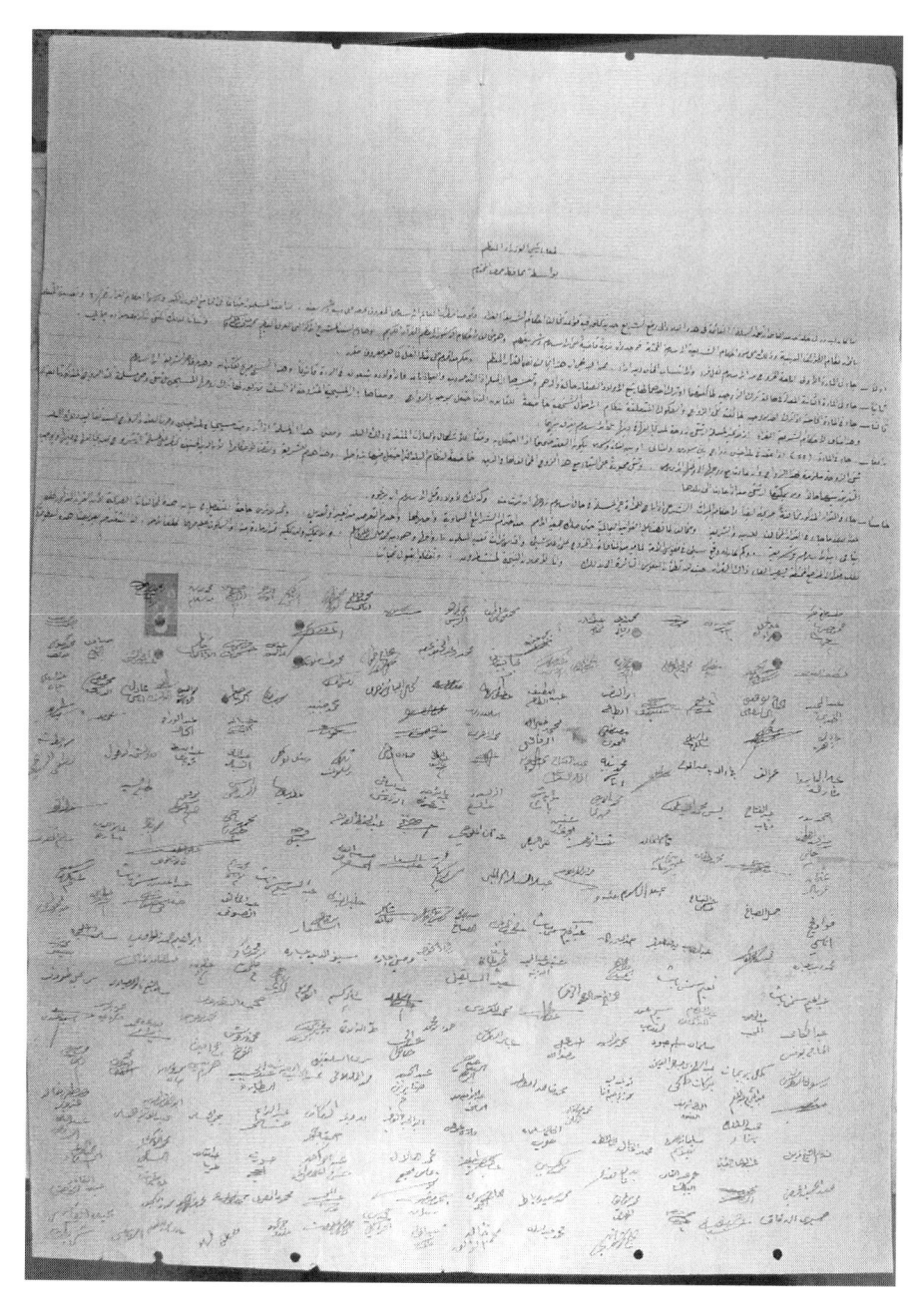

Figure 2 The Homs petition to the Syrian interior ministry (forwarded by the governor of Homs, 11 February 1939). *Courtesy of the Historical Documents Centre, Damascus.*

married non-Muslim woman converted to Islam she would remain under the authority of – indeed, married to – a non-Muslim husband. The article recognising marriages contracted by Syrians and Lebanese abroad could also permit a Muslim woman to be married to a non-Muslim man, 'even if she returned to her Islamic fatherland [wa-in ʿādat ilā wataniha al-islāmī]'. But 'the true religion warns the Muslim woman against marrying anyone who differs from her in her religion, obliges their immediate separation, and does not permit her to remain with him if she returns to her country'.

Finally, the petition also claimed – without a specific citation – that the decree would permit a non-Muslim woman whose husband had converted to Islam, and any non-Muslim children, to inherit from him.[90] Neither decree explicitly stipulates this; presumably it was seen as a logical result of the amended Article 23, mentioned also by al-Qassab.

In their religious argumentation, then, the two documents are rather similar. However, in the justifications that they invoke to support their arguments, and in their form, they are very different. The relationship between form and content is instructive, and illuminates the wider historical context within which these documents were produced.

The first is a letter, typed on several pages of standard-sized paper carrying the letterhead of the Damascus Association of 'Ulama', signed on that organisation's behalf by its president. It presented itself as expressing the association's authoritative opinion, with no reference to how that opinion was reached – that is, to its own creation. The second is a petition, handwritten on a single large sheet of paper in a clear, scribal hand. It, too, was a collective opinion, but not an 'anonymous' one expressed through the intermediary of a bureaucratic organisation and its president: it was signed by some two hundred individuals. Moreover, the Homs petition described its own production: surprised by the promulgation by 'the responsible authorities in this country'[91] of legislation that contravened Islamic law,

> the Muslims held a meeting in the great Nuri mosque and studied the provisions of decree 60 and its amendments relating to the fixing of the status of the religious communities [al-tawāʾif al-dīniyya] in the light of the provisions of the respected Islamic shariah. They found it to be a mortal blow [darbatan qādiyatan] to Islam and their shariah...

This difference is also visible in the reference points each document took in support of its arguments. The shariah, the Qur'an and existing precedents in Islamic law were collectively the key reference point for both. But for the Homs petition they were virtually the sole reference point – the only justification external to Islamic law that they proffered was a single reference to international law, when they asserted that the decree's content was 'contrary to the religion and the shariah, and contrary to what international laws including the charter of the League of Nations have decreed'. Importantly, there is only the vaguest reference to the state in the Homs petition – it referred only to the 'responsible authorities in this country [*al-sulta al-qā'ima fī hādhihi al-bilād*]'; it was addressed to the minister with the request that he 'forward it to the relevant authorities [*al-marāji' al-mukhtassa*]' so the decree could be abrogated.

Al-Qassab's letter, by contrast, reached for any number of justifications external to Islamic law. Although it argued on the basis of the truth of Islam as a revealed religion, it argued for that religion's unique and dominant position in Syria on the grounds that the country was, as the 'verified, official records of the census [*quyūd al-ihsā' al-rasmiyya al-muthbata*]' showed, 'inhabited by a Muslim majority' – a majority, moreover, which protected 'minorities'. (The Homs petition mentioned neither a majority nor minorities.) As we saw above, al-Qassab's letter referred much more specifically to the League of Nations Charter, which, it noted, was the justification for the French presence in Syria. Where the Homs petition aimed to influence the 'relevant authorities', the association addressed the Syrian government with specific demands regarding Syrian state activities, particularly the functioning of the courts. It is notable that the Homs petition did not mention the revised Article 27, instituting a higher jurisdiction in personal status matters – which, as I observed above, would assert the secular state's authority over all religious jurisdictions. The Association of 'Ulamā', by contrast, strongly objected to this article, for this reason. A concern with the state is thus not just implicit but explicit in their letter. While the Homs petition contented itself with protesting against articles of the decree that challenged the dominance of Islamic norms in social life, the Association of 'Ulamā' far more actively asserted Islam's role as the 'defining authority' of the state. Indeed, it justified itself by using arguments that could make sense, and could exist, only in the context of a nation-state.

The Homs petition, in its form and reference points, if not in its specific subject, could have been written a century or two earlier: a petition to authority from the city's 'ulamā' and notables, assuming the right to speak on behalf of local society on the basis of their own personal authority. Its religious argumentation assumed Islam's position as the 'norm-definer' in Syria not because Muslims formed the numerical majority, but because Islam is the true religion. By contrast, the form and reference points of the association's letter are unimaginable outside the modern context of the nation-state. The association was self-consciously operating in that context, as one modern bureaucratic institution addressing, and seeking to influence, another: the Syrian state. It did so in the 'official' form used by the state: a typed letter on headed paper, from one bureaucratic official (the association's president) to another (the Syrian interior minister). Moreover, the association was addressing the Syrian state partly on the latter's terms. The Syrian state's legal existence derived from the League of Nations; the association invoked the League Charter. The Wilsonian ideal of the self-determination of peoples meant that nation-states had to represent their populations; the association – citing that most 'state' of instruments, the census – claimed to speak for a majority of the Syrian population. Independent nation-states had to offer protection to their minorities; Islam, said the Association, had always done so. As the French had projected the new category of minority into the past to describe their involvement in the Ottoman Empire, so too al-Qassab projected it into the past, taking the modern category as a synonym for *dhimmi*, the 'protected' non-Muslim communities under Muslim rule. But for much of the Islamic past, dhimmis were not in the minority.[92]

Opposition to the personal status reform decrees spread far more widely than the 'ulama', of course: the French sent in the troops to put down mass unrest on the streets, not to interrupt the meetings of the Damascus Association of 'Ulama'. Nonetheless, comparing these two documents is extremely useful for showing how the developing nation-state context had created the conditions for the emergence of a self-defined 'majority' in Syria.[93] At the same time, it reminds us that people did not automatically see themselves as a majority simply because the conditions for them to do so were now in place. The drafters of the Homs position felt no need to refer to themselves as representing any such thing, and al-Qassab, who did use the term, may have been unusual in doing so. Although an active and influential figure, his intellectual profile (as a reformist former student of Muhammad 'Abduh, active in Arab nationalist circles since the early 1900s) was atypical among the Damascene 'ulama' his letter claimed to speak for, and his self-consciously modern terminology may have been his alone.[94] This raises another question: is it accurate to consider opposition to the reform decrees as a 'majority' mobilisation?

If there is a majority in the opposition to Decrees 60 and 146, it is surely a Sunni Muslim one: the most strident protests came from Muslims (not only 'ulama') and related to the effect the legislation would have on the status of the Muslim community. Puaux eventually defused the situation by issuing a decree suspending the decrees' application to 'Muslims', and received many messages from Muslim groups expressing satisfaction and gratitude for this.[95]

Syrian Christians certainly felt that Sunni Islam had successfully imposed itself on the Syrian state. When the Syrian government's commission on the question issued its conclusion that the reform was contrary to Islamic law,[96] the Beirut newspaper *al-Bashir* published a heartfelt editorial under the headline 'Must we despair? [*Faut-il désespérer?*]'.[97] Arguing, with emphatic bold type, for a secular civil law that would 'permit a common national life based on the essential **equality** of **personal rights**', the newspaper wrote that

> For too long, **Muslim law** was arbitrarily **imposed** on **non-Muslims**; this is what created the profound cleavage [*le fossé profond*] that divided the nation, and what constitutes the whole historic problem of **minorities**.

Today, the Syrian Commission, with a brutal audacity, **calls this problem into question** and with a word cancels out the progress made [*le chemin parcouru*] in the last twenty years towards fraternal rapprochement: '**The Muslims alone form the Nation ... The others are communities**'.

(Here again we see the contemporary issue of minorities projected into the past as a 'historic problem'.) The implications of the commission's stance were so grave for non-Muslims, and Muslim non-Sunnis, that the newspaper asked 'if we should despair of the idea of the Syrian nation'.

As it became clear that the High Commission would accept the Syrian commission's conclusions, however grudgingly, the Catholic patriarchs of the French mandate territories sent a letter to the High Commissioner that was later also published in *al-Bashir*. They, too, argued strongly – and perhaps a touch disingenuously – for a 'neutral', secular state with a civil law. Unsurprisingly, they particularly emphasised the concepts of liberty, equality and fraternity. Liberty, in the sense of freedom of conscience – notably the freedom to change religion. Equality, for both individuals and communities: 'Equality, which has been included in the treaty projects and the protocols that have followed them, to the point that the words "majority" and "minority" were systematically deleted – [words] resuscitated today to justify dictatorial and exclusivist claims'.[98] And fraternity, to argue that opponents of the reforms were wrong to claim that they would divide the majority from the minorities and break the links of fraternity in Syria. Instead, true fraternity depended on the reform:

> only a supraconfessional legislation, balancing and fixing the personal statuses of the diverse religious communities of our countries can make it easier for these communities to live each alongside the others and meld them, with order, in a mutual sympathy and in national unity.

The Christian clergy, at least, argued – explicitly, and actually using the terms – that the suspension for Muslims of Decrees 60 and 146 would leave the Christian communities as permanently disadvantaged minorities within a state dominated by a Muslim majority: 'We cannot accept', they said, 'that in Syria the Sunni majority should impose the legal prescriptions of the Qur'an on the Christian minorities.' And again, defending the (civil) higher jurisdiction which al-Qassab had particularly condemned: 'Would it be normal, in all frankness, that in case of conflict – always possible – a majority community should impose its law and its solution on a minority community?'

By 1939, it is clear that the Christian patriarchs did perceive the contest to define and control the practices of a state whose encroachment on the lives of the population was steadily increasing as a contest between a 'majority', on one hand, and 'minorities', on the other. But the dissenting member of the Syrian government's commission on the question, the legal scholar and ('non-political') politician Yusuf al-Hakim, perceived the matter slightly differently. In his memoirs he reiterated the view he had stated at the time: that a civil law presented sufficient benefits to Syria's status as a state worthy of independence that all religious groups should for the greater good accept the limitations on their particular privileges. But he did not see the successful blocking of the reform as a majority imposing its will on the state, and the minorities. Indeed, he wrote of the support that his dissenting opinion had received from 'those who love renewal and progress' belonging to all communities.[99] They included 'a great number of senior 'ulama' and highly-educated persons both Muslim and Christian'. Such people had, like al-Hakim, held off from 'coming between the two factions competing for rule among the many political parties'. For al-Hakim, the 'religious demonstrations' against the reform decrees were a mobilisation that one of those factions (the nationalist opposition, allied with certain 'ulama') had called out in order to embarrass the other (the Bloc government). In other words, it was not the mobilisation of a coherent 'majority', but a piece of factional politics that successfully drew out mass support by somewhat underhand methods – as befitted parties which were 'all alike in believing that ["]the end justifies the means"'.

Among other reasons, this view is worth taking seriously because it does not assume that communities acted as monolithic blocs in political affairs. A constant concern of this book has been to avoid such reductive assumptions, and to understand them when they are made in the sources: for example, when French officials apply such thinking to Syrians. They certainly did this during the personal status controversy, especially as regards Muslims, whose opposition to the reform was usually attributed to all Muslims without exception. Gabriel Puaux went so far as to speak of the 'totalitarian pretensions of Sunnism'.[100]

In fact, Puaux's depiction of the opposition was at best a persistent mischaracterisation. As we saw above, he claimed that the Bloc summoned up opposition from the 'ulama' more or less on a whim, whereas the 'ulama' who opposed the reform actually opposed the Bloc for (among other things) agreeing to it. Puaux's interpretation underestimates the capacity for independent action of the 'ulama' and overestimates the Bloc's ability, by this stage, to manipulate them. Just as likely is that activist 'ulama' like al-Qassab chose to use this issue – where they had a natural political advantage – to put pressure on a discredited government that had proven unable to defend Syrian interests.

Seeing the 'ulama' as a tool wielded by the Bloc in order to stir up the masses, however, had certain advantages for the High Commission. It allowed Muslims as a whole to be presented as a passive, monolithic group beholden to the whims of a few politicking nationalists – and as basically fanatical, easily whipped up into a fury over religious issues. It also obscured the startling fact that the mandatory authorities, in all their careful preparations for the reform decrees, seem never to have asked Sunni religious leaders for their opinion.

Whereas the opinions of Christian patriarchs, and to a lesser extent Druze, ʿAlawi or Ismaʿili religious leaders, were canvassed and taken seriously, the voices of Sunni religious figures are almost absent from the High Commission records on the subject – right up until the moment when their opposition suddenly scotched the reform. There is no equivalent to Cardinal Tappouni, the Syrian-Catholic patriarch, who alone seems to have played a more important role in French considerations (and left a deeper personal trace on the archives relating to the reform) than all Sunni ʿulama'.[101] Just as the High Commission, for reasons we have already explored, treated the Christian clergy as the political leaders of their community, the French seem to have assumed that the Syrian government in place (whether before or after the arrival in power of the National Bloc in 1936) spoke, by default, for the 'Muslims' – on religious as well as on political matters. The magnitude of this error became apparent as the ʿulama' made the running in the opposition to the reform, leaving the Bloc government no alternative but to ostentatiously repudiate a text it had previously, albeit secretly, accepted. Of course, the Syrian government may itself have hoped that the ʿulama' would follow wherever it led, especially in the period of nationalist rule. We have already seen that the Bloc's stand over personal status law reform, while seeking to channel religious opposition to the French, also sought (however lamely) to assert the position of parliament – an institution of the secular state – as the sole legitimate source of law in Syria.

This unwillingness to acknowledge the political dynamic between the ʿulama' and the Syrian government highlights another noticeable aspect of Puaux's characterisation of the opposition: his determination to abstract the issue of personal status reform from any consideration of its political context. Puaux claimed that the Bloc itself incited opposition out of some impish desire to 'creat[e] difficulties for the mandatory power', without explaining why the Bloc might wish to do so.[102] In fact, by 1939 the public mood in much of Syria was extremely hostile to the mandatory power for a number of rather good reasons, among them the French refusal to ratify the treaty, the loss of Alexandretta, and French officials' readiness to undermine the government's authority. If members of the Bloc government shared this popular anger, the party could not, having staked everything on (and attained power by) signing a treaty with France, simply come out in opposition to the mandatory power. The Bloc's chief political rivals in this period, the nationalists loosely grouped around ʿAbd al-Rahman al-Shahbandar, benefited mightily from not being subject to the same constraint. But that popular anger caused by French actions gradually made the position of the Bloc untenable, hence Mardam Bek's decision to use the issue of personal status reform as a way to recover some of his lost political credit. By considering the opposition to the reform in isolation, and by attributing it to 'Muslims' in general, Puaux glossed over French responsibility for the reform's failure. That responsibility was both direct and indirect. Direct, in that the High Commission had seemingly made no effort to canvass the views of an extremely influential group that had an obvious interest in any change to legislation in this area, and duly led the opposition to it. And indirect, in that French obstructiveness had undermined the Bloc on so many issues that popular anger against both the imperial power and the supine nationalist government had reached a pitch where any one issue could have blown up into unrest.

But opposition to the reform evidently cannot be understood separately from its context. In February and March of 1939 the Syrian interior ministry received reports of protests from all over the country, often relating to the 'nidhām al-tawā'if'. But when people demonstrated their anger over the reform, they protested also about a range of other issues. If the 'ulama' of Aleppo or students of Islamic law in Homs protested about personal status in particular, the staff and students of civil secondary schools in Homs were more concerned about challenges to Syrian state authority in peripheral areas: they sent telegrams demanding action over an attack on the principal of the Tajhiz school in Latakia and the burning of the Syrian flag in the Jazira.[103] Notables and students in Dar'a on the Jordanian border wrote 'to disapprove of the communities law' – Decree 60 – but also 'to support the unity of the country, and to demand the ratification of the 1936 treaty'.[104] In Homs again, a demonstration of school students began at the Tajhiz, but then proceeded to the Orthodox and Jesuit secondary schools and also drew some participation from the general population; they made their way to the Government House, 'calling for the downfall of colonialism, criticizing the communities law [nidhām al-tawā'if]'.[105]

Although this last document does not specifically confirm that students from the other schools actually joined the demonstration, it is likely that they did. Souheil Chebat, who grew up in Damascus in this period, described joining a demonstration that had come to his (Orthodox) school from the Damascus Tajhiz and proceeded to other communal schools; being a small child, he was carried on the shoulders of an older boy, and went home hoarse with shouting. In this case, too, the demonstrators' chanting addressed more than one issue:

> Tahyā al-wataniyya – Islām wa masīhiyya
> Iskandarūn 'arabiyya – tasqut al-suhyūniyya
> [Long live nationalism – Muslims and Christians
> Alexandretta is Arab – down with Zionism]

(At the time, he did not know what 'Zionism' was.) That particular demonstration was a little earlier than the protests over the personal status controversy, but it followed the same pattern as some of them, and illustrates both the range of targets for nationalist protests and the diverse communal backgrounds of the people who joined them.[106]

There is no way of knowing whether in other circumstances the Bloc might have successfully convinced, co-opted or coerced the 'ulama' into accepting a reformed personal status law. But it certainly can be argued that the 'Muslim majority' that mobilised against personal status reform exists clearly only if that opposition is examined in isolation. Once we place it back in its context, the 'majority' is suddenly much less distinct. On any of the other burning issues of the day, the 'majority' might well have constituted itself somewhat differently. It is almost certainly true, for example, that by 1939 a majority of Syrians would have agreed with the sentiment 'down with colonialism!', and would have had a clear idea of how that sentiment should lead to a redefinition of the state: namely, as an independent nation-state free of French tutelage. That numerical majority was not, however, restricted to a single culturally-defined group. Likewise, Yusuf al-Hakim publicly supported the personal status reform against both popular opposition and his fellow members of the Syrian government's commission, al-Qassab among them. But he was nonetheless a Syrian nationalist, albeit a non-partisan one. Apportioning the blame for the failure of nationalist rule in his memoirs, he identified many weaknesses on the Syrian side, but placed ultimate responsibility on France's failure to ratify the treaty and adoption of many policies seen as harmful to the nationalist cause (including the '*nidhām al-tawā'if*' he had himself defended).[107] Al-Hakim did not belong to the 'majority' invoked by al-Qassab in his letter to the Syrian government, but he did belong to that other majority: Syrians who wanted Syria to be independent.

Conclusion

In this affair as in others, it is more analytically useful to understand the 'majority' as an effective ideological fiction, used for their own political ends by a coalition of influential actors, than as a real sociological grouping. The different parts of this coalition sought and achieved different things: for anti-Bloc nationalist politicians like 'Abd al-Rahman al-Shahbandar, a transient political aim (forcing the compromised Bloc out of government); for Muslim 'ulama' such as Kamil al-Qassab, a longer-term strategic goal (imposing their political ideology as the 'state norm'). It is not hard to see how in a different political conjuncture this coalition could have broken down – and with it the idea of a permanent 'majority'.

Nonetheless, the personal status debacle proved the fiction's power. The French backed down over the reform, but only as it touched 'Muslims'. Paradoxically, by accepting the definition of the 'majority' given by opponents of the reform, they reinforced the minority status of the other communities. Because the reforms applied only to non-Muslims, Christian patriarchs certainly had the sense that Sunni Muslims had imposed themselves as the dominant community within the state, and left Christians as subordinate minorities: 'we cannot accept', they wrote, though they had to, that 'a state be created where minorities are fixed [*établies*] in civic inferiority, where the Christian minorities are placed in tutelage under a theocratic Muslim regime [*sous un pouvoir théocratique musulman*]'.[108] If the latter description was an exaggeration, the perception of being a minority fixed in civic inferiority was real enough.

But the power of the concept of 'majority' went even further. Whereas Puaux's temporary suspension of Decree 60 applied specifically to Sunni Muslims, the new decree permanently suspending it applied to 'the Muslims'. All other Muslim communities were thereby collapsed into the Sunni 'ulama's definition of Islam. So, while the maintenance of Decree 60's provisions for Christian and Jewish communities fixed them in a legally subordinate position, their suspension for 'Muslims' stripped Muslim communities other than the Sunnis of their legal existence as a distinct community.[109] Ironically, this measure, taken by the French in order to resolve an acute but temporary crisis, permanently effaced the institutional distinctions within the 'Muslim' community that it had been French policy since the occupation to reinforce. They were thus legally incorporated into a religiously-defined majority that many of them had spent much of the mandate period trying to escape. If Christians faced an institutionally subordinate recognition as minorities, among non-Sunni Muslims such deliberate non-recognition – in the context of the developing institutions of a modern state, which would no longer accept the flexible practices of the Ottoman period – may have been an even greater spur to the development of minority feeling.

By the later 1930s the nation-state structure in Syria was sufficiently well established for the concept of majority to become meaningful for Syrians themselves; hence its being invoked by opponents of the personal status law reform. We can see how the same structural developments had also (and probably a little earlier) made the category of minority meaningful; we can see, too, how until those changes had taken place the two terms were not meaningful, were not used by any actors involved, and are of questionable analytical value for scholars. This does not mean, however, that when studying the period in which the concepts of majority and minority had become meaningful scholars can deploy them without caution. Rather, once those concepts have become meaningful, we should seek to understand who used them and why, and not simply reproduce them, or for that matter apply them to groups which did not themselves use them. Over the question of personal status law reform, as over the question of minority guarantees in the treaty, political actors who sought to redefine the communities they belonged to as 'minorities' also sought to restructure them politically – in their internal structure, in their relationship to the wider society, in their relationship to the state. The same goes for those claimed to speak for a 'majority', but the stakes were arguably higher: that claim implied a redefinition of the state in its relationship with the whole population, majority and minorities alike.

Notes

1. Hourani, *Syria and Lebanon*, pp. 225–6. These words are also quoted by Khoury, *Syria and the French Mandate*, p. 567.
2. Khoury, *Syria and the French Mandate*, p. 577.
3. This applies more or less equally to Hourani, *Syria and Lebanon*; Longrigg, *Syria and Lebanon*; and Khoury, *Syria and the French Mandate*. Shambrook, *French Imperialism in Syria*, mentions personal status only with reference to the fall of the Haffar government (p. 257).
4. Khoury, *Syria and the French Mandate*; Shambrook, *French Imperialism in Syria*.
5. This is the case with Hourani, *Syria and Lebanon*.
6. The subject is also absent from the recent, wide-ranging volumes on the mandates edited by Nadine Méouchy and Peter Sluglett.
7. The general information on personal status law in this and the following paragraphs is drawn from documents in AD-SL Boxes 591, 592 and 593. Particularly useful are two substantial High Commission documents on the topic: a fifty-page study produced by the High Commissioner's delegate to the Contrôle Générale des Wakfs in 1928 (AD-SL Box 591, dossier *Statut personnel. Documentation*. Document entitled *Réforme du statut personnel*, dated February 1928), and a fourteen-page note produced by the same department – renamed the Contrôle des Wakfs et de l'Immatriculation foncière – in 1934 (AD-SL Box 592, dossier *Statut personnel. Dossier général. Note sur les questions relatives au Statut Personnel*, stamped Gennardi and dated 24/5/1934). I have included page references for these long, page-numbered documents, which I cite frequently.
8. One jurisdictional confusion that evidently did *not* trouble the French was that arising from the existence of the 'mixed courts' set up in the Ottoman Empire to try cases involving foreigners (including, as time went by, Ottomans who had taken foreign citizenship) and still in existence under the mandate. This issue, which had proved a tremendous obstacle to Ottoman legal reform, is almost never mentioned in the French documents I have read on personal status law reform, even though the mixed courts were presumably also affected.
9. A French official noted that:

> Christian and Israelite plaintiffs used their right [*faculté*] of submitting cases to the Muslim tribunals so widely that the competence of the religious jurisdictions (patriarchates and rabbinates) was soon restricted to cases relative to the matrimonial regime; the canonical law of the community fell into desuetude, and Muslim law – now applied to the generality of cases between non-Muslims – was by this means introduced into custom. It is precisely these customary dispositions that the patriarchates or confessional tribunals apply today in

settlement of cases their members may submit to them may submit to them [*au règlement des litiges dont ils peuvent être saisis par leurs ressortissants*].

(AD-SL Box 591, dossier *Statut personnel. Documentation*. Document entitled *Réforme du statut personnel*, dated February 1928, quote at 3–4.) That is, in order to reduce the 'loss-by-attrition' of their legal authority to the Muslim courts, the non-Muslim communities had gradually adopted Muslim legal norms. The extremely widespread phenomenon of Christians and Jews preferring to have cases heard before the cadi had been irritating communal leaders ever since the Islamic conquest.

10. AD-SL Box 591, dossier *Statut personnel. Documentation*. Document entitled *Réforme du statut personnel*, dated February 1928, pp. 9–10.
11. Details are given below.
12. On the Protestants, see AD-SL Box 593, dossier *Le Statut personnel et la Communauté Protestante*, notably the letter signed by four senior members (Arab and Armenian) of the 'Synode protestant libano-syrien' to HC (27/5/1936) listing the various acts of the Ottoman government granting recognition to Protestants as a personal status community. For the 'Epiphanios dispute' and its implications see AD-SL Box 593, dossier *Le Statut personnel des communautés religieuses et la question de l'Eglise orientale orthodoxe de Mgr Epiphanios*.
13. This and following: AD-SL Box 591, dossier *Statut personnel. Documentation*. Document entitled *Réforme du statut personnel*, dated February 1928, quotes at 12–13.
14. Under existing law, in fact, such property was technically registered as belong to the head of the community (at least for the Christian churches). This created serious problems if the head of the community died intestate, since existing law relied on the Ottoman sultan to appoint an acting successor, but the sultanate had been abolished. For such a case, and the French solution to it, see details of the death and succession of Syrian-Catholic Patriarch Ephrem II Rahmani in 1929, in AD-SL Series B, Box 16 dossier 317: *Cardinal Tappouni*.
15. AD-SL Box 592, dossier *A/s. du Statut Personnel* (handwritten). On customs privileges: *Information N°10* (5/1/1933). On special privileges of senior Greek Orthodox clergy, including the right to be judged 'before special jurisdictions composed partly of laymen and partly of ecclesiastics, meeting at the Seat of the Patriarchate' in civil matters and 'by their peers the Orthodox prelates meeting under the presidency of the Patriarch' in criminal matters: Zacharie (Greek Orthodox Metropolitan, Beirut) to HC (1/12/1932).
16. AD-SL Box 592, dossier *Statut personnel. Dossier général*, subdossier *Le statut personnel catholique*. Lagarde to Martel, 2/11/1938. Lagarde was junior minister at the MAE, and had until recently served as a senior official in Syria. A longer commentary on the Apostolic Delegate's proposals can be found in a ten-page *Note* by the Contrôle des Wakfs et de l'immatriculation foncière (10/10/1938) – same box, not filed in a dossier.

17. AD-SL Box 592, dossier *Statut personnel. Dossier Général*. Enclosure, *Note sur le statut personnel*, with letter to French Minister in Iraq (1/4/1939).
18. Both the 1928 document *Réforme du statut personnel* and the 1934 *Note sur les questions relatives au Statut Personnel*, cited above, use these words.
19. AD-SL Box 593, dossier *Juridictions religieuses. Statut personnel. Privilèges patriarcaux*, subdossier *Statut personnel. Juridictions religieuses [1927–28]. Note concernant l'arrêté sur les juridictions religieuses* (unattributed; Paris, 12/10/1926 – stamped 16/11/1926 on first page).
20. Berkes calls it 'the decisive moment in favour of secularism': *The Development of Secularism*, p. 467.
21. This and following quote: AD-SL Box 593, dossier *Juridictions religieuses. Statut personnel. Privilèges patriarcaux*, subdossier *Statut personnel. Juridictions religieuses [1927–28]. Note concernant l'arrêté sur les juridictions religieuses* (unattributed; Paris, 12/10/1926 – stamped 16/11/1926 on first page).
22. This and following quote from AD-SL Box 592, dossier *Statut personnel. Dossier général. Note sur les questions relatives au Statut Personnel*, stamped Gennardi and dated 24/5/1934, quotes at p. 7. Other factual information in this paragraph derives from the cited documents.
23. AD-SL Box 593, dossier *Juridictions religieuses. Statut personnel. Privilèges patriarcaux*, subdossier *Statut personnel. Juridictions religieuses [1927–28]. Note concernant l'arrêté sur les juridictions religieuses* (unattributed; Paris, 12/10/1926 – stamped 16/11/1926 on first page).
24. AD-SL Box 592, dossier *Statut personnel. Dossier général. Note sur les questions relatives au Statut Personnel*, stamped Gennardi and dated 24/5/1934, pp. 7–8.
25. AD-SL Box 592, dossier *Statut personnel. Dossier général. Note sur les questions relatives au Statut Personnel*, stamped Gennardi and dated 24/5/1934, p. 8.
26. These quotes and information in the rest of the paragraph from AD-SL Box 593, dossier *Juridictions religieuses. Statut personnel. Privilèges patriarcaux*, subdossier *Statut personnel. Juridictions religieuses [1927–28]. Note concernant l'arrêté sur les juridictions religieuses* (unattributed; Paris, 12/10/1926 – stamped 16/11/1926 on first page).
27. The long document on *Réforme du statut personnel* cited above was produced by the High Commissioner's delegate for the Contrôle Général des Wakfs under Ponsot, in February 1928. The Lebanese government took up the issue for itself in 1930 with a presidential decree-law (N°6, of 3/2/1930 – text available in AD-SL Box 592, dossier *A/s. du Statut Personnel*). This, too, provoked opposition: see, e.g., same location, Ponsot to MAE (10/3/1933), and the enclosed translation of article from *Osservatore Romano* and statement to Lebanese President of Christian patriarchs meeting at Bkerké.
28. AD-SL Box 592, dossier *Statut personnel. Dossier général. Note sur les questions relatives au Statut Personnel*, stamped Gennardi and dated 24/5/1934, quote at p. 13.

29. This and following quote from AD-SL Box 592, dossier *Statut personnel. Dossier général. Note exposant le point de vue de Monsieur le Haut-Commissaire au sujet du règlement des questions relatives au Statut Personnel* (7/6/1934).
30. One striking example is the report commissioned in September 1933 from the Lebanese judge and legal scholar Choucri Cardahi by Paul Boncour, the French Minister for Foreign Affairs, and entitled *En marge de la protection des minorités. La question du statut personnel; son évolution dans les pays du Proche Orient* (AD-SL Box 591, dossier *Statut personnel. Documentation*). This report was later published in *L'Asie française* (325, Dec. 1934, pp. 317–27), which did not mention that it had been commissioned by the MAE.
31. Also the Lebanese state, since the decree applied to the mandate territories as a whole.
32. This and following quote from AD-SL Box 592, dossier *Statut personnel. Dossier général. Note exposant le point de vue de Monsieur le Haut-Commissaire au sujet du règlement des questions relatives au Statut Personnel* (7/6/1934).
33. AD-SL Box 592, dossier *Statut personnel. Dossier général*. Letter, MAE to Martel (1/5/1935). The quotes come from the Italian legislation, a decree of 29/5/1929, directly cited in translation over two pages of this letter (Articles 3 and 9, respectively).
34. Some representative examples can be found in AD-SL Box 591, dossier *Statut personnel. Documentation*, including subdossiers on Egypt and Iraq. The latter contains issues of the *'Iraq Government Gazette* forwarded to Beirut by the French Legation to Iraq, with relevant items in the list of contents on the front page marked in blue pencil: for *IGG* No. 9 (28/2/1932) it is *Regulations of the Jewish Community – No. 36 of 1931*; a less directly relevant example is *IGG* No. 32 (2/8/1931), where *Official Holidays Law – No. 72 of 1931* is marked. The latter example illustrates just how wide the scope of personal status law could be.
35. AD-SL Box 591, dossier *Statut personnel. Documentation*. Document entitled *Réforme du statut personnel* (February 1928), p. 19.
36. AD-SL Box 592, dossier *Statut personnel. Dossier général. Note sur les questions relatives au Statut Personnel*, stamped Gennardi and dated 24/5/1934, pp. 9–13.
37. AD-SL Box 593, dossier *Statut personnel des communautés. Cas des réfugiés russes*. See especially note by Mazas, legislative counsellor (1/5/1936) and letter, d'Aumale (French Consul General in Palestine) to HC's delegate-general (16/6/1936).
38. See below.
39. The text of the decree can be found in AD-SL Box 592, dossier *Statut personnel. Dossier général*, subdossier *Statut dex [sic] communautés religieuses. Textes*. Another decree of the same day (61/LR) annulled all personal status legislation prior to Decree 60/LR once this and its related texts had come into effect.
40. This and following quote from AD-SL Box 592, dossier *A/s. du Statut Personnel*. Ponsot to MAE (21/4/1933).

41. The text can be found in AD-SL Box 592, dossier *Statut personnel. Dossier général*, subdossier *Statut dex* [sic] *communautés religieuses. Textes*.
42. See annexe I of the decree, listing 'communities enjoying *de jure* or *de facto* recognition'.
43. Titles I and II of the decree, respectively.
44. Berkes, *The Development of Secularism*, p. 158; Masters, *Christians and Jews*, chs 3–4.
45. Within Lebanon only, the decree also gave a special matrimonial regime to Protestants, not recognised as a personal status community (Article 22).
46. AD-SL Box 593, dossier *Application du Statut Personnel des Communautés religieuses [et la communauté musulmane –] Changement de religion et divorce*. Copy of letter from Ata Bey Ayoubi, Syrian PM, to HC's delegate in Damascus (20/5/1936), included with letter from HC's delegate to HC's delegate-general (22/5/1936).
47. Copies of all three can be found in AD-SL Box 593, dossier *Statut personnel. Dossiers particuliers*, subdossier *Statut personnel des sectes dissidentes de l'islam*, as enclosures with a letter from Schoeffler to Puaux (27/8/1940). One was from the 'traditional' religious authorities, the *shuyūkh 'aql* of Baakline, another from a group calling itself the Druze Reform Club (*al-Nādī al-islāhī al-darzī*). A third is unattributed.
48. AD-SL Box 592, dossier *Statut personnel. Dossier général*. Puaux to French Minister in Iraq (1/4/1939), enclosure *Note sur le statut personnel*.
49. AD-SL Box 593, dossier *Le Statut personnel et la Communauté Arménienne orthodoxe*. Papken I (Catholicos coadjuteur de Cilicie), to Meyrier, acting HC (12/5/1936), enclosure *Observations sur l'Avant-Projet*.
50. AD-SL Box 592, dossier *Statut personnel. Dossier général*. Martel to MAE (2/2/1938); Puaux to French Minister in Iraq (1/4/1939), enclosure *Note sur le statut personnel*.
51. Hourani, *Syria and Lebanon*, p. 218.
52. The text can be found in AD-SL Box 592, dossier *Statut personnel. Dossier général*, subdossier *Statut dex* [sic] *communautés religieuses. Textes*.
53. Article 6 simply tasked the High Commissioner's secretary-general with executing the decree.
54. AD-SL Box 592, dossier *Statut personnel. Dossier général*. Puaux to French Minister in Iraq (1/4/1939), enclosure *Note sur le statut personnel*.
55. AD-SL Box 592, dossier *Statut personnel. Dossier général*. Information N° 69/S (13/2/1939).
56. AD-SL Box 592, dossier *Statut personnel. Dossier général*. Information N° 66/S (13/2/1939); al-Hakim, *Sūriyya wal-intidāb al-faransī*, p. 287.
57. AD-SL Box 592, dossier *Statut personnel. Dossier général*. Information N° 66/S (13/2/1939). However, another delegation – this one including 'ulama' – visited Mardam Bek the same day to demand not just the suspension but the abrogation of the reform.

58. This and following from AD-SL Box 592, dossier *Statut personnel. Dossier général*. Puaux to French Minister in Iraq (1/4/1939), enclosure *Note sur le statut personnel*.
59. *Décision N° 69* of 11/3/1939, in AD-SL Box 592, dossier *Statut personnel. Dossier général*, subdossier *Statut dex [sic] communautés religieuses. Textes*.
60. AD-SL Box 592, dossier *Statut personnel. Dossier général*. Puaux to French Minister in Iraq (1/4/1939), enclosure *Note sur le statut personnel*.
61. AD-SL Box 592, dossier *Statut personnel. Dossier général*. Puaux to French Minister in Iraq (1/4/1939), enclosure *Note sur le statut personnel*. According to Yusuf al-Hakim, Puaux's exalted rhetorical style led some Syrians to compare him with an evangelical pastor: *Sūriyya wal-intidāb al-faransī*, p. 286.
62. Al-Hakim, *Sūriyya wal-intidāb al-faransī*, pp. 287–90. I discuss the rejection of the reform in more detail below.
63. AD-SL Box 592, dossier *Statut personnel. Dossier général*. Undated *Procès-Verbal* for the commission's session of 28/3[/1939].
64. Decree N°53/LR of 30/3/1939. Text available in AD-SL Box 592, dossier *Statut personnel. Dossier général*, subdossier *Statut dex [sic] communautés religieuses. Textes*.
65. AD-SL Box 592, dossier *Statut personnel. Dossier général*. Telegram, MAE to HC (30/3/1939).
66. This and following quote: AD-SL Box 592, dossier *Statut personnel. Dossier général*. Telegram, Puaux to MAE (31/3/1939).
67. This information, and the quotation, are from AD-SL Box 592, dossier *A/s. du Statut Personnel* (handwritten), subdossier *Congrès des patriarches pour l'étude des questions de statut personnel*. Letter, d'Aumale to MAE; undated, but this copy is marked 'Communiqué Beyrouth, le 11 Mars 1931'. The Armenian Orthodox had been in dispute with the British for more than a year over this.
68. Text available in AD-SL Box 592, dossier *Statut personnel. Dossier général*, subdossier *Statut dex [sic] communautés religieuses. Textes*.
69. This account is based on AD-SL Box 593, dossier *Statut personnel. Dossiers particuliers*, subdossier *Statut personnel des sectes dissidentes de l'islam. Note pour Monsieur le Secrétaire général* (30/4/1937), by the legislative counsellor, Mazas. All quotes are from this document. Mazas gives AH dates for the deaths of Husayn and Asma, 1330 and 1349 respectively; the CE dates are 1912 and 1930–1.
70. The French official reporting this judgement adds the qualifier that the court affirmed this 'if not in quite the terms employed here, at least very clearly'.
71. This tribunal had been set up by Decree 2978 of 5/12/1924, and was only competent to judge on personal status cases emanating from ecclesiastical courts *other* than the shariah courts. Note the difference, then, between this and the 'higher jurisdiction' envisaged by Decree 146 in 1938, whose competence did extend over the shariah courts, hence the fierce opposition to it. Decree 146, meanwhile, made no reference to the existing *tribunal des conflits*: in their attempt to reduce areas of potential conflict and overlapping competence between jurisdictions, the French

Personal Status Law Reform [205

had introduced a new one! A French official had to write to the High Commission to ask what would be the relationship between the new body and the old: AD-SL Box 592, dossier *Statut personnel. Dossier général. Note pour Monsieur le Conseiller législatif* from Meyrier (? – hard to read), 16/1/1939; enclosed letter, Fournier (Judicial counsellor of Syrian Republic, Inspector-General of Justice) to HC's delegate in Damascus (22/12/1938). The sheepish response was that Decree 146 'contented itself with envisaging the <u>future</u> institution' of a higher jurisdiction: same location, *Note* by Mazas, legislative counsellor (25/1/1939). This gives the impression that nobody had even thought of this problem and no-one knew what to do about it, so best to pretend it wasn't there. Which, because of the opposition to the decree – and notably to this measure – was soon the case.

72. In a later case relating to the Druzes the High Commission also accepted this principle of territoriality: see AD-SL Box 593, dossier *Statut personnel. Dossiers particuliers*, subdossier *Statut personnel des sectes dissidentes de l'islam*. Documents contained in *bordereau d'envoi*, HC to Inspecteur Général des Wakfs (29/7/1940); *Note pour Monsieur le Chef du Cabinet Politique* (7/8/1940); letter, HC to HC's assistant delegate for autonomous territory of Jabal Druze (9/8/1940).

73. French translations of various Ottoman legal texts cited in favour of a separate Druze status were forwarded to the French delegation in Damascus by Fakhri Kanafani in 1934, evidently with the backing of a number of Druze notables and religious leaders; carbon copies of his letter (dated 10/1/1934) and the texts were forwarded to Martel by the delegate as enclosures with a long letter (6/2/1934) discussing the general principles and their implications for other communities, but not the specifics of the Kanafani case. The conflicting precedents are also outlined in AD-SL Box 593, dossier *Statut personnel. Dossiers particuliers*, subdossier *Statut personnel des sectes dissidentes de l'islam*. HC's delegate to Syrian Republic to Martel (6/3/1936). The delegate requests instructions on the matter.

74. AD-SL Box 593, dossier *Statut personnel. Dossiers particuliers*, subdossier *Statut personnel des sectes dissidentes de l'islam*. Undated (1934) copy of letter, Syrian Minister of the Interior to French counsellor for the interior, enclosed with letter, HC's delegate to Syrian Republic to Martel (13/7/1934).

75. AD-SL Box 593, dossier *Statut personnel. Dossiers particuliers*, subdossier *Statut personnel des sectes dissidentes de l'islam*. Fain to HC's assistant delegates in Aleppo, Homs, Dayr al-Zur and inspector of special services (*Inspecteur des S.S.*) for Damascus and Hawran sanjaks (20/12/1935) enclosing copy of letter, assistant counsellor of HCt/HC's assistant delegate for autonomous Sanjak of Alexandretta (10/2/1934). NB: this and all the replies on the subject cited below are archive copies rather than originals.

76. The 'Alawi community already had such recognition in the Alaouites, but evidently not in the rest of Syria. The governor of the Alaouites was not among the addressees.

77. This and following from AD-SL Box 593, dossier *Statut personnel. Dossiers*

particuliers, subdossier *Statut personnel des sectes dissidentes de l'islam*. Fain to HC's assistant delegates in Aleppo etc. (20/12/1935). Enclosed copy of letter, assistant counsellor of HCt/HC's assistant delegate for autonomous Sanjak of Alexandretta (10/2/1934).

78. This and following from AD-SL Box 593, dossier *Statut personnel. Dossiers particuliers*, subdossier *Statut personnel des sectes dissidentes de l'islam*. HC's assistant delegate for sanjaks of Homs and Hama to HC's delegate to Syrian Republic (21/1/1936).
79. This and following from AD-SL Box 593, dossier *Statut personnel. Dossiers particuliers*, subdossier *Statut personnel des sectes dissidentes de l'islam*. Trojani, special services officer/chief of A'zaz post to HC's assistant delegate for vilayet of Aleppo (26/1/1936).
80. This and following from AD-SL Box 593, dossier *Statut personnel. Dossiers particuliers*, subdossier *Statut personnel des sectes dissidentes de l'islam*. Tuillier, special services officer/chief of Idlib post to HC's assistant delegate for vilayet of Aleppo (10/1/1936).
81. AD-SL Box 593, dossier *Statut personnel. Dossiers particuliers*, subdossier *Statut personnel des sectes dissidentes de l'islam*. Grall, inspector of special services for sanjaks of Damascus and Hawran to HC's delegate to the Syrian Republic (16/1/1936).
82. Even in the French case there have been many exceptions to the prized republican uniformity, e.g., in Alsace and Algeria. But the importance of this uniformity is as a norm towards which practice, at least to some extent, strives.
83. It should be noted that the synagogues of Damascus, Aleppo and Beirut were considered as three *separate* communities under Decree 60 (annexe I). This may reflect the absence of a 'church' hierarchy among the Jewish community.
84. Thomas Hylland Eriksen, 'Linguistic hegemony and minority resistance', *Journal of Peace Research* (1992), 29(3): 313–32, discusses many of these issues.
85. These and following quotes from MWT, *wathā'iq al-dawla*, sijill 2, *wizārat al-dākhiliyya*, 74: al-Qassab to Syrian minister of interior (8/2/1939).
86. This phrasing went down particularly badly with Syrian Christian leaders, who pointed out that Christians and Jews were just as much 'chez eux' in Syria as Muslims – though they ignored its clear reference to the division in Islamic law between *dār al-islām* and *dār al-harb*.
87. One such case was that of Wadiah bent Abdallah Loutfi, a Greek Catholic who converted to Islam and thereby obtained a divorce from her husband. Documents detailing the case from the period December 1935–May 1936 were filed under both 'minorities' and 'personal status', so to speak: in AD-SL Box 494, dossier *Traité Franco-Syrie – Application – Question des minorités*, and in AD-SL Box 593, dossier *Application du Statut Personnel des Communautés religieuses* [hw: *et la communauté musulmane –*] *Changement de religion et divorce*.
88. MWT, *wathā'iq al-dawla*, sijill 2; *wizārat al-dākhiliyya*. 16/5381: governor of Homs to Syrian interior ministry (11/2/1939).

89. This and following quotes from petition enclosed with MWT, *wathā'iq al-dawla*, sijill 2; *wizārat al-dākhiliyya*. 16/5381: governor of Homs to Syrian interior ministry (11/2/1939).
90. This refers to children who were majors at the time of his conversion, since children who were minors would have followed him.
91. This and following quotes from petition enclosed with MWT, *wathā'iq al-dawla*, sijill 2; *wizārat al-dākhiliyya*. 16/5381: governor of Homs to Syrian interior ministry (11/2/1939).
92. Compare Gelvin's point (in *The Modern Middle East*, pp. 137–8) about *al-Haqa'iq*, a periodical published by Damascus 'ulama' just before the First World War that called for the creation of 'an Islamic political party to compete in the arena of mass politics':

> That the ulama associated with *al-Haqa'iq* would even think of founding an Islamic political party to guarantee the 'progress' of the 'nation' demonstrates the extent to which the nineteenth-century cultural, social and political transformation had influenced religious doctrines and institutions in the Ottoman Empire.

93. A summarised version of my discussion of these documents appeared as a 'Quick study' in *International Journal of Middle Eastern Studies* (2010), 42(1): 10–12.
94. I thank Thomas Pierret for this point.
95. Representative samples can be found in AD-SL Box 592, dossier *Suspension statut personnel*.
96. Yusuf al-Hakim, a member of the commission, lists the Association of 'Ulama's seven theses accurately in his memoirs (*Sūriyya wal-intidāb al-faransī*, p. 289) and states that the majority of the commission agreed with them – unsurprisingly, since Kamil al-Qassab now sat on it.
97. This and following from AD-SL Box 592, dossier *Statut personnel. Dossier général.* Cutting from *al-Bashir*, 24/3/[1939]. All emphases in original. NB: *al-Bashir* was a bilingual publication: this editorial was in French, but Arabic predominated.
98. This and following: AD-SL Box 592, dossier *Suspension statut personnel*. Letter to HC (29/3/1939); copy of *al-Bashir* (4/4/1939). The letter is an unsigned copy; an editor's note in the issue of *al-Bashir* says it was presented by a conference grouping all Catholic patriarchs and bishops of Syria and Lebanon 'without exception'.
99. This and following from al-Hakim, *Sūriyya wal-intidāb al-faransī*, p. 290.
100. AD-SL Box 592, dossier *Statut personnel. Dossier général.* Puaux to MAE (22/3/1939).
101. Tappouni, who was made a cardinal around this time, also featured especially often in the archives relating to the treaty negotiations. His weight in French considerations was disproportionate given the modest size of his flock relative to several other Christian communities.

102. AD-SL Box 592, dossier *Statut personnel. Dossier général.* Puaux to French Minister in Iraq (1/4/1939), enclosure *Note sur le statut personnel.*
103. MWT, *wathā'iq al-dawla*, sijill 2; *wizārat al-dākhiliyya.* 76: letter from governor of Aleppo to Ministry of Interior (18/3/1939), forwarded to Prime Minister's office (21/3/1939); 19/5384: petition forwarded to interior ministry by governor of Homs (14/2/1939); 27/5392: telegrams from Homs forwarded to interior ministry by governor of Homs (27/2/1939). The *Tajhīz* schools were civil secondary schools, whose pupils would have been predominantly Muslim. Other instances of this word will not be italicised.
104. MWT, *wathā'iq al-dawla*, sijill 2; *wizārat al-dākhiliyya.* 29/5394: letter from governor of Hawran to interior ministry (14/3/1939) covering two letters of protest (not present).
105. MWT, *wathā'iq al-dawla*, sijill 2; *wizārat al-dākhiliyya.* 30/5395: letter from governor of Homs to interior ministry (18/3/1939).
106. Personal communication from Souheil Chebat. This demonstration took place in the winter of 1937 or 1938, when he was eight or nine years old.
107. Al-Hakim, *Sūriyya wal-intidāb al-faransī*, pp. 299–301.
108. AD-SL Box 592, dossier *Suspension statut personnel.* Letter to HC (29/3/1939); copy of *al-Bashir* (4/4/1939).
109. Al-Hakim, *Sūriyya wal-intidāb al-faransī*, p. 290, note 1.

CONCLUSION

MINORITIES, MAJORITIES AND THE WRITING OF HISTORY

The week before I submitted the doctoral thesis on which this book is based, I met an American historian in the library where I was fretting over my footnotes. One day we went for lunch, and she asked me a question: what, in a single sentence, is the argument of your thesis? Somewhere around the fourteenth subordinate clause of my answer I had to accept that I was no longer in the realm of a single sentence, and gave up. I should think about an answer, she told me, since that question often came up in job interviews.[1]

That night, long after midnight, I was walking home from the library down a quiet Oxford street when I suddenly realised that I had the answer. In fact, I could get it down to four words, short enough to fit on a t-shirt: *Objective conditions, subjective categories*. Or, in the full sentence version: The nation-state form creates the objective conditions in which people begin to consider themselves as majorities and minorities; however, these remain subjective categories.

This book has sought to demonstrate that 'minorities' emerged in Syria during the mandate period, as a result of the development of the nation-state form. As state authority spread across the territory, it bound the population more closely together as a single unit under a single set of institutions within fixed borders. For some groups within the population, this fixed them in a state structure where they were a minority; it gave others a sense of belonging to, and the scope for acting as, a 'majority' within the state. As the presence of the state in the everyday life of the population intensified, the institutional relationship between population and state was redefined; because the state now claimed to represent the population, whichever group could constitute itself as the majority could claim the right to define that relationship. Others had more limited rights (whether formally or informally defined), and were constituted as minorities. It was this transformation of the state that created the objective conditions within which Syrians began to understand their society as being made up of minorities and a majority. Precisely how they chose to define those groups, and what political implications they drew from their definition, was an open question: the categories themselves remained subjective.

As I have argued, this makes it unwise to understand French policy simply in terms of minorities and majorities. The French, who so actively sought to institutionalise divisions within Syrian society, did not initially do so on the grounds that certain communities were minorities. However, when the state structures that they put in place – and Syrians sought to control – made that category meaningful, the French sought to harness it. In ways that would serve their own ends, they tried to limit its application to certain groups, and define its legal content. The logic of the nation-state form, however, meant that the category escaped simple definition by the imperial power. On one level, it was defined by a body of international law over which France had very limited influence. On another, there was nothing to stop Syrians using or rejecting it on their own terms. Syrians from groups the French did not want to call minorities adopted the term to describe themselves; others whom the French did seek to define as minorities proclaimed themselves part of the majority.

If we look at the emergence of minorities from the other direction, we also see that they are not exceptional groups within modern nation-states: if they are marginal, it is only in the sense that a margin defines a page. The existence of separatist movements shows us state authority in the act of spreading; when such movements based their claims on a cultural identity different to that of the state, they highlighted the cultural identity that the state itself now adopted – or at least, had attributed to it. As the definition of borders turned some communities into minorities, it also permitted the definition of the majority. The application to Syria of the international law on minorities marked Syria's status in the internationally recognised order as a nation-state becoming independent, at least nominally; within Syria, the definition of legally-protected 'minorities' served to define the majority, and its relationship to the state that now claimed to represent it. In many ways, the history of the nation-state is the history of minorities: that is, the history of the processes that lead certain groups to be defined as 'minorities'.

Other, equally valid subjects suggest themselves for case studies like the ones I have presented here: language is an obvious one, touched on tangentially in several places throughout this book. All of the examples I have presented are Syrian, but the phenomena I elucidate can easily be identified elsewhere. This book has sought to offer a specific case study, while also providing an analytical framework that can be applied to other cases in order to understand the changes that affect the architecture of community[2] under the multiple pressures of modern state development. By doing so, it has also shown how historicising the category of minority itself (and its twin, majority) opens new perspectives on that development – perspectives that are concealed when minorities are simply assumed to exist, as such.

If minorities are not marginal to the history of modern states, how has their history been marginalised? First of all, one can identify a 'majority view': one where the writing of history contributes, knowingly or not, to the same process of defining a majority that has run through this book as the corollary to the definition of minorities. Those who claim to speak for a majority – not a claim I accept uncritically, as will be clear to the reader by now – are most concerned with that majority's history, understood as a nation's history. By writing 'national' history they affirm the majority's existence in the present and project it back into the past; in doing so, they also assimilate the history of the state to that of the nation. Of course, this is not only true of professional historians. Politicians, journalists, novelists, television producers, teachers and many others, not all of them directly part of the state, all make more or less elaborate references to a national past: this is part of the everyday maintenance that nations require. Present-day minorities enter the picture only to the extent that their history touches that of the majority: to return to our Syrian example, consider the Armenian immigrant who threatens the fatherland, or indeed who demonstrates the moral qualities (tolerance, hospitality) of a Syrian nation to which he remains fundamentally foreign. Both can be found in the works of the great Syrian historian Muhammad Kurd ʿAli; but the Armenian refugee as a Syrian is a rare bird.[3] Foreigners may adopt this majority viewpoint by default, either because they too focus on the history of the 'nation' (even when approaching it more critically as the history of a particular nationalism) or because they unquestioningly apply categories transferred from their own historical context.

The 'minority viewpoint' is the flip side of the majority viewpoint, and constitutes a self-marginalisation. Members of these communities who want to rehabilitate a history effaced from national histories; foreigners who, *a priori*, see minorities in the society they study: they take for granted that their community has always been a minority, relative to a dominant community always constituted as a majority. The majority and the state which is assumed to represent it enter their narrative only to the extent that their history touches that of the minority under study. In other words, by depicting the history of the minority they seek to define it in the present and project it back into the past: national history writ small, as it were, in which one may detect a concern to justify a claim to a future state. By seeing the minority history as separate from the majority history, such accounts may reinforce rather than overcome its marginalisation. Meanwhile, by associating domination with the majority and subordination with the minority, even in order to make a (laudable) protest against injustice, they may also obscure the real forms of domination that are common to both.[4]

In this analysis, both majority and minority histories impose present categories and preconceptions on the past in ways that pose serious obstacles to our understanding. It would be futile, not to mention impossible, to try and eliminate our consciousness of the present from our understanding of the past: history is, precisely, applying a present consciousness to the past. We view the past through the prism of the present, in the hope that this will help us understand the present through the prism of the past. Nonetheless, it is possible to maintain a critical awareness of our own position, and the categories and preconceptions it brings with it. I have tried to suggest one way of doing this here, by historicising a concept that historians and others routinely use to describe past and present societies.[5] Such a critical awareness can help us avoid taking for granted, wrongly, that conditions obtaining in contemporary states and societies obtained in earlier ones. At the same time, it can help us reach a fuller understanding of how the contemporary world was formed. And it may offer a means of defence when history is abused, as it always will be, for divisive political ends.

Notes

1. This was Diana Davis, of UC Davis, and I would like to thank her.
2. Watenpaugh (*Being Modern in the Middle East*, p. 26) borrows this phrase from Geoff Eley and Ronald Grigor Suny.
3. Muhammad Kurd ʿAli, *Khitat al-Shām*, vol. 3, 3rd edn (Damascus: Maktabat al-Nūri, 1983 [1928]), pp. 163–5, and *Mudhakkirāt*, vol. 3 (Damascus: Matbaʿat al-Taraqqi, 1949), pp. 685–6. Their refugee origin has marked the Armenians out (not only from the 'outside') as a non-Syrian group – further removed from the 'majority' than members of many other Syrian minorities – long after most of them became Syrian citizens comfortable speaking Arabic: Nicola Migliorino, '"*Kulna suriyyin?*" The Armenian community and the state in contemporary Syria', in *La Syrie au quotidien. Cultures et pratiques du changement*, special issue of *Revue des mondes musulmans et de la Méditerranée* (2006), 115–16: 97–115.
4. Both may be deliberate as well as unwitting, of course.
5. Mazower, *Salonica*, and Norman Davies and Roger Moorhouse, *Microcosm: Portrait of a Central European City* (London: Jonathan Cape, 2002) suggest another: each writes the history of a city in a way that extracts that history from the nationalist accounts that have claimed it, while examining the effects on the city and its people of competing nationalisms.

SELECT BIBLIOGRAPHY

Archival Sources

(i) Ministère des Affaires Etrangères, Centre des archives diplomatiques (Nantes), fonds Syrie-Liban

Reference in text as AD-SL Box 123, dossier *title*, subdossier *title*. Document (date). Thus:

AD-SL Box 568, dossier *Tcherkess*, subdossier *Armement des villages tcherkess de Boueidan, Blei, Bourak*. HC's delegate to State of Syria (Veber) to HC's delegate to Contrôle Général des Wakfs (23/2/1928).

Not all dossiers are properly inventoried and not all documents are in dossiers. Sometimes, therefore, the folder information is sketchy. To save space, where a document such as a *Note* or an intelligence service *Information* has a number, I identify it by that number and the date only. Since not all – not many! – signatures are legible, names are often not given.

All cited documents are from the *1er versement* unless stated. The rare exceptions are from Série B, the 'nominative dossiers' on individuals – these are identified in the reference.

(ii) Service Historique de l'Armée du Terre (Vincennes), sub-series 4 H (Levant, 1917–1946)

Reference in text as SHAT 4 H Box 123, dossier 1: *title*, subdossier *title*. Document (date). Thus:

SHAT 4 H Box 168, dossier 1: *Opérations des troupes du territoire de l'Euphrate dans la Haute-Djézireh (occupation du Bec de Canard) 1927–1930*, subdossier *Organisation des Postes du Bec de Canard et occupation de [ces postes]. Note sur l'action politique menée dans la Région Nord de Djézireh* . . . (1/12/1926)

The same points apply here as above, although in general the organisation of documents within the box is clearer. Notably, as a rule each dossier within a box is numbered.

(iii) Markaz al-wathā'iq al-tārikhiyya (Damascus), state documents collection
Reference in text as MWT, *wathā'iq al-dawla*, sijill [inventory] number; section – subsections. Document number (description and date where necessary). Thus:
MWT *wathā'iq al-dawla*, sijill 2; *wizārat al-dākhiliyya – al-amn al-'ām – taqārīr*. 1: letter from Khayrī Ridā, qā'immaqām of Kurd Dagh, to minister of interior (25/4/1934).
In the Syrian archives, the same call number may group several related documents (e.g., correspondence on a specific topic). In this case I have given the range of dates and a general description where citing the whole group, the individual date where citing a single document. Sometimes there are two overlapping sequences of numerotation – in some cases I have given both numbers for ease of triangulation.

(iv) Private papers of Albert Zurayq
These documents were kindly made available to me by Souheil Chebat, Damascus.

Newspapers and Periodicals

(i) In Arabic
Except where stated, Arabic titles were consulted at the Asad Library, Damascus.
al-Ayyām, Damascus.
Alif Bā', Damascus.
al-Muqtabas, Damascus.
al-Qabas, Damascus (all references from articles reprinted in al-Rayyis 1994).
al-Yawm, Damascus. NB: *al-Yawm* was published during *al-Ayyām*'s periods of suspension in order to bypass the suspension order; issues of *al-Yawm* carried two numbers, one for the title's own sequential numerotation and one for that issue's place in the numerotation of *al-Ayyām*.

(ii) In French
Journal officiel de la République française – Débats parlementaires – Débats de l'Assemblée Nationale, Paris.
L'Asie française, Paris. NB: *L'Asie française* published longer articles with and without individual bylines, and shorter uncredited 'Chroniques' (news articles). Unless an author is cited in my footnotes, articles are uncredited. Credited articles are not cited individually in the bibliography. The bulletin was usually published monthly (every two months between July and October), but appeared irregularly during the First World War: three issues in 1915, four in 1916, etc.

Select Bibliography

Reference Works

These standard multi-volume reference works are mostly included because specific entries from them are cited, as historical sources, in Chapter 1. Single-volume and/or single-authored dictionaries and encyclopaedias are listed under *Books and Articles*.

(i) Lexicographical Dictionaries

Grand Larousse de la langue française (Paris 1975).
Hachette Dictionnaire de la langue française (Paris 1876).
Le Robert dictionnaire historique de la langue française (Paris 1992/1998).
Le Robert dictionnaire de la langue française (Paris 1985).
Oxford English Dictionary online (www.oed.com).

(ii) Encyclopaedias

Encyclopaedia Britannica, 11th edn (Cambridge: Cambridge University Press, 1910–11) and 14th edn (London: Encyclopaedia Britannica Co., 1929).
Encyclopedia of Islam, CD-ROM edition (Leiden: Brill 1999–).
Encyclopaedia of the Social Sciences (New York: Macmillan 1930–5).
International Encyclopedia of the Social Sciences (New York: Macmillan & Free Press, 1968).
International Encyclopedia of the Social & Behavioral Sciences (Oxford: Elsevier, 2001).

Books and Articles

For all articles cited in online versions, date of viewing should be taken as 31 January 2011.

Abrams, L. and D. J. Miller, 'Who were the French colonialists? A reassessment of the parti colonial, 1890–1914', *The Historical Journal* (1976), 19(3): 685–725.
Aldrich, Robert, *Greater France. A History of French Overseas Expansion* (London: Palgrave, 1996).
Altuğ, Seda and Benjamin Thomas White, 'Frontières et pouvoir d'État. La frontière turco-syrienne dans les années 1920 et 1930', *Vingtième siècle. Revue d'histoire* (2009), 103: 91–104.
Anderson, Benedict, *Imagined Communities: Reflections on the Origin and Spread of Nationalism*, rev. edn (London: Verso, 1991).
Anderson, Benedict, 'Nationalism', in Joel Krieger (ed.), *The Oxford Companion to Politics of the World*, 2nd edn (Oxford: Oxford University Press, 2001).
Andréa, Général Charles, *La révolte druze et l'insurrection de Damas 1925–1926* (Paris: Payot, 1937).
Andrew, C. M. and A. K. Kanya-Forstner, 'The French "colonial party": its composition, aims and influence, 1885–1914', *The Historical Journal* (1971), 14(1): 99–128.

Andrew, C. M. and A. S. Kanya-Forstner, 'The Groupe Colonial in the French Chamber of Deputies, 1892–1932', *The Historical Journal* (1974), 17(4): 837–66.

Antonius, George, *The Arab Awakening* (London: Hamish Hamilton, 1938).

Arendt, Hannah, *The Origins of Totalitarianism*, paperback edn (London: André Deutsch, 1986). NB: Edition information is unclear in this book, but it appears to be an unrevised paperback of the 1973 edition, unchanged from the 3rd edition (1968) except for the addition of new prefaces.

Ayalon, Ami, *Reading Palestine: Printing and Literacy, 1900–1948* (Austin, TX: University of Texas Press, 2004).

Ayalon, Ami, *The Press in the Arab Middle East: A History* (Oxford: Oxford University Press, 1995).

Bābīl, Nasūh, *Sihāfa wa siyāsa. Sūriyya fil-qarn al-'ishrīn* (*Press and Politics. Syria in the Twentieth Century*), 2nd edn (Beirut: Riad al-Rayyes, 2001).

Balibar, Étienne, 'The nation form: history and ideology', in Balibar and Wallerstein, *Race, Nation, Class*, pp. 86–106.

Balibar, Étienne and Immanuel Wallerstein, *Race, Nation, Class. Ambiguous Identities*, trans. Chris Turner (London: Verso, 1991).

Bancel, Nicolas, Pascal Blanchard and Françoise Vergès, *La République coloniale. Essai sur une utopie* (Paris: Albin Michel, 2003).

Banks, Marcus, *Ethnicity: Anthropological Constructions* (London: Routledge, 1996).

Barber, Peter and Tom Harper, *Magnificent Maps: Power, Propaganda and Art* (London: The British Library, 2010). Exhibition catalogue.

Barkey, Karen, *Empire of Difference: The Ottomans in Comparative Perspective* (Cambridge: Cambridge University Press, 2008).

Barkey, Henri J. and Graham E. Fuller, *Turkey's Kurdish Question* (Lanham, MD: Rowman & Littlefield, 1998).

Batatu, Hanna, *Syria's Peasantry, the Descendants of its Lesser Rural Notability, and their Politics* (Princeton, NJ: Princeton University Press, 1999).

Bayly, C. A., *The Birth of the Modern World, 1780–1914: Global Connections and Comparisons* (Oxford: Blackwell, 2004).

Beauplan, Robert de, *Où va la Syrie? Le mandat sous les cèdres* (Paris: J. Tallandier, 1929).

Beinin, Joel, *Workers and Peasants in the Modern Middle East* (Cambridge: Cambridge University Press, 2001).

Ben-Dor, Gabriel, 'Ethnopolitics and the Middle Eastern state', in Esman and Rabinovich (eds), *Ethnicity, Pluralism, and the State*, pp. 71–92.

Bengio, Ofra and Gabriel Ben-Dor (eds), *Minorities and the State in the Arab World* (Boulder, CO: Lynne Rienner Publishers, 1999).

Benot, Yves, *Massacres coloniaux 1944–1950: la IVe République et la mise au pas des colonies françaises*, paperback edition with new afterword (Paris: La Découverte, 2001).

Berger, Maurits, 'Regulating tolerance: protecting Egypt's minorities', in Baudoin

Dupret (ed.), *Standing Trial: Law and the Person in the Modern Middle East* (London: I. B. Tauris, 2004), pp. 345–71.

Berkes, Niyazi, *The Development of Secularism in Turkey* (Montreal: McGill University Press, 1964).

Berstein, Gisèle and Serge Berstein, *La Troisième République. Les noms, les thèmes, les lieux* (Paris: MA Éditions, 1987).

Bianquis, Anne-Marie (ed.), *Damas. Miroir brisé d'un Orient arabe* (Paris: Autrement, 1993).

Blanchard, Pascal and Sandrine Lemaire (eds), *Culture impériale. Les colonies au cœur de la République, 1931–1961* (Paris: Autrement, 2004).

Blanchard, Pascal and Sandrine Lemaire (eds), *Culture coloniale. La France conquise par son empire 1871–1931* (Paris: Autrement, 2003).

Bloch, Marc, *L'Étrange défaite* (Paris: Gallimard, 1990 [1946]).

Bloxham, Donald, *The Great Game of Genocide. Imperialism, Nationalism, and the Destruction of the Ottoman Armenians* (Oxford: Oxford University Press, 2005).

Blumi, Isa, 'Contesting the edges of the Ottoman Empire: rethinking ethnic and sectarian boundaries in the Malësore, 1878–1912', *International Journal of Middle East Studies* (2003), 35(2): 237–56.

Borne, Dominique and Henri Dubief, *Nouvelle histoire de la France contemporaine 13. La Crise des années 30, 1929–1938* (Paris: Seuil, 1989).

Boudon, Raymond and François Bourricaud, *A Critical Dictionary of Sociology* (London: Routledge, 1989).

Bou-Nacklie, N. E., 'Les Troupes Spéciales: religious and ethnic recruitment, 1916–46', *International Journal of Middle East Studies* (1993), 25(4): 645–60.

Bozarslan, Hamit, 'États et modes de gestion du probléme kurde', in *Les Kurdes et les États*, special issue of *Peuples méditerranéens* (1994), 68–69: 185–214.

Brandell, Inga (ed.), *State Frontiers: Borders and Boundaries in the Middle East* (London: I. B. Tauris, 2006).

Brandell, Inga and Annika Rabo, 'Arab nations and nationalism: dangers and virtues of transgressing disciplines', *Orientalia Suecana* (2003), LI–LII: 35–46.

Braude, Benjamin, 'Foundation myths of the *millet* system', in Braude and Lewis, *Christians and Jews in the Ottoman Empire*, vol. 1, pp. 69–88.

Braude, Benjamin and Bernard Lewis (eds), *Christians and Jews in the Ottoman Empire: The Functioning of a Plural Society. Vol. 1: The Central Lands* and *Vol. 2: The Arab Lands* (New York: Holmes & Meier, 1982).

Breuilly, John, *Nationalism and the State*, 2nd rev. edn (Manchester: Manchester University Press, 1993).

Bulliet, Richard W., 'Process and status in conversion and continuity', in Michael Gervers and Ramzi Jibran Bikhazi (eds), *Conversion and Continuity: Indigenous Christian Communities in Islamic Lands, Eighth to Eighteenth Centuries* (Toronto: Pontifical Institute of Mediaeval Studies, 1990), pp. 1–12.

Bulliet, Richard W., *Conversion to Islam in the Medieval Period: An Essay in Quantitative History* (Cambridge, MA: Harvard University Press, 1979).

Bullock, Alan, Stephen Trombley and Bruce Eadie, *The Harper Dictionary of Modern Thought* (London: Harper & Row, 1988).
Burke, Edmund, 'Orientalism and world history: representing Middle Eastern nationalism and Islamism in the twentieth century', *Theory and Society* (1998), 27(4): 489–507.
Burke, Edmund, 'A comparative view of French native policy in Morocco and Syria, 1912–1925', *Middle Eastern Studies* (1973), 9(3): 175–86.
Cagaptay, Soner, *Islam, Secularism, and Nationalism in Modern Turkey. Who is a Turk?* (London: Routledge, 2006).
Calderwood, Howard B., 'International affairs: The proposed generalization of the minorities régime', *The American Political Science Review* (1934), 28(6): 1088–98.
Cashmore, Ellis Ernest, Michael Banton and Heribert Adam, *Dictionary of Race and Ethnic Relations*, 4th edn (London: Routledge, 1996).
Chidiac, Edmond, 'Les intérêts communs syro-libanais (1920–1950)', in Méouchy (ed.), *France, Syrie et Liban*, pp. 259–71.
Choksy, Jamsheed K., *Conflict and Cooperation. Zoroastrian Subalterns and Muslim Elites in Medieval Iranian Society* (New York: Columbia University Press, 1997).
Choueiri, Youssef M. (ed.), *State and Society in Syria and Lebanon* (Exeter: University of Exeter Press, 1993).
Choueiri, Youssef M., *Arab History and the Nation-State: A Study in Modern Arab Historiography 1820–1980* (London: Routledge, 1989).
Clark, Bruce, *Twice a Stranger: How Mass Expulsion Forged Modern Greece and Turkey* (London: Granta, 2006).
Clarke, Paul and Joe Foweraker (eds), *Encyclopedia of Democratic Thought* (London: Routledge, 2001).
Cleveland, William L., 'The Arab nationalism of George Antonius reconsidered', in Jankowski and Gershoni (eds), *Rethinking Arab Nationalism*, pp. 65–86.
Cleveland, William L., *A History of the Modern Middle East*, 3rd edn (Oxford: Westview Press, 2004).
Cohen, Amnon, 'On the realities of the millet system: Jerusalem in the sixteenth century', in Braude and Lewis, *Christians and Jews in the Ottoman Empire*, vol. 2, pp. 7–18.
Cohen, Mark R., *Under Crescent and Cross. The Jews in the Middle Ages* (Princeton, NJ: Princeton University Press, 1994).
Cohen, Ronald, 'Ethnicity: problem and focus in anthropology', *Annual Review of Anthropology* (1978), 7: 379–403.
Colley, Linda, *Britons: Forging the Nation, 1707–1837*, 2nd edn (London: Yale University Press, 2005).
Commins, David, *Historical Dictionary of Syria* (Lanham, MD: Scarecrow Press, 1996).
Commins, David, 'Religious reformers and Arabists in Damascus, 1885–1914', *International Journal of Middle East Studies* (1984), 18(4): 405–25.

Coquery-Vidrovitch, Catherine and Charles-Robert Ageron, *Histoire de la France coloniale III. Le déclin. 1931 à nos jours* (Paris: Armand Colin, 1991).

Dalrymple, William, *From the Holy Mountain. A Journey in the Shadow of Byzantium* (London: HarperCollins, 1997).

Davie, May, 'Les Orthodoxes entre Beyrouth et Damas: une *millet* chrétienne dans deux villes ottomanes', in Choueiri (ed.), *State and Society in Syria and Lebanon*, pp. 32–45.

Davies, Norman and Roger Moorhouse, *Microcosm: Portrait of a Central European City* (London: Jonathan Cape, 2002).

Davison, Roderic H., 'Turkish attitudes concerning Christian–Muslim equality in the nineteenth century', in Hourani *et al.* (eds), *The Modern Middle East*, pp. 61–81 (first published 1954).

Davison, Roderic H., *Essays in Ottoman and Turkish History, 1774–1923: The Impact of the West* (London: Saqi Books, 1990).

Davison, Roderic H., 'The advent of the principle of representation in the government of the Ottoman empire', in Davison, *Essays*, pp. 96–111 (first published 1968).

Davison, Roderic H., 'The *millets* as agents of change in the nineteenth-century Ottoman empire', in Braude and Lewis (eds), *Christians and Jews in the Ottoman Empire*, vol. 1, pp. 319–37.

Dawn, C. Ernest, 'From Ottomanism to Arabism: the origin of an ideology', in Hourani *et al.* (eds), *The modern Middle East*, pp. 375–93 (first published 1973).

Dawn, C. Ernest, 'The origins of Arab nationalism', in Khalidi *et al.* (eds), *The Origins of Arab Nationalism*, pp. 3–30.

Deguilhem, Randi, 'State civil education in late Ottoman Damascus: a unifying or a separating force?', in Philipp and Schaebler (eds), *The Syrian Land*, pp. 221–50.

Deringil, Selim, *The Well-protected Domains: Ideology and the Legitimation of Power in the Ottoman Empire, 1876–1909* (London: I. B. Tauris, 1998).

Dodge, Toby, *Inventing Iraq: The Failure of Nation Building and a History Denied*, paperback edition with new preface (London: Columbia University Press, 2005).

Dodge, Toby, 'International obligation, domestic pressure and colonial nationalism; the birth of the Iraqi state under the mandate system', in Méouchy and Sluglett (eds), *The British and French Mandates*, pp. 143–64.

Elias, Elias Hanna, *La presse arabe* (Paris: Maisonneuve et Larose, 1993).

El-Saleh, Mohammed Ali, 'Les aspects économiques généraux de la relation mandataire: France, Syrie et Liban 1918–1946', in Méouchy (ed.), *France, Syrie et Liban*, pp. 197–210.

Elvin, Mark, 'A working definition of "modernity"?', *Past and Present* (1986), 113: 209–13.

Eriksen, Thomas Hylland, 'Linguistic hegemony and minority resistance', *Journal of Peace Research* (1992), 29(3): 313–32.

Esman, Milton J. and Itamar Rabinovich (eds), *Ethnicity, Pluralism, and the State in the Middle East* (Ithaca, NY: Cornell University Press, 1988). Their own contribution is 'The study of ethnic politics in the Middle East', pp. 3–24.

Findley, Carter V., 'The acid test of Ottomanism: the acceptance of non-Muslims in the late Ottoman bureaucracy', in Braude and Lewis (eds), *Christians and Jews in the Ottoman Empire*, vol. 1, pp. 339–68.

Firro, Kais M., 'Ethnicizing the Shi'is in mandatory Lebanon', *Middle Eastern Studies* (2006), 42(5): 741–59.

Firro, Kais M., *Inventing Lebanon: Nationalism and the State under the Mandate* (London: I. B. Tauris, 2003).

Firro, Kais M., 'The Druze in and between Syria, Lebanon and Israel', in Esman and Rabinovich (eds), *Ethnicity, Pluralism, and the State*, pp. 185–97.

Fournié, Pierre, 'Le Mandat à l'épreuve des passions françaises: l'affaire Sarrail (1925)', in Méouchy (ed.), *France, Syrie et Liban*, pp. 125–68.

Fournié, Pierre, 'La représentation des particularismes ethniques et religieux en Syrie et au Liban', in Pascal Blanchard, Stéphane Blanchoin and Nicolas Bancel (eds), *L'autre et nous: «Scènes et types». Anthropologues et historiens devant les représentations des populations colonisées, des «ethnies», des «tribus» et des «races» depuis les conquêtes coloniales* (Paris: ACHAC, 1995), pp. 137–41.

Fournié, Pierre and Jean-Louis Riccioli, *La France et le Proche-Orient 1916–1946. Une chronique photographique de la présence française en Syrie et au Liban, en Palestine, au Hedjaz et en Cilicie* (Tournai: Casterman, 1996).

Fournié, Pierre and François-Xavier Trégan, 'Outils documentaires sur le mandat français', Méouchy and Sluglett (eds), *The British and French Mandates*, pp. 45–53.

Francis, E. K., 'Minority groups – a revision of concepts', *British Journal of Sociology* (1951), 2(3): 219–29, 254.

Friedman, Jonathan, 'The past in the future: history and the politics of identity', *American Anthropologist*, new series (1992), 94(4): 837–59.

Fromkin, David, *A Peace to End all Peace. The Fall of the Ottoman Empire and the Creation of the Modern Middle East*, paperback edition (London: Phoenix Press, 2000).

Fuccaro, Nelida, 'Minorities and ethnic mobilisation: the Kurds in northern Iraq and Syria', in Méouchy and Sluglett (eds), *The British and French Mandates*, pp. 579–95.

Fuccaro, Nelida, 'Ethnicity and the city: the Kurdish quarter of Damascus between Ottoman and French rule, c. 1724–1946', *Urban History* (2003), 30(2): 206–24.

Gaborieau, Marc, 'La tolérance des religions dominées dans l'Inde traditionnelle: ses prolongements modernes au Népal et au Pakistan', in *La Tolérance. Colloque international de Nantes, mai 1998. Quatrième centenaire de l'édit de Nantes* (Rennes: Presses universitaires de Rennes, 1999).

Gawrych, George W., 'Tolerant dimensions of cultural pluralism in the Ottoman Empire: the Albanian community, 1800–1912', *International Journal of Middle East Studies* (1983), 15(4): 519–36.

Gellner, Ernest, 'Nationalism', *Theory and Society* (1981), 10(6): 753–76.

Gelvin, James L., *The modern Middle East. A history* (Oxford: Oxford University Press, 2005).
Gelvin, James L., 'Modernity *and* its discontents: on the durability of nationalism in the Arab Middle East', *Nations and Nationalism* (1999), 5(1): 71–89.
Gelvin, James L., *Divided Loyalties: Nationalism and Mass Politics in Syria at the Close of Empire* (London: University of California Press, 1998).
Gelvin, James L., 'The other Arab nationalism: Syrian/Arab populism in its historical and international contexts', in Jankowski and Gershoni (eds), *Rethinking Nationalism in the Arab Middle East*, pp. 231–48.
Gelvin, James L., review of Khalidi *et al.* (eds), *The Origins of Arab Nationalism*, in *British Journal of Middle Eastern Studies* (1993), 20(1): 100–2.
Gershoni, Israel, 'Rethinking the formation of Arab nationalism in the Middle East, 1920–1945: old and new narratives', in Jankowski and Gershoni (eds), *Rethinking Arab Nationalism*, pp. 3–25.
Girardet, Raoul, *L'Idée coloniale en France de 1871 à 1962*, paperback edition with new preface and addenda (Paris: Table Ronde, [1979?]).
Gleason, Philip, 'Minorities (almost) all: the minority concept in American social thought', *American Quarterly* (1991), 43(3): 392–424.
Göçek, Fatma Müge, 'Ethnic segmentation, western education, and political outcomes: nineteenth century Ottoman society', *Poetics Today* (1993), 14(3): 507–38.
Goswami, Manu, *Producing India. From Colonial Economy to National Space* (Chicago, IL: University of Chicago Press, 2004).
Greenshields, T. H., '"Quarters" and ethnicity', in G. H. Blake and R. I. Lawless (eds), *The Changing Middle Eastern City* (London: Croom Helm, 1980), pp. 120–40.
Gunter, Michael M., *Historical Dictionary of the Kurds* (Oxford: Scarecrow Press, 2004).
Halliday, Fred, 'The formation of Yemeni nationalism: initial reflections', in Jankowski and Gershoni (eds), *Rethinking Arab Nationalism*, pp. 26–41.
al-Hakim, Yūsuf, *Sūriyya wal-intidāb al-faransī: dhikriyat IV* (*Syria and the French Mandate: Memoirs IV*) (Beirut: Dār al-Nahār lil-Nashr, 1983). NB: this is almost certainly a second or later edition; I have been unable to find details of the first.
Hanioğlu, M. Şükrü, 'The Young Turks and the Arabs before the revolution of 1908', in Khalidi *et al.* (eds), *The Origins of Arab Nationalism*, pp. 31–49.
Hanna, 'Abdallah, 'Pour ou contre le mandat français. Réflexions fondées sur des enquêtes de terrain', Méouchy (ed.), *France, Syrie et Liban*, pp. 181–8.
Hanna, 'Abdallah, *'Abd al-Rahmān al-Shahbandar (1879–1940). 'ilm nahdawī wa rajul al-wataniyya wal-taharrur al-fikrī* (*'Abd al-Rahman al-Shahbandar (1879–1940). Nahda Thought, the Man of Nationalism, and Intellectual Emancipation*) (Damascus: al-Ahālī, 2000).
Hanna, 'Abdallah, *al-haraka al-'ummāliyya fī sūriyya wa lubnān, 1900–1945* (*The Labour Movement in Syria and Lebanon, 1900–1945*) (Damascus: Dār Dimashq, 1973).

Hassoun, Amer Bader ('Āmir Badr Hassūn), *The Book of Syria. Photos from the Syrian life / Kitāb Sūriyya. Suwar min al-hayāt al-sūriyya / Le livre de la Syrie. Images de la vie syrienne* (Damascus: privately published, 2005).

Haut Commissariat de la République française à Beyrouth, *La Syrie et le Liban sous l'occupation et le mandat français 1919–1927* (Paris: Berger-Levrault, 1927).

Haut Commissariat de la République française à Beyrouth, *La Syrie et le Liban en 1922* (Paris: Emile Larose, 1922).

Hirschman, Charles, 'The meaning and measurement of ethnicity in Malaysia: an analysis of census classifications', *The Journal of Asian Studies* (1987), 46(3): 555–82.

Hirschman, Charles, 'The making of race in colonial Malaya: political economy and racial ideology', *Sociological Forum* (1986), 1(2): 330–61.

Hirschon, Renée (ed.), *Crossing the Aegean: An Appraisal of the 1923 Compulsory Population Exchange between Greece and Turkey* (Oxford: Berghahn, 2003).

Hobsbawm, E. J., *Nations and Nationalism since 1780. Programme, Myth, Reality*, 2nd edn (Cambridge: Cambridge University Press, 1992).

Hobsbawm, E. J., *The Age of Empire 1875–1914* (London: Weidenfeld & Nicolson, 1987).

Hodgson, Marshall G. S., *The Venture of Islam. Conscience and History in a World Civilization. Vol. 1: The Classical Age of Islam* and *Vol. 3: The Gunpowder Empires and Modern Times* (London: University of Chicago Press, 1974).

Honvault, Juliette, 'La coopération nationaliste avec le pouvoir mandataire: ambiguïtés et éthique politique chez l'émir 'Adil Arslān lors des négociations d'Ankara sur le Sandjak d'Alexandrette', in Méouchy (ed.), *France, Syrie et Liban*, pp. 211–27.

Hourani, Albert H., *A History of the Arab Peoples* (London: Faber & Faber, 1991).

Hourani, Albert H., *Arabic Thought in the Liberal Age 1798–1939*, reissued with new preface (Cambridge: Cambridge University Press, 1983).

Hourani, Albert H., *Minorities in the Arab World* (London: Oxford University Press, 1947).

Hourani, Albert H., *Syria and Lebanon: A Political Essay* (Oxford: Oxford University Press, 1946).

Hourani, Albert H., Philip S. Khoury and Mary C. Wilson (eds), *The Modern Middle East: A Reader* (London: I. B. Tauris, 1993).

Hurewitz, J. C., *Diplomacy in the Near and Middle East. A Documentary Record. Vol. 1: 1535–1914* (Princeton, NJ: D. Van Nostrand, 1956).

Husry, Khaldun S., 'The Assyrian Affair of 1933', *International Journal of Middle East Studies* (1974), 5(2): 161–76, and (1974), 5(3): 344–60.

al-Idilbī, Ulfat, *Dimashq ya basmat al-huzn (Damascus, Oh Smile of Sorrow)* (Damascus: Dar Tlass, 1989).

Inalcik, Halil and Donald Quataert, *An Economic and Social History of the Ottoman Empire, 1300–1914* (Cambridge: Cambridge University Press, 1994).

Jankowski, James and Israel Gershoni (eds), *Rethinking Nationalism in the Arab Middle East* (New York: Columbia University Press, 1997).

Select Bibliography

Jovelet, Louis (pseudonym for Robert Montagne), *L'évolution sociale et politique des 'pays arabes', 1930–1933* (Paris: P. Geuthner, 1933).

Kamenetsky, Christa, 'Folklore as a political tool in Nazi Germany', *Journal of American Folklore* (1972), 85(337): 221–35.

Karakasidou, Anastasia, *Fields of Wheat, Hills of Blood: Passages to Nationhood in Greek Macedonia, 1870–1990* (London: University of Chicago Press, 1997).

Karpat, Kemal H., *The Politicization of Islam. Reconstructing Identity, State, Faith, and Community in the Late Ottoman State* (Oxford: Oxford University Press, 2002).

Karpat, Kemal H., 'The status of the Muslim under European rule: the eviction and settlement of the Çerkes', in *Studies on Ottoman Social and Political History: Selected Articles and Essays* (Leiden: Brill, 2002 [1984]), pp. 647–75.

Karpat, Kemal H., 'The Ottoman ethnic and confessional legacy in the Middle East', in Esman and Rabinovich (eds), *Ethnicity, Pluralism, and the State*, pp. 35–53.

Karpat, Kemal H., '*Millets* and nationality: the roots of the incongruity of nation and state in the post-Ottoman era', in Braude and Lewis, *Christians and Jews in the Ottoman Empire*, vol. 1, pp. 141–69.

Kayali, Hasan, *Arabs and Young Turks: Ottomanism, Arabism and Islamism in the Ottoman Empire, 1908–1918* (London: University of California Press, 1997).

Kedourie, Elie, 'Ethnicity, majority, and minority in the Middle East', in Esman and Rabinovich (eds), *Ethnicity, Pluralism, and the State*, pp. 25–31.

Kedward, Rod, *La vie en bleu: France and the French since 1900*, paperback edition (London: Penguin, 2006).

Kessel, Joseph, *Les fils de l'impossible* (Paris: Christian Bourgois Editeur, 1990 [1970]).

Khadduri, Majid, 'The Alexandretta Dispute', *The American Journal of International Law* (1945), 39(3): 406–25.

Khalidi, Rashid, 'Concluding remarks', in Méouchy and Sluglett (eds), *The British and French Mandates*, pp. 695–704.

Khalidi, Rashid, 'The origins of Arab nationalism: introduction', in Khalidi *et al.* (eds), *The Origins of Arab Nationalism*, pp. vii–xix.

Khalidi, Rashid, 'Ottomanism and Arabism in Syria before 1914: a reassessment', in Khalidi *et al.* (eds), *The Origins of Arab Nationalism*, pp. 50–69.

Khalidi, Rashid, 'Arab nationalism: historical problems in the literature', *The American Historical Review* (1991), 96(5): 1363–73.

Khalidi, Rashid, Lisa Anderson, Muhammad Muslih and Reeva S. Simon (eds), *The Origins of Arab Nationalism* (New York: Columbia University Press, 1991).

Khoury, Gérard D., *Une tutelle coloniale: le mandat français en Syrie et au Liban. Ecrits politiques de Robert de Caix* (Paris: Éditions Bélin, 2006).

Khoury, Gérard D., 'Les conditions d'instauration du Mandat français au Proche-Orient après la Première guerre mondiale', in Méouchy (ed.), *France, Syrie et Liban*, pp. 75–89.

Khoury, Philip S., 'The paradoxical in Arab nationalism. Interwar Syria revisited', in Jankowski and Gershoni (eds), *Rethinking Arab Nationalism*, pp. 273–87.

Khoury, Philip S., 'Syrian urban politics in transition: the quarters of Damascus during the French mandate', in Hourani *et al.* (eds), *The Modern Middle East*, pp. 429–65 (first published 1984).

Khoury, Philip S., 'Abu Ali al-Kilawi: a Damascus *qabaday*', in Edmund Burke, III (ed.), *Struggle and Survival in the Modern Middle East* (London: I. B. Tauris, 1993), pp. 179–90.

Khoury, Philip S., *Syria and the French Mandate: The Politics of Arab Nationalism, 1920–1945* (London: I. B. Tauris, 1987).

Khoury, Philip S., *Urban Notables and Arab Nationalism: The Politics of Damascus 1860–1920* (Cambridge: Cambridge University Press, 1983).

Khuri, Fuad I., *Imams and Emirs: State, Religion and Sects in Islam* (London: Saqi Books, 1990).

King Jr, Morton B., 'The minority course', *American Sociological Review* (1956), 21(1): 80–3.

Kirişci, Kemal, 'Migration and Turkey: the dynamics of state, society and politics', in Reşat Kasaba (ed.), *The Cambridge History of Turkey, Vol. 4: Turkey in the Modern World* (Cambridge: Cambridge University Press, 2008), ch. 7.

Klein, Janet, 'Kurdish nationalists and non-nationalist Kurdists: rethinking minority nationalism and the dissolution of the Ottoman Empire, 1908–1909', *Nations and Nationalism* (2007), 13(1): 135–53.

Klein, Janet, 'Conflict and collaboration: rethinking Kurdish–Armenian relations in the Hamidian period, 1876–1909', *International Journal of Turkish Studies* (2007), 13(1–2): 153–66.

Krämer, Gudrun, 'Moving out of place: minorities in Middle Eastern urban societies, 1800–1914', in Peter Sluglett (ed.), *The Urban Social History of the Middle East, 1750–1950* (Syracuse, NY: Syracuse University Press, 2008).

Krieger, Joel (ed.), *The Oxford Companion to Politics of the World* (Oxford: Oxford University Press, 2001).

Kumaraswamy, P. R., 'Problems of studying minorities in the Middle East', *Alternatives: Turkish Journal of International Relations* (2003), 2(2): 244–64.

Kurd 'Ali, Muhammad, *Khitat al-Shām* (*Domains of Syria*), vol. 3, 3rd edn (Damascus: Maktabat al-Nūri, 1983 [1928]).

Kurd 'Ali, Muhammad, *Mudhakkirāt* (*Memoirs*), vol. 3 (Damascus: Matba'at al-Taraqqi, 1949).

Laurens, Henry, 'Le Mandat français sur la Syrie et le Liban', in Méouchy (ed.), *France, Syrie et Liban*, pp. 409–15.

Lenormant, François, *Une persécution du christianisme en 1860*, facsimile edition (Paris: W. Remquet, n.d. [1860]).

Lewis, Norman, *Nomads and Settlers in Syria and Jordan, 1800–1980* (Cambridge: Cambridge University Press, 1987).

Longrigg, Stephen H., *Syria and Lebanon under French Mandate* (London: Oxford University Press, 1958).

Lust-Okar, Ellen Marie, 'Failure of collaboration: Armenian refugees in Syria', *Middle Eastern Studies* (1996), 32(1): 53–68.

Maestracci, Noël, *La Syrie contemporaine: tout ce qu'il faut savoir sur les territoires placés sous mandat français*, 2nd edn (Paris: Charles-Lavauzelle, 1930).

Makdisi, Ussama, *The Culture of Sectarianism: Community, History, and Violence in Nineteenth-century Ottoman Lebanon* (London: University of California Press, 2000).

Makdisi, Ussama, 'Ottoman Orientalism', *The American Historical Review* (2002), 107(3). Accessed online at: http://historycooperative.press.uiuc.edu/journals/ahr/107.3/ah0302000768.html.

al-Malazi, Souheil (Suhayl al-Malāzī), *al-Tabāʿa wal-sihāfa fi Halab* (*Printing and Press in Aleppo*) (Damascus: Dār Yaʿrub lil-dirāsāt, 1996).

al-Mallūhī, Mahyār ʿAdnān, *Muʿjam al-jarāʾid al-sūriyya 1865–1965* (*Encyclopedia of Syrian Newspapers 1865–1965*) (Damascus: Oula, 2002).

Manz, Beatrice F., 'Multi-ethnic empires and the formulation of identity', *Ethnic and Racial Studies* (2003), 26(1): 70–101.

Maʾoz, Moshe, 'Communal conflicts in Ottoman Syria during the reform era: the role of political and economic factors', in Braude and Lewis (eds), *Christians and Jews in the Ottoman Empire*, vol. 2, pp. 91–105.

Marceau, Akil, 'Les droits des minorités et les Kurdes', in *Les Kurdes et les États*, special issue of *Peuples méditerranéens* (1994), 68–69: 267–79.

Marcus, Abraham, *The Middle East on the Eve of Modernity. Aleppo in the Eighteenth Century* (New York: Columbia University Press, 1989).

Mascle, Jean, *Le Djebel Druze*, 3rd edn (Beirut: Les Lettres françaises, 1944).

Masters, Bruce, *Christians and Jews in the Ottoman Arab World: The Roots of Sectarianism* (Cambridge: Cambridge University Press, 2001).

Mazower, Mark, *No Enchanted Palace: The End of Empire and the Ideological Origins of the United Nations* (Princeton, NJ: Princeton University Press, 2009).

Mazower, Mark, *Salonica, City of Ghosts: Christians, Muslims, and Jews, 1430–1950* (London: HarperPerennial, 2005).

Mazower, Mark, 'Minorities and the League of Nations in interwar Europe', *Daedalus* (1997), 126(2): 47–63.

McDougall, James, *History and the Culture of Nationalism in Algeria* (Cambridge: Cambridge University Press, 2006).

McDowall, David, *A Modern History of the Kurds*, 3rd rev. edn (London: I. B. Tauris, 2004).

McDowall, David, *The Kurds: A Nation Denied* (London: Minority Rights Group, 1992).

Meeker, Michael E., *A Nation of Empire: The Ottoman Legacy of Turkish Modernity* (Berkeley, CA: University of California Press, 2002).

Méouchy, Nadine (ed.), *France, Syrie et Liban 1918–1946. Les ambiguïtés et les dynamiques de la relation mandataire* (Damascus: Institut français d'études arabes de Damas, 2002). Méouchy's own contribution, apart from the thematic introduction, is 'Les mobilisations urbaines et rurales à l'époque mandataire. Remarques préliminaires', pp. 315–23.

Méouchy, Nadine and Peter Sluglett (eds) (with/avec la collaboration amicale de Gérard Khoury and Geoffrey Schad), *The British and French Mandates in Comparative Perspectives / Les mandats français et anglais dans une perspective comparative* (Leiden: Brill, 2004).

Meyer, James H., 'Immigration, return, and the politics of citizenship: Russian Muslims in the Ottoman empire, 1860–1914', *International Journal of Middle East Studies* (2007), 39(1): 15–32.

Meyers, Barton, 'Minority group: an ideological formulation', *Social Problems* (1984), 32(1): 1–15.

Migliorino, Nicola, '"*Kulna suriyyin?*" The Armenian community and the state in contemporary Syria', *La Syrie au quotidien. Cultures et pratiques du changement*, special issue of *Revue des mondes musulmans et de la Méditerranée* (2006), 115–116: 97–115.

Mitchell, Timothy, *Rule of Experts. Egypt, Techno-politics, Modernity* (London: University of California Press, 2002).

Mizrahi, Jean-David, 'La France et sa politique de mandat en Syrie et au Liban (1920–1939)', in Méouchy (ed.), *France, Syrie et Liban*, pp. 35–65.

Mizrahi, Jean-David, *Genèse de l'État mandataire. Services des Renseignements en Syrie et au Liban dans les années 1920* (Paris: Publications de la Sorbonne, 2003).

Moaz, 'Abd al-Razzaq, 'The urban fabric of an extramural quarter in 19th-century Damascus', in Philipp and Schaebler (eds), *The Syrian Land*, pp. 165–83.

Montagne, Robert, 'French policy in North Africa and in Syria', *International Affairs* (1937), 16(2): 263–79.

Montagne, Robert, 'Le traité franco-syrien', *Politique étrangère* (1936), 1(5): 34–54.

Mottahedeh, Roy P., *Loyalty and Leadership in an Early Islamic Society* (Princeton, NJ: Princeton University Press, 1980).

Nielsen, Jørgen S., 'Contemporary discussions on religious minorities in Muslim countries', *Islam and Muslim-Christian Relations* (2003), 14(3): 325–35.

Nisan, Mordechai, *Minorities in the Middle East: A History of Struggle and Self-expression* (Jefferson, NC: McFarland, 1991).

Öktem, Kerem, 'Nationalism and territory in the post-Ottoman space', RAMSES working paper 2/06, European Studies Centre, University of Oxford (2006). Accessed online at http://www.sant.ox.ac.uk/esc/ramses/oktem.pdf.

Olson, Robert W., 'The Kurdish rebellions of Sheikh Said (1925), Mt. Ararat (1930), and Dersim (1937–8): their impact on the development of the Turkish air force and on Kurdish and Turkish nationalism', *Die Welt des Islams*, new series (2000), 40(1): 67–94.

Olson, Robert W. and William F. Tucker, 'The Sheikh Sait rebellion in Turkey (1925): a study in the consolidation of a developed uninstitutionalized nationalism and the rise of incipient (Kurdish) nationalism', *Die Welt des Islams*, new series (1978), 18(3/4): 195–211.

O'Shea, Maria T., 'Between the map and the reality. Some fundamental myths of Kurdish nationalism', in *Les Kurdes et les États*, special issue of *Peuples méditerranéens* (1994), 68–69: 165–83.

Owen, Roger and Şevket Pamuk, *A History of the Middle East Economies in the Twentieth Century* (London: I. B. Tauris, 1998).

Pandey, Gyanendra, *The Construction of Communalism in Colonial North India*, 2nd edn with a new afterword (New Delhi: Oxford University Press, 2006).

Pedersen, Susan, 'Back to the League of Nations', review essay, *The American Historical Review* (2007) 112(4), available at: http://www.historycooperative.org/journals/ahr/112.4/pedersen.html.

Perez, Jean, 'Les compagnies méharistes au Levant (1921–1941)', *Revue historique des armées* (2003), 233: 79–96.

Philipp, Thomas and Birgit Schaebler (eds), *The Syrian Land: Processes of Integration and Fragmentation. Bilād al-Shām from the 18th to the 20th Century* (Stuttgart: Franz Steiner Verlag, 1998).

Piterberg, Gabriel, 'The tropes of stagnation and awakening in nationalist historical consciousness. The Egyptian case', in Jankowski and Gershoni (eds), *Rethinking Arab Nationalism*, pp. 42–61.

Poulton, Hugh, *Top Hat, Grey Wolf and Crescent. Turkish Nationalism and the Turkish Republic* (London: Hurst, 1997).

Provence, Michael, *The Great Syrian Revolt and the Rise of Arab Nationalism* (Austin, TX: University of Texas Press, 2005).

Provence, Michael, 'A nationalist rebellion without nationalists? Popular mobilizations in mandatory Syria 1925–1926', in Méouchy and Sluglett (eds), *The British and French Mandates*, pp. 673–92.

Provence, Michael, 'An investigation into the local origins of the Great Revolt', in Méouchy (ed.), *France, Syrie et Liban*, pp. 377–93.

Quataert, Donald, *The Ottoman Empire 1700–1922*, 2nd edn (Cambridge: Cambridge University Press, 2005).

Rabbath, Edmond, *Unité syrienne et devenir arabe* (Paris: Marcel Rivière, 1937).

Rabinovich, Itamar, 'The compact minorities and the Syrian state, 1918–1945', *Journal of Contemporary History* (1979), 14(4): 693–712.

Rabinovich, Itamar, 'Arab political parties: ideology and ethnicity', in Esman and Rabinovich (eds), *Ethnicity, Pluralism, and the State*, pp. 155–72.

Raymond, André, *Grandes villes arabes à l'époque ottomane* (Paris: Sindbad, 1985).

al-Rayyis, Najīb, *Sūriyyat al-istiqlāl (1936–1946). Al-aʿmāl al-mukhtāra 3 (Syria and Independence (1936–46). Selected works 3)* (London: Riad el-Rayyes, 1994).

al-Rayyis, Najīb, *Sūriyyat al-intidāb (1928–1936). Al-aʿmāl al-mukhtāra 2 (Mandate Syria (1928–1936). Selected works 2)* (London: Riad el-Rayyes, 1994).

al-Rayyis, Najīb, *Yā dhalām al-sijn (1920–1952). Al-aʿmāl al-mukhtāra 1 (O Prison Shadows (1920–1952). Selected works 1)* (London: Riad el-Rayyes, 1994).

Reilly, James A., 'Inter-confessional relations in nineteenth-century Syria: Damascus, Homs and Hama compared', *Islam and Christian-Muslim Relations* (1996), 7(2): 213–24.

al-Rifāʿī, Shams al-Dīn, *Tārīkh al-siḥāfa al-sūriyya, al-juzʾ al-thānī: al-intidāb al-faransī ḥattā al-istiqlāl, 1918–1947* (History of the Syrian Press, Part 2: The French Mandate to Independence, 1918–1947) (Cairo: Dār al-Maʿārif, 1969).

Robb, Graham, *The Discovery of France* (London: Picador, 2007).

Robertson, David, *A Dictionary of Modern Politics* (London: Europa, 1993).

Rodrigue, Aron, 'Difference and tolerance in the Ottoman Empire. Interview by Nancy Reynolds', *Stanford Electronic Humanities Review* (1996), 5.1. Accessed online at: http://www.stanford.edu/group/SHR/5-1/text/rodrigue.html.

Rogan, Eugene, *Frontiers of the State in the late Ottoman Empire: Transjordan, 1850–1921* (Cambridge: Cambridge University Press, 1999).

Rogan, Eugene, 'Instant communication: the impact of the telegraph in Ottoman Syria', in Philipp and Schaebler (eds), *The Syrian Land*, pp. 113–28.

Rondot, Pierre, 'Syrie 1929, itinéraire d'un officier', in Bianquis (ed.), *Damas*, pp. 95–104.

Saadeh, Sofia, 'Greater Lebanon: the formation of a caste system?', in Choueiri (ed.), *State and Society in Syria and Lebanon*, pp. 62–73.

Sack, Dorothée, 'The historic fabric of Damascus and its changes in the 19th and at the beginning of the 20th century', in Philipp and Schaebler (eds), *The Syrian Land*, pp. 185–202.

Saint Point, Valentine de, *La vérité sur la Syrie: par un témoin* (Paris: Cahiers de France, 1929).

Salibi, Kamal, *A House of Many Mansions: The History of Lebanon Reconsidered* (London: I. B. Tauris, 1988).

Schad, Geoffrey, 'Toward an analysis of class formation in Syria: Aleppo's textile industrialists and workers during the mandate', in Méouchy (ed.), *France, Syrie et Liban*, pp. 291–305.

Schaebler, Birgit, 'State(s) power and the Druzes: integration and the struggle for social control (1838–1949)', in Philipp and Schaebler (eds), *The Syrian Land*, pp. 331–67.

Scham, Alan, *Lyautey in Morocco: Protectorate Administration, 1912–1925* (Berkeley, CA: University of California Press, 1970).

Scott, James C., *Seeing like a State: How Certain Schemes to Improve the Human Condition have Failed* (London: Yale University Press, 1998).

Scott, James C., *Domination and the Arts of Resistance: Hidden Transcripts* (London: Yale University Press, 1990).

Scruton, Roger, *A Dictionary of Political Thought*, 2nd edn (London: Macmillan, 1996).

Seale, Patrick, *Asad of Syria: The Struggle for the Middle East* (London: I. B. Tauris, 1988).

Shambrook, Peter, 'Bypassing the nationalists: Comte Damien de Martel's

"administrative" reforms of January 1936', in Méouchy (ed.), *France, Syrie et Liban*, pp. 229–33.
Shambrook, Peter, *French Imperialism in Syria, 1927–1936* (Reading: Ithaca Press, 1998).
Shlaim, Avi, *War and Peace in the Middle East. A Concise History*, revised and updated paperback edition (London: Penguin, 1995).
Simon, Reeva S., 'The imposition of nationalism on a non-nation state. The case of Iraq during the interwar period, 1921–1941', in Jankowski and Gershoni (eds), *Rethinking Arab Nationalism*, pp. 87–104.
Sluglett, Peter, 'Will the real nationalists stand up? The political activities of the notables of Aleppo, 1918–1946', in Méouchy (ed.), *France, Syrie et Liban*, pp. 273–90.
Sluglett, Peter, 'Les mandats/the mandates: some reflections on the nature of the British presence in Iraq (1914–1932) and the French presence in Syria (1918–1946)', in Méouchy and Sluglett (eds), *The British and French Mandates*, pp. 103–27.
Stein, Leonard, *Syria* (London: E. Benn, 1926).
Stone, Norman, *Europe transformed 1878–1919*, 2nd edn (Oxford: Blackwell, 1999).
Taboada-Leonetti, Isabelle, 'Stratégies identitaires et minorités: le point de vue du sociologue', in Carmel Camilleri *et al.* (eds), *Stratégies identitaires* (Paris: Presses universitaires de France, 1998), pp. 43–84.
Tachjian, Vahé, *La France en Cilicie et en Haute-Mésopotamie. Aux confins de la Turquie, de la Syrie et de l'Irak (1919–1933)* (Paris: Karthala, 2004).
Takla, Youssef S., 'Corpus juris du mandat français', in Méouchy and Sluglett (eds), *The British and French Mandates*, pp. 63–100.
Tauber, Eliezer, 'The struggle for Dayr al-Zur: the determination of borders between Syria and Iraq', *International Journal of Middle East Studies* (1991), 23(3): 361–85.
Tejel Gorgas, Jordi, 'Les Kurdes de Syrie, de la "dissimulation" à la "visibilité"?', *La Syrie au quotidien. Cultures et pratiques du changement*, special issue of *Revue des mondes musulmans et de la Méditerranée*. (2006), 115–116: 117–33.
Thomas, Martin C., 'Albert Sarraut, French colonial development, and the communist threat, 1919–1930', *The Journal of Modern History* (2005), 77(4): 917–55.
Thomas, Martin C., 'Bedouin tribes and the imperial intelligence services in Syria, Iraq and Transjordan in the 1920s', *Journal of Contemporary History* (2003), 38(4): 539–61.
Thomas, Martin C., 'French intelligence-gathering in the Syrian mandate, 1920–40', *Middle Eastern Studies* (2002), 38(1): 1–32.
Thompson, Elizabeth, *Colonial Citizens: Republican Rights, Paternal Privilege and Gender in French Syria and Lebanon* (New York: Columbia University Press, 2000).
Thompson, Elizabeth, 'Ottoman political reform in the provinces: the Damascus Advisory Council in 1844–45', *International Journal of Middle East Studies* (1993), 25(3): 457–75.

Tilly, Charles, *Coercion, Capital and European States, AD 990–1992*, revised paperback edition (Oxford: Blackwell, 1992).

Turlington, Edgar, 'The settlement of Lausanne', *The American Journal of International Law* (1924), 18(4): 696–706.

Valensi, Lucette, 'Inter-communal relations and changes in religious affiliation in the Middle East (seventeenth to nineteenth centuries)', *Comparative Studies in Society and History* (1997), 39(2): 251–69.

Van Bruinessen, Martin, 'Kurdish society and the modern state: ethnic nationalism versus nation-building', in van Bruinessen, *Kurdish Ethno-nationalism versus Nation-building States. Collected Articles* (Istanbul: Isis Press, 2000), pp. 43–65 (first published 1991).

Van Bruinessen, Martin, 'Nationalisme kurde et ethnicités intra-kurdes', *Les Kurdes et les États*, special issue of *Peuples méditerranéens* (1994), 68–69: 11–37.

Van Bruinessen, Martin, 'Genocide in Kurdistan? The suppression of the Dersim rebellion in Turkey (1937–38) and the chemical war against the Iraqi Kurds (1988)', in George J. Andreopoulos (ed.), *Conceptual and Historical Dimensions of Genocide* (Philadelphia, PA: University of Pennsylvania Press, 1994), pp. 141–70.

Vatikiotis, P. J., 'Non-Muslims in Muslim society: a preliminary consideration of the problem on the basis of recent published works by Muslim authors', in Esman and Rabinovich (eds), *Ethnicity, Pluralism, and the State*, pp. 54–70.

Watenpaugh, Keith D., 'Steel shirts, white badges, and the last *qadabāy*: fascism, urban violence and civic identity in Aleppo under French rule', in Méouchy (ed.), *France, Syrie et Liban*, pp. 325–47.

Watenpaugh, Keith D., *Being Modern in the Middle East. Revolution, Nationalism, Colonialism, and the Arab Middle Class* (Princeton, NJ: Princeton University Press, 2006).

Watenpaugh, Keith D., 'Towards a new category of colonial theory: colonial cooperation and the *survivors' bargain* – the case of the post-genocide Armenian community of Syria under French mandate', in Méouchy and Sluglett (eds), *The British and French Mandates*, pp. 597–622.

Watenpaugh, Keith D., 'Middle-class modernity and the persistence of the politics of notables in inter-war Syria', *International Journal of Middle Eastern Studies* (2003), 35(2): 257–86.

Watts, Nicole, 'Relocating Dersim: Turkish state-building and Kurdish resistance, 1931-1938', *New Perspectives on Turkey* (2000), 23: 5–30.

Weber, Eugen, *The Hollow Years: France in the 1930s* (London: Sinclair-Stevenson, 1995).

Weber, Eugen, *Peasants into Frenchmen: The Modernization of Rural France, 1870–1914* (London: Chatto & Windus, 1977).

Weulersse, Jacques, 'Aspects permanents du problème syrien: la question des minorités', *Politique Etrangère* (1936), 6: 29–39.

Weygand, Général Maxime, 'Le mandat syrien: quelques réflexions – quelques précisions', *La Revue de France* 1927, May–June: 241–58.

White, Benjamin Thomas, 'Addressing the state: the Syrian 'ulama' protest personal status law reform, 1939', *International Journal of Middle Eastern Studies* (2010), 42(1): 10–12.

White, Benjamin Thomas, 'The Kurds of Damascus in the 1930s: development of a politics of ethnicity', *Middle Eastern Studies* (2010), 46(6): 901–17.

White, Benjamin Thomas, 'The nation-state form and the emergence of 'minorities' in Syria', *Studies in Ethnicity and Nationalism* (2007), 7(1): 64–85.

Wright, Quincy, 'The bombardment of Damascus', *The American Journal of International Law* (1926), 20(2): 263–80.

Yapp, M. E., *The Near East since the First World War. A History to 1995* (London: Longman, 1996).

Yapp, M. E., *The Making of the Modern Near East 1792–1923* (London: Longman, 1987).

Zisser, Eyal, 'Who's afraid of Syrian nationalism? National and state identity in Syria', *Middle Eastern Studies* (2006), 42(2): 179–98.

Zisser, Eyal, 'The 'Alawis, lords of Syria: from ethnic minority to ruling sect', in Ofra Bengio and Gabriel Ben-Dor (eds), *Minorities and the State in the Arab World*, pp. 129–45.

Zubaida, Sami, 'Contested nations: Iraq and the Assyrians', *Nations and Nationalism* (2000), 6(3): 363–82.

Zürcher, Erik J., *Turkey: A Modern History*, 3rd edn (London: I. B. Tauris, 2004).

Zürcher, Erik J., 'The vocabulary of Muslim nationalism', *International Journal of the Sociology of Science* (1999), 137: 81–92.

Unpublished Papers and Theses

Bokova, Lenka, 'La révolution syrienne contre le mandat français', doctoral thesis, Université de Paris VII, 1988.

Méouchy, Nadine, 'Les Formes de conscience politique et communautaire au Liban et en Syrie à l'époque du mandat français 1920–1939', doctoral thesis, Université de Paris IV-Sorbonne, 1989.

Owen, Roger, unpublished paper presented to Harvard University History department, February 2005.

Sato, Noriko, 'Concealing otherness. Ambivalent position of Syrian Orthodox Christians', paper presented at British Society for Middle Eastern Studies annual conference, Durham, 12–14 September 2005.

Tejel Gorgas, Jordi, 'Le mouvement kurde de Turquie en exil. Continuités et discontinuités du nationalisme kurde sous le mandat français en Syrie et au Liban (1925–1946)', doctoral thesis (n.d. [2003]), École des hautes études en sciences sociales/ Université de Fribourg.

Yacoub, Joseph, *La question assyro-chaldéenne, les Puissances européennes et la SDN (1908–1938)*, unpublished doctoral thesis, Université de Lyon II.

INDEX

Abdülhamid II (Ottoman sultan), 29
Alaouites (autonomous statelet), 11, 12, 16n32, 79, 82, 88, 148, 154, 162
'Alawis, 45, 61, 70, 142, 145, 148
  in armed forces, 45, 54–5
  and personal status law, 182
  petitioning French authorities, 87–8
  separatist movement, 72–3
  unofficial recognition in Ottoman Empire, 164
Aleppo, 4, 78, 97n32, 150
  state of, 11
Alexandretta, Sanjak of, 12, 57, 70, 79, 154, 155n6, 162
  Turkish identity in, 149
Alif Bā' (newspaper), 72
  on population, territory and state, 75–82
Anatolia
  contest of nationalisms in, 136
Anderson, Benedict, 34, 37, 84
Anglo-Iraqi treaty, 56, 135, 141
Arabism, 71; *see also* nationalism, Arab
archives, French, 5, 107
  gaps in, 5, 7, 15n14, 55–6
  insistence on Syrian disunity, 6
  Kurds in, 112
archives, Syrian, 7, 92

Arendt, Hannah, 41n57
Armenians, 48, 79, 142, 211
  in armed forces, 113
  cooperation with Kurds, 114
  Dashnak party, 114
al-Asad, Hafiz, 83
L'Asie française (bulletin of the Comité de l'Asie française), 10, 135
  campaign regarding Franco-Syrian treaty, 140–1
  insistence on Syrian disunity, 137, 138
  language of 'minorities' in, 134–43
association (as principle of colonial rule), 45, 50, 112–13, 116
Assyrians, 76, 110, 140–1, 147
Atatürk, Kemal, 29, 74
Austro-Hungarian Empire
  national identity in, 32
autonomist movements, 84, 87–91
  and identitarian feeling, 87, 90
al-Ayyām (newspaper)
  on population, territory and state, 75–82

Babil, Nasuh (journalist), 79–81, 84, 93
Bakdash, Khalid, 119
Balkans, 32, 35, 132
Barmada, Mustafa, 176

[233]

Bedouin, 89, 102
    Contrôle Bédouin, 12
Berkes, Niyazi, 28, 58
Bloc, National *see* National Bloc
Boehm, Max Hildebert, 38n5, 38n8
borders, 102, 180
    as defining minorities, 118, 177, 210
    formation of, 35, 41n55, 77, 83, 107;
        see also Syria, territorial definition of
    see also Syrian–Turkish border
Bou-Nacklie, Nacklie, 45
Briand, Aristide, 134
British mandate
    Iraq under, 140–1
    as reference point in Syrian politics, 135, 178
British–Iraqi treaty *see* Anglo-Iraqi treaty
Burke, Edmund, 45

Cagaptay, Soner, 107
Catholics, 166
    concerns about representation, 151
    Syrian-Catholics, 148
Christians, 35, 51, 55, 55–6, 145, 192–3
    as clients of France, 51, 53, 58, 76, 195
    elimination from Anatolia, 106
    in Jazira, 76, 86
    migrants from Turkey, 76–7, 142
    preferred interlocutors of French, 195
    seeking legal protection as minorities, 143–6, 192–3
    and separatist movements, 73
    as subordinate minorities, 197–8
    see also Patriarchs
Circassians, 52, 53, 89–90, 131, 139, 146–8, 149
    in armed forces, 52, 54
    petitioning French authorities, 145, 151
citizenship, 33–4, 36, 150
colonialism, 137
    French, 15n13
    protests against, 196

Comité de l'Asie française *see* L'Asie française
'common law communities', 165; *see also* personal status law reform
communications
    in nation-state-building, 35
'compact minorities', 54–5, 61; *see also* Druzes *and* 'Alawis
Congress of Berlin (1878), 132
Contrôle Bédouin, 12
courts *see* legal system

Damascus, 72, 74, 87, 144, 156n24, 166, 176, 196
    Kurdish quarter, 115–17
    state of, 11
Damascus Association of 'Ulama', 175, 185, 188, 190, 192
Darbisiyya incident, 113
de Beauplan, Robert, 43, 46
de Caix, Robert, 46, 135
de Gaulle, Charles, 104
de Jouvenel, Henry, 10, 168
de Martel, Damien, 10, 56, 59, 139, 143, 169
Decree 60, 171
Dentz, Henri, 5
Deringil, Selim, 28
Dersim, 107, 114
Druzes, 54–5, 61, 70, 142, 145
    'Druze' revolt, 89
    exceptional status in Ottoman Empire, 164–5, 179, 180
    Lebanese, 173

education, 90, 149
    Circassian medium, 146, 149
    in formation of nation-state identity, 33
    in mandate charter, 133
Emin Agha, 108, 110–11
Encyclopaedia of the Social Sciences, 22, 30, 38n4

ESS see *Encyclopaedia of the Social Sciences*
Euphrates (district), 70, 92

Faysal I (King of Iraq), 50
France
　mission civilisatrice, 137
　as 'protector of minorities', 56, 59, 133, 140
　Third Republic, 11
　Vichy Regime in, 5, 10
Franco-Syrian treaty, 56, 133–4, 135, 142, 144–8, 169
　and *L'Asie française*, 141
　destruction of records regarding, 7
　drafting of text, 139
　negotiations over, 142
　nonratification of, 197
　policy towards minorities in, 148–51
Franklin-Bouillon Agreement (Ankara Agreement), 103, 105
French mandate, 43–4
　legal basis, 49
　policy of divide and rule, 44, 45–7, 53, 60, 118
　Syrian state as instrument of, 86, 184
　undermining Syrian government authority, 82, 196
　see also association (as principle of colonial rule)
Froidevaux, Henri, 135, 137

Gelvin, James, 50, 71
Ghanimé, Latif, 131, 144, 146, 148
Ghazi I (King of Iraq), 92
Giannini, Monsignor, 144
Gouraud, General Henri, 10, 134
Greece
　population exchange with Turkey, 23–4, 27
Greek Orthodox, 58
Greeks, 156n20
　as minority in Turkey, 27

Hajo Agha, 104, 108, 110, 115
al-Hakim, Yusuf, 55, 74, 175, 194, 197
al-Hammam (village), 105
Hanna, ʿAbdallah, 82
Haute-Djézireh see Jazira
Hayy al-Akrād see Damascus, Kurdish quarter
High Commission (French), 107, 116, 163, 165, 167–9, 179, 194
　as 'the authority' (*al-Sulta*), 81, 87, 98n46
　survey of practice regarding personal status law, 182–5
Hourani, Albert, 45

identitarian movements, 87, 90, 91, 210
al-Idilbi, Ulfat, 54
IESS see *International Encyclopedia of the Social Sciences*
International Court of Justice, 132
International Encyclopedia of the Social Sciences, 25, 26
Iraq, 71, 76, 92, 110, 111, 138, 147
　admitted to League of Nations, 138
　British mandate in, 56, 103, 113, 135, 140–1
　protection of minorities in, 141
　US invasion (2003), 103
Islam
　as defender of minorities, 187, 188, 192
　Ottoman Empire not recognising division in, 164
　as source of legitimation in Ottoman Empire, 32
Ismaʿilis, 51, 89, 145
　and personal status law, 182
　unofficial recognition in Ottoman Empire, 164
al-ʿIssa, Yusuf, 52, 59

Jabal Druze, 11, 12, 73, 79, 148, 154, 162

Jazira, 12, 76–82, 101, 117, 119, 142, 154, 162
  subordination to National Bloc government, 86
Jesuits, 88
Jews, 39n14, 145
  lay hostility towards religious courts among, 164
  in Salonica, 35, 48

Khoury, Philip, 45
Khoybun ('Independence') committee, 114
Kurd 'Ali, Muhammad, 211
Kurds, 53, 58, 70, 145
  autonomous Kurdish zone, 112
  cooperation with Armenians, 114
  cultural and political activity in Syria, 115, 116–17
  employed in border posts, 113
  French surveillance of, 114–15, 116
  incorporation in Turkish Republic, 107
  in Iraq, 140
  in Jazira, 76, 86
  in Kurd Dagh, 120
  'Kurdish question', 112
  'minoritisation' of, 112–17
  taking refuge in Syria, 107–11, 113, 118

Latakia, 11
Lausanne, Treaty of, 104
League of National Action, 119
League of Nations, 24, 37, 44, 56, 57, 91, 132, 136
  Article 22 of Covenant, 49
  Permanent Mandates Commission, 137
League of Nations Mandate for Syria and Lebanon, 133
  Article 6, 50, 133
  Article 22, 139
Lebanon, 4, 11, 51, 79, 87, 179

legal system in Syria
  jurisdiction of state courts, 149, 179–80
  Kanafani case, 179–81
  Ottoman, 150
  see also shariah law
Longrigg, Stephen, 45
Lyautey, Marshal Hubert, 50

majority
  not basis of state legitimation, 31, 34
  and formation of nation-state, 37
  as rhetorical device, 25, 191, 197
  term used in political discourse, 3
Makdisi, Ussama, 4, 33
al-Malazi, Souheil, 8
mandate charter see League of Nations Mandate for Syria and Lebanon
Mardam Bek, Jamil, 174, 175
  resignation, 162, 195
Mardin, 76
Maronites, 70
millet system, 13, 17n36, 33, 45, 47–9, 173
  contrasted with minority, 59
  French understanding of, 47–9, 50–1
  not including Muslims, 54
  persistence of millet identities, 56–60
minority
  in *L'Asie française*, 136, 138
  in colonies, 132
  constituted through definition of border, 118, 177–8
  contrasted with millet, 59
  emergence in public discourse, 21–5, 27, 28, 30, 31, 37, 44, 60, 131, 134, 198
  exceptionalism, 4
  fixation of boundaries of, 148
  in Franco-Syrian treaty, 142, 144–8, 169
  integral to nation-state, 4, 27, 30–1, 90, 94, 118, 184

in international law, 23–5, 49, 52–3, 132–4, 135, 142–3, 150, 210
'need not be a numerical minority', 26
in post-war Europe, 22, 23, 132
and separatism, 69, 94
Supreme Allied Council and adoption of term, 132
usage of term in French archives, 2, 46–7
usage of term by Syrians, 143–52
Muslims
and French citizenship, 36
'majority' against personal status law reform, 197

National Bloc, 86, 91, 92, 101, 116, 119, 147, 151
blocking 1933 Franco-Syrian treaty, 139
fall of Bloc government, 162
opposing personal status law reform, 175–6, 194, 195
nationalism, 70–1
Arab, 71, 95n4
in Anatolia, 136
'mystical' territorial claims of, 74, 78, 84
reaction to separatism, 73–4
Syrian Arab, 8–9, 13, 53, 57, 119
among Syrian Christians, 59
and Syrian newspapers, 8–9, 71, 74, 75–82, 83–4
nation-state
abstracted from history, 83
authority of, 34–6
development of creates minority identities, 90, 184, 209
and identity, 30–1, 71, 90, 192, 211
imposed on Syria, 72
modern notion of, 2
requiring 'continuous maintenance', 84
and separatist movements, 70–1
'sons of the country', 77
Nazism, 38n5

nizam (social order), 39n31
Nouri, Monsignor Ignace, 56, 131, 143
Nusaybin, 105

Ottoman Empire, 2, 27, 31, 37, 44, 45, 82, 83, 87
breakup of, 106
diversity in, 48
legal system in, 150, 163
legitimation not based on majority rule, 31
Muslim majority in, 32–3
not recognising divisions in Islam, 164, 179
Ottomanism, 32–3
and separatism, 32
suppression of 'allogenous populations', 136

Palestine, 178
parti colonial (colonial lobby in France), 135
Patriarchs, 6, 146, 152, 179, 193
personal status law, 163–6; *see also* personal status law reform
personal status law reform
challenge to French authority over, 176
Decree 60/LR (13 March 1936), 171–3, 178, 181, 188, 198
Decree 146/LR (18 November 1938), 174–5, 188
demonstrations against, 176, 196
early attempts at reform, 168–9
language of 'minorities' in, 169
marriage, 174–5, 181, 182–3, 187, 188–90
not applied to Muslims, 177, 198
opposition by Sunnis, 192
in other countries, 170–1, 178
reform as extension of state authority, 178, 184
reforms abandoned, 177, 192
secularising intent, 170

personal status law reform (*cont.*)
 standardisation of practice, 183–4
 survey of local practices, 181–4
 'ulama' not consulted about reforms, 194–5
petitions, 87–8, 89, 91, 117
 against personal status law reform, 146–8, 175, 185–92
Poidebard, Father Antoine, 111
Ponsot, Henri, 10, 108, 139, 169
Provence, Michael, 46
Puaux, Gabriel, 10, 85, 166, 175, 185, 194–6, 198

Qamishli, 76, 78, 85, 104, 105
 flag incident in, 101
al-Qassab, Kamil, 185

Rabbath, Edmond, 143, 148–52
al-Rayyis, Najib, 9, 57, 74
Reform Edict (1856 Ottoman), 58; *see also* tanzimat
representative government, 28–9, 30–3

Sabri, 'Uthman, 115
Sarrail, General Maurice, 10, 109, 168
Seale, Patrick, 45, 82
separatism, 69–100, 210
 in the Alaouites, 72–3
 among linguistic and religious mainstream, 91, 92
 not automatically associated with minorities, 94
 and Christians, 73
 'precise opposite of', 91
 and Sunnis, 69–70
Service des Renseignements (SR), 108
shariah law, 163, 164
 abolished in Turkey, 167
 challenged by personal status law reform, 184
 common law based on, 165
Shaykh Sa'id rebellion, 107, 108, 110, 113

Shi'is, 57
 in Lebanon demanding Syrian unity, 91
 and personal status law, 183
Sluglett, Peter, 72
South Africa
 black 'minority' in, 26
SR *see* Service des Renseignements
state
 access to state jobs, 149
 'a state happened' (*sār fī dawla*), 82
 jurisdiction of legal system, 149–50
 maintenance of as superseding ideology, 93
 religious legitimation of, 29, 31–3, 49
 state versus religious authority, 170, 178
 symbols of authority of, 80–1
 symbols of as focus for discontent, 85–6
state, non-national, 23; *see also* nation-state
Sunnis, 57, 181
 accused of 'totalitarian pretensions', 194
 ethnolinguistic division among, 51
 nationalism considered purely an affair of, 88
 not considered a personal status community, 165
 not consulted about personal status law reform, 194–5
 as numerical majority in Syria, 1, 3, 180, 197
 opposition to personal status law reform, 192
 separatism among, 69–70
 subordinating Christians, 197
Sykes–Picot agreement, 50
Syria
 administrative subdivision of, 13
 bilād al-Shām ('natural Syria'), 83, 86
 as defined in Mandate Charter, 11

Index

territorial definition of, 2–3, 12, 71–1, 87, 92; *see also* Syrian–Turkish border
Syrian-Catholics, 148
Syrian–Turkish border, 101, 103–5, 105–11, 112–17, 118
   build-up of state authority on, 104–5, 106, 113
   exclusion zone, 109–11, 115

Tahan, Patriarch Alexandros III, 58
tajzi'a see *tamzīq*
tamzīq ('dismemberment' of Syrian territory), 11, 72
tanzimat, 29, 33–4, 36
Tappouni, Monsignor Ignace Gabriel I, 59, 146, 195
   prominence in French archives, 195, 207n101
Tcherkess *see* Circassians
Tilly, Charles, 30, 90
Transjordan, 135
Turkish Republic, 44, 106
   abolition of shariah courts, 167
   formation of, 23, 32, 106
   incorporation of Kurds, 107
   population exchange with Greece, 23, 27

'ulama'
   not consulted about personal status law reform, 194–5
   relationship with National Bloc, 194–5
   see also Damascus Association of 'Ulama'

Watenpaugh, Keith, 4
Weber, Eugen, 36
Weygand, General Maxime, 10, 168

Yazidis, 141
   and personal status law, 182
   unofficial recognition in Ottoman Empire, 164
Young Turks, 136

Zisser, Eyal, 45